D1045212

ALSO BY STEPHEN JOEL TRACHTENBERG

Write Me a Letter!: The Wit and Wisdom of Stephen Joel Trachtenberg
Reflections on Higher Education
Thinking Out Loud
Speaking His Mind
The Art of Hiring in America's Colleges and Universities

BIG MAN ON CAMPUS

A University President Speaks Out on Higher Education

STEPHEN JOEL TRACHTENBERG

with Tansy Howard Blumer

Onondaga Free Library

A TOUCHSTONE BOOK
Published by Simon & Schuster
NEW YORK LONDON TORONTO SYDNEY

TOUCHSTONE
A Division of Simon & Schuster, Inc.
1230 Avenue of the Americas
New York, NY 10020

First Touchstone hardcover edition June 2008

TOUCHSTONE and colophon are registered trademarks of Simon & Schuster, Inc.

For information about special discounts for bulk purchases, please contact Simon &
Schuster Special Sales at 1-800-456-6798 or business@simonandschuster.com.

DESIGNED BY JOY O'MEARA

Manufactured in the United States of America

1   3   5   7   9   10   8   6   4   2

Library of Congress Cataloging-in-Publication Data
Trachtenberg, Stephen Joel.
Big man on campus : a university president speaks out on higher education /
Stephen Joel Trachtenberg with Tansy Howard Blumer.
p.   cm.
1. Education, Higher—United States.   I. Blumer, Tansy Howard.   II. Title.
LA228.T69 2008
378.73—dc22
2007039377

ISBN-13: 978-1-4165-5719-7
ISBN-10:   1-4165-5719-9

To teachers and learners everywhere,
especially Francine, Adam, and Ben, who never stop educating me

CONTENTS

PREFACE

On an airplane flight between Washington, D.C., and Denver, Colorado, a man sitting next to me asked what line of work I was in. We had a lot of time, so I told him I manage a large community that sits on more than forty acres of land in the middle of one of the nation's most interesting cities. I said that the community is based on a model begun in the Middle Ages and many of our traditions are derived from that time, including the rather odd appearance from time to time of people wearing ceremonial gowns and handing out ornate sheepskin documents. I watch over 5,500 residents living in numerous housing units on the site and help plan the activities of 10,000 others commuting to and from the site each day.

My workforce runs a fitness center, a hospital, two hotels, a multitude of restaurants, and various theaters where we sponsor performances by musicians, politicians, visiting heads of state, comedians, actors, and dancers. We have a number of athletic teams that compete nationwide. Accountants, lawyers, and investment brokers watch over the money we receive for our efforts. I told him I have a police force, the largest payroll in the city after the federal and local governments, and, most important, more than 1,400 experts lecturing on every subject under the sun and doing research on matters with implications for the betterment of mankind. We have librarians and computer experts who find things for members of the community to read and study. We have our own newspapers and our own TV and radio production facilities. Most of our residents stay for four years. Our enterprise is so popular that I have to hire people to decide who of the thousands who apply will be invited to be a part of our community. In my line of work,

I have my share of critics, but I am pleased to say I also have a number of supporters, many of whom give me money to use for my programs. Supportive or not, many people have an opinion about how I should be doing my job.

My flight companion listened intently to my job description. Then he asked, "So, are you the mayor of a big city or something?"

AMERICANS REVERE their universities and root for local basketball and football teams even when they haven't attended the university. But I think they should become better informed about these fascinating institutions, which contribute a great deal to society and also seek a great deal from it. Universities ask for our children and our understanding. They ask that we be sympathetic to—and tolerant of— academic freedom and free speech in a very special way. They ask that we be participants but at the same time give them a lot of room to do things that may seem overly critical and unwelcoming. They ask for a considerable portion of the national treasure. This is not true just of the public universities; it is true of all tax-exempt universities with research programs funded by the federal government assisting students who receive financial aid.

We need an educated, informed electorate that understands universities as human institutions and their leaders as people dancing and juggling as fast as they can to make universities flourish in the face of great challenges. In the coming years, our universities will need even more sympathy and understanding on the part of Americans because the cost of running them will not go down. They will be competing with the debt we are incurring in Afghanistan and Iraq, the cost of Social Security and other benefits for the baby boomers, health care, the cost of integrating immigrants into the body politic, and the cost of upkeep of the environment and the infrastructure.

I want you to understand what it is like to be a university president and what a university is like from the inside out. But I have not written a textbook. That is not my style and probably not what you would enjoy reading anyway. Instead, I have written a very personal and a bit unconventional book about my life as a university president. It is meant to give pleasure as well as make you think about these institutions with increased concern and empathy. Maybe it will even cause some readers to reach for a checkbook and donate to some worthy university. Welcome to my world.

Stephen Joel Trachtenberg
Washington, D.C.

BIG MAN ON CAMPUS

1.

ENROLLMENT IS LIFE

After announcing that I would step down from the presidency of The George Washington University—a prestigious university with an enrollment of about 20,000 located in downtown Washington, D.C.—I took an hour off to sit in front of the university's Gelman Library with a cup of coffee and watch the passing parade of professors and young men and women students. It was a very soothing, very beautiful experience and gave me a great sense of satisfaction about my tenure as president. I thought about the surprising, challenging, and wonderful thirty years I have led while serving as president of two universities. I marveled at the notion that an admittedly quirky guy like me has managed to lead such a rewarding professional life in the traditional world of academe. I recalled some of the many interesting and often daunting issues I have dealt with during my career. I thought about my worries for the future of American higher education and the challenge of instituting innovation and efficiency in an environment where change is threatening to many. It was then that I decided I could write a book about all this—for all the people who have ever wondered what makes a university tick and what its president does all day.

Years ago I read about a little college of art in Connecticut that closed because it could no longer stay afloat fiscally. The *Hartford*

Courant published an article about the demise of the college and quoted a faculty member who said, "I noticed that my classes were getting smaller and smaller and I thought that was a *good* thing because I was able to teach to smaller and smaller groups of students. It never occurred to me that it could be a sign that the school might have to fold. I was astounded!" Although the innocence of this comment might seem rather stunning to a university administrator, it is really not unusual for people to react this way because most of them believe that colleges and universities are here forever. They don't fail like railroads or airlines or dot-com companies. Or do they?

In my last year as president of GW, there was an opinion piece in the student newspaper written by a young woman who said she thought the enrollment was too large. She proposed that we reduce it by about 2,000 students but hold the faculty and the facilities constant. I wrote to her and asked, "If we were to reduce the student body as you proposed and the average student represents $30,000 per year to the university, what number does that result in?" She wrote back, "$60 million." I guess the figure shocked her a little, so she generously added this comment: "You don't have to do it all at once; you can phase it in over the next ten years." The fact is that $60 million subtracted from a university's operating budget because of a reduction in enrollment would have to be immediately replaced, or the university would quickly head the way of that little college in Connecticut. Even if the student had conceded the need to eliminate programs and people to compensate for the loss of tuition income, what might she have wanted the administration to eliminate? Laboratories? Health services? Athletic programs? Buildings and grounds? The faculty? The university police force? Dormitories and food service? Academic programs? The administration?

Universities are very special places. Their structure and their customs are rooted in earlier times, and we are trying to preserve these ancient institutions while living in the twenty-first century, but we cannot ignore or hold at arm's length all aspects of modern life. In fact, according to John Sexton, president of New York University, "There are 85 institutions in the world today that exist as they did 500 years

ago. [These are] the English Parliament, the Papacy, eight Swiss can-
tons—and of the 75 remaining, 70 are universities."

We have to pay the electric bill. We have to buy computers and
more books for the library. We have to provide faculty and staff with
health and dental plans, day care for their children, and salaries that
allow them to live in contemporary America. Universities are not like
their medieval predecessors. And they are not mom-and-pop shops.
They are big, businesslike endeavors, and the president has to be able
to hold a businesslike perspective at the same time that he or she understands and supports the deepest values and ambitions of the people
within who are committed to scholarship and learning.

The United States has had a lock on high-quality higher education
for a long time, during which people from all over the world have wanted
to come to American universities. But the interest in our universities suffered a bit of a decline, exacerbated after 9/11, when we threw up walls
to screen international students because of security concerns. The clock
stopped, and people from other nations came to the conclusion that they
did not necessarily have to go to an American university. They found
plausible alternatives in Australia, Canada, New Zealand, or elsewhere.
Meanwhile, many countries like China and India are rapidly building
their own new universities.

America currently has many unmet needs. Forty-five million of us
have no health care, and even if we ignore ethical issues, we will have
to deal with that problem because it is a drag on the economy and a
potential public health hazard. There are other looming obligations.
These include the retiring baby boomers and the inadequate Social
Security program; our infrastructure—disintegrating bridges, tunnels,
and roads that were built for the smaller traffic loads of earlier years—
that desperately needs to be repaired; and urban and rural schools that
are in need of an overhaul. Universities are very expensive to run, and
they will ultimately be called upon to become more efficient in the use
of their resources. Current billion-dollar university endowment campaigns draw the attention of politicians. In 2006, when a scandal arose
at American University, which is also in Washington, D.C., Senator
Charles Grassley of Iowa, the ranking member of the Senate Finance

Committee, labeled that university the "poster child of excess" because the president was said to be drinking $100 bottles of wine and otherwise indulging himself at the university's expense. All of this occurred while the board of trustees was allegedly negligent in its oversight of the university's operations and administration.

Recently we saw students acting badly at Gallaudet University, also in Washington, D.C., which is the country's only university for the deaf. These students were dissatisfied with the selection of Dr. Jane K. Fernandes, the university's provost, to serve as the next president of the university. Fernandes is a deaf person, but she was not "deaf enough" for the Gallaudet student body, which apparently has unwritten rules for how to be deaf. She grew up speaking and reading lips—not signing, as some students seem to feel is mandatory for membership in the culture of deafness—and, in breach of the students' notion of deaf authenticity, she attended mainstream public schools and universities rather than schools for the deaf. Although the Gallaudet Board of Trustees had already approved the choice of Fernandes to be the president, the student protests that followed closed the school and ultimately led to a revote by the board repudiating its earlier selection. This was the second time in an eighteen-year period that the students had succeeded in shutting down the school over the issue of the new president's deafness, an unhappy legacy for the school to have to overcome in the years ahead.

Fernandes was deprived of the presidency before she was even inaugurated. The outgoing Gallaudet president, I. King Jordan, had been put into office eighteen years earlier, after the students, with the support of faculty, alumni, and friends of the university, rejected the selection of a hearing president and shut the campus over the issue. As a result, Jordan became the first deaf president of the school. After the Fernandes incident, Jordan was moved to write in an editorial, "When I announced that I was stepping down as president . . . I spoke of the health of the university and said that Gallaudet was well positioned for the future. Sadly, this may no longer be the case" (*The Washington Post*, January 22, 2007).

Most of the university's operating budget comes from the U.S. Congress—that is, from the tax dollars of the American taxpayer. When the

Gallaudet students threw their tantrum over the choice of their next president, they were saying in effect, "We own this university and will get what we want by shutting it down." In a civilized university, you simply don't decide who the president is by making it impossible to function.

These students—and some of their professors, apparently—seemed to have forgotten that our countrymen tend to be committed to both democracy and due process, even if we don't always agree with the outcome. One example of this is the country's accession to the Supreme Court's decision regarding the outcome of the 2000 presidential election. No one took to the streets to close down the government or the Supreme Court. Instead, the people demonstrated their belief in the rule of law and accepted the outcome. But in the Gallaudet situation, the board of trustees allowed anarchy to reign and, under pressure from the students, cravenly reversed its presidential appointment. Because Gallaudet is dependent on taxpayers' money, if I were in Congress, I would have said during the protest, "If the students don't go back to class and there isn't some orderly process for deciding on the president, I am going to start cutting appropriations. And then we can let them take over the place and we'll see how they manage to pay the bills."

The Gallaudet protestors showed absolutely no respect for their university or the protocols of the academy. And the faculty of Gallaudet failed in its important obligation to teach their students how to behave like university-educated people. Not surprisingly, following these shameful events, the Middle States Commission on Higher Education said it would delay the university's accreditation renewal. According to an article in *The Washington Times* (February 22, 2007), the commission cited, among the reasons for the delay, its "concerns about the functionality of Gallaudet's governance system." An old and trusted institution of higher learning has been severely damaged by this disgraceful episode, and Congress would be justified in imposing sanctions to protect the institution.

In June 2007, several months after these shocking events at the university, the Middle States Commission on Higher Education placed the university on probation, a melancholy proof of the seriousness of the institution's problems. I am not surprised that the university's accreditor took a harder look as a result of these events and found even more things that were troublesome about the institution. It is not difficult to understand that an interested third party viewing the institution from the outside would see the need for a more in-depth review. I also don't doubt the purity of heart of the people at Gallaudet who disrupted the school and forced it to close, citing their strongly felt disagreement with the choice of a new president. However, they simply did not understand how things are done in universities. In this case, it would have been useful for them to learn the rules of engagement in an institution of higher learning.

In my judgment, Congress's interest in higher education will continue to increase and senators will keep watching what is happening on our campuses. For one thing, they might see Harvard's endowment going over $35 billion at the same time it is said that the school is considering yet another fund-raising campaign. The questions facing Harvard should be, When is enough enough? When does a university have the resources it needs? Surely Harvard is aware that its endowment is larger than the Gross Domestic Product of some countries. There may be a case for more, but if so, it must be made so all can see it. Harvard's leadership might well be concerned that suddenly there could be questions from Congress about the appropriateness of a tax-exempt status for such a huge accumulation of wealth. I think Harvard is trying to appear virtuous by stopping its early-admissions program and by deciding that the university will no longer give scholarships but instead give outright grants to people whose families make under $40,000 per year. They must realize, however, that this last declaration is insignificant because the number of people affected by these initiatives at Harvard is minuscule. In any case, I think we may see congressional hearings on the issue of allowing tax-exempt status for wealthy universities. This is a serious question, one that can have a devastating effect on many universities in our country that are more modestly situated.

IN AMERICA, where there is no natural-born nobility, we have generally strived to achieve rank on our own, and one way to become a member of the "American elite" has come from being associated with one of the prestigious American universities. One such group of prestigious institutions includes the Ivy League, MIT, and Stanford University. If you have graduated from one of these institutions, that fact can have a defining effect on your entire life. But this has become somewhat less true as the country has become more heterogeneous and more interesting overall during the last several decades. We are seeing increasing numbers and distinguishing kinds of elite state universities, and there is now more excellence available to a much larger section of the population.

The average tenure of a university president is currently about eight years. This is an important piece of data. Universities often take a full year or more to carefully go through a search process to identify a new president, and in no time they have to do it all over again! In the first year of office, the person is getting to know the job. In the last year, the person is preparing to leave. That leaves only six years in which to get something done. Surely that is not enough time for a university president to formulate a vision of what an institution should be doing and do what is necessary to bring that vision to reality.

BEING A university president has a Sisyphean quality to it; you keep rolling boulders up the hill, and they keep rolling back down on you. But once in a while, you actually get a boulder or two up to the top and are able to get it over the other side. The Talmud says, "You cannot in your lifetime achieve all the things you are committed to doing, but this does not relieve you of the burden to keep trying." This is a good description of the life of a university president. In my case, being the president drew on every talent, every skill, every capacity I developed in my lifetime. Moreover, no two days were ever the same. In the course of a day, I could be sitting with the vice president of advancement trying to devise a fund-raising strategy and then with the vice president for business trying to figure out what the tuition ought to be for next year and how to make budget allocations. Later in the day, I might be in a meeting with the vice president for academic affairs talking about curriculum changes and new degree programs. Or I might be in conversation with the general counsel to discuss legal matters affecting universities and focus on a few high-profile cases important to my university. Or I could have been with the vice president for student affairs talking about drinking or smoking on campus or the proper role of athletics versus the highest academic ambitions. Each day had its challenges, its rewards, and its hard knocks. And the next day, the fun started all over again, full of new issues along with issues that kept coming back again and again no matter what I did.

How should we be supporting university presidents so that they can accomplish the goals for which they were recruited? We need board members, neighbors, students, and faculty who are more aware of the president's role and the importance of some of the issues universities face. I believe that universities seem so well-established that people think they can be criticized and kicked around and have resources extracted without realizing that there needs to be a give-back and that universities need to be nurtured and supported consistently.

A lot of philanthropy goes into universities, but it is important to remember that 80 percent of endowment assets in the country are held by only 16 percent of the universities. GW is a big university with an operating budget of less than a billion dollars a year. There are thousands of people on the payroll and thousands of students as well as hundreds of thousands of living graduates. Yet the economic model of the university is very similar to that of a theater. People arrive at the box office, buy a ticket, and give the ticket to the usher on their way to see the show. The bills of the theater are paid for by the box-office receipts. Likewise, 90 percent of GW's bills are paid by tuition—at the box office! We are a tuition-driven institution.

When thinking about tuition, people are often misled by the media, which make much over the list price of tuition and do not recognize the various pricing plans that universities have developed in order to build greater justice and equity into the system. Universities want a broad socioeconomic spectrum of students and do not want the inability to pay full price to be a barrier to admission for qualified students. The fact is that students in America can arrange to get an education with very little of their own money. Unfortunately, the poorest students often do not get the counseling and guidance they need to take full advantage of the availability of financial aid. If I had a magic wand, I would fix this situation by improving the ability of high school counselors to help students negotiate the financial aid maze.

Tuition is a very complicated business because many people think of it as the cost of getting something. But really it is the *price*, not the cost, that is important. For example, certain *costs*—such as products and services—are basically the same for all universities. But the *price* differs at different institutions. Independent universities have higher tuitions because they don't get the subvention that the state institutions do. At public institutions, the price of tuition is a political decision. The governor and the legislature can decide what price they want to charge, and they can make that price work by giving the institution the underwriting it needs to pay its bills. A private university is an economic being, its tuition price driven by the cost of running the institution—tuition plus its other sources of income. Harvard, with its endowment of $35 billion, could, if it wished, do away with tuition altogether. By contrast, GW, along with hundreds of other colleges and universities in our country, despite the appearance of solid resources, would have to close its doors if it did not have tuition income. The perilous reality faced by many a university president is this: *enrollment is life.*

The price of tuition is further complicated by the amount of financial aid provided by an institution. Only students who can afford to pay the full tuition are likely to be charged the sticker price. The needier students are generally subsidized in some way. The infinite number and type of pricing schemes of American universities could fill a book of their own.

UNIVERSITY PRESIDENTS are increasingly in the news. The experience of Lawrence Summers at Harvard is one dramatic example of this. During his tenure as Harvard's president, Summers made a number of remarks at various occasions that touched on sensitive issues that offended some groups, including affirmative action advocates, women, and environmentalists. In 2005, while attending a conference sponsored by the National Bureau of Economics Research (NBER) on Diversifying the Science and Engineering Workforce, it was suggested that factors other than socialization could explain the disproportionate numbers of men and women in high-end science and engineering positions. Summers hypothesized that the possibility could be men's higher capacity in relevant innate abilities. This was misconstrued by some to mean that he was suggesting that men are more intelligent than women. Summers's speculation became public, an outcry occurred on the Harvard campus, and the national news media fanned the flames of disputation. This, along with previous controversial statements by Summers, is believed to have been the primary factor in his departure from the presidency after a period of unease. In his case, one faction of the faculty—that of the School of Arts and Sciences—was able to drive him out of office in spite of the positive reviews he got from other large groups of faculty.

Situations like these are not unusual; they have been going on for some time. In recent years, there has been a lot of turnover in university presidencies, and there will be a lot more. People are stepping down as a matter of course, but also because of some difficult situation that is in the spotlight. These are important jobs. In the coming years, there will be tremendous flux, particularly in community colleges. Where will the university presidents of the future come from?

These are not good times for university presidents. Their brief average tenure is a disaster for the individuals, and not much better for their institutions. For example, Jeffrey Lehman left Cornell University after two years, Edward Hundert left Case Western Reserve after four, Charles Karelis was out at Colgate after less than two, Evan Dobelle was out at the University of Hawaii after three, and Lawrence Summers of Harvard was forced out after five. Perhaps a special example of presidential brevity is Trinity College in Hartford, Connecticut, which had four presidents and one acting president between 2000 and 2006.

The circumstances leading to the resignations or dismissals of these presidents were all different. But the results for the universities were similar; a void at the top, the cost and labor of a premature search, and an uneasy succession. I wonder if Harvard would be what it is today had James Bryant Conant, Nathan M. Pusey, and Derek C. Bok not served consecutively for a total of nearly sixty years, from 1933 to 1991, with roughly equal tenures. It is hard to imagine that Harvard, absent three generations of their steady leadership, would have grown to be such a great American institution. After my nineteen years at GW, it would be wonderful for the university to have the next president serve an equally long term and then for his successor to do the same. Whether that would turn GW into Harvard is hard to say; Harvard had a head start.

THE MORE I thought about the transition from my administration to the next and listened to what was being said about all the high expectations for my successor, the more I thought it would be a good idea for me to talk to the board of trustees and make a plea for humane treatment for him. And so I plunged in during one of my last board meetings and asked for several important considerations.

First, I warned the board not to project onto him expectations that no human being can live up to. About 250 years ago, Edward, the second Baron Thurlow, observed that corporations have neither a body to be kicked nor a soul to be damned. In that sense, my university, like any university, is a corporation. But I hoped the board, the faculty, and the students would resist the temptation to see the new president as the university made flesh, with a kickable soul and a damnable body. He is not the soul or heart of the university, but its leader.

The new president talked to the board about growing the endowment. I was glad to hear that but asked the board members not to make him the battering ram of fund-raising. The president of any university must energetically and wholeheartedly participate in fund-raising. But it is not the president's only job, and the board, deans, and senior faculty have a shared responsibility in the fund-raising endeavor. Unfortunately, this responsibility is often forgotten or ignored, especially by the faculty. They generally prefer just to ask the president for money.

I urged the board not to expect my successor to be omniscient. No one is! I reminded them of the scandal involving the lacrosse players at Duke University—the scandal that turned out to be a lot more like prosecutorial misconduct than the sexual assault that was first alleged. When the events—whatever they were—first came to light, many people blamed Richard Brodhead, the president of Duke, for not intervening and preventing an off-campus party where there were a keg and two strippers. How, I asked, was President Brodhead supposed to know the party was even going on? He's not a mind reader, and Duke is not a police state with spies employed to phone in the latest intelligence about Saturday night revelries. A university president is not clairvoyant. Granted, students, not to mention faculty and staff, can often lack judgment and be up to no good. But knowing about this ahead of time is impossible; presumably, omniscience resides in only one place, and He is not a university president.

I further asked the board to keep in mind that leading a university is daunting, bordering on overwhelming. The president is supposed to be a good businessman and a pretty fair accountant. He also needs to be an intellectual with such rich and broad interests that he can talk on any topic with any professor. He needs to be in touch with the lives and concerns of students. And he needs to have a vision for the institution and a clear focus on how to achieve that vision. But he really can't play all roles at once or equally well at all times; I suggested that they let him play those roles in which he excels, let him delegate to others with necessary competencies, and offer help when they believe it is needed.

I told them that they, along with the faculty and staff of the institution, need to nurture and protect their president, especially in the first years. After nearly thirty years as a university president, I have learned an obvious lesson: I needed the board most when times were tough or critics were gathering. Smooth sailing doesn't require an oar, but when you're up the creek, you really do want a paddle; actually, several.

HAVING MADE this plea to the board, I began to think of what I might say to the new president about what I have been doing for so many years. He wasn't likely to ask for a tutorial, but it was useful to think about what I believe are the greatest problems he will face while also reminiscing about the many satisfactions—and, yes, joys—I experienced in the job.

There is no doubt in my mind: money is the biggest challenge facing the modern university president. Finding it, asking for it, raising it, using it efficiently, keeping it safe, investing it wisely, defending allocations, charging and justifying tuition, and challenging established notions about it—all money-related topics perpetually vex and confound a sitting president.

The second most enduring challenge I faced as a university president was working with faculty. As individuals, faculty members are mostly quite splendid—lovely, actually. The kind of people you want as friends or neighbors or married to your children! But the problems arise when they gather as a group, clutching their copies of *Robert's Rules of Order*, pledged to oppose any perceived threat to the status quo that may be suggested by their president.

As president, I spent hours at my desk every day, reading not just the mail addressed to me personally but communications of many other kinds, and there were times when I felt as if I were drowning in the complaints of my fellow human beings. To be fair, I did sometimes get a letter indicating satisfaction with some aspect of the university, but a fair share were from entitled neighbors, dissatisfied faculty, unhappy alums, and disappointed students and parents. Yes, they were in the small minority—the large majority of them don't write to me at all—but still I thought I should advise the new president to get ready for the onslaught. I do concede, however, that grousing and grumbling appear to be endemic in society and not just a university-related issue.

A president must possess an ironic streak, including when listening to students—with no knowledge of history—explaining how the world has come to this sorry state. Times like that—and times when a literary allusion used in conversation with a student falls flat due to the student's relative ignorance—make me worry about the absence of a common understanding of what a college education should include. A BA from one school often bears no relationship to the BA from another. I am not the only one worried about this; all colleges wrestle with the curriculum question.

I would encourage my successor to have regular office hours for students and to attend their performances, discussions, athletic events, and informal gatherings whenever possible. Talking to and observing students became one of the most important and enjoyable things I did as president. Surely, my willingness to be with and enjoy students is part of the legacy of the wonderful teachers I myself had over the years.

One of the many reasons why this new GW president was chosen was because of his previous experience as an administrator in a large and successful research-oriented university. Increasing the research orientation of universities is a nationwide trend; as a result, the rewards for teaching at our institutions of higher education are often replaced with more powerful incentives to do research. One of the nice things about my university is that the institution still cares about teaching. But, like many other universities, we don't seem to care quite as passionately as we used to, and I am apprehensive about the future of all universities who emphasize research while deemphasizing the incentives for classroom activity.

College and university rating systems are springing up all over. *U.S. News & World Report* was first to print such a ranking. The result, while it may seem useful to prospective students and their parents, has had a startling effect on the expenditure of university resources to attract students and on decision making about admissions programs and systems. While universities can't do much about this situation, except perhaps refuse to participate, it is an area of concern for university presidents because, among other things, it drives up costs and ramps up students' expectations of housing accommodations and other amenities.

2.

YOUNG ENOUGH TO STILL
DO SOME DAMAGE

When debating with myself about concluding my GW presidency, I thought of the ancient Greek farmer whose son
triumphed in the Olympics. The crowd cheered him and
carried him on their shoulders. But when a second son also won his
competition, the crowd cried out, "Die now!" In other words, the father
was at the pinnacle of happiness and things couldn't possibly get better. It's a wonderful story. But there are a lot of things to do in academe
and a lot of room for improvement. I have a lot of energy for the fray,
and I know things can get even better. I certainly hope I haven't left
anyone with the impression that when I gave up the GW presidency, I
was retiring. I left university administration to step up to the faculty and
enjoy the restoration of my First Amendment rights. I looked forward
to teaching, writing, consulting, and being active in many ways.

A lot of people said they were sorry I was leaving; that was nice to
hear. Some were less kind. But so it goes. Many people said, "You look
so well—so young—you should stay a few more years." So I thought,
What? I have to look sick or old in order to start some new departures?
People say a lot of things. But the truth is, three unbroken decades as
president is itself a perfectly plausible reason for my saying "It's time to

do something else while I'm still young enough to still do some damage." Having said that, I started wondering about what that might be. It was hard to think about leaving something I have loved doing for so long and find something new that I could love as much.

In getting to that decision in 2007, this Brooklyn-born and -bred only son of two Jewish immigrants passed through several of the nation's best academic institutions and was shaped and inspired by many influential teachers, professors, and several of the giants in the field of education. The path I took began with P.S. 254 and James Madison High School in Brooklyn, New York, continued with a BA from Columbia, a JD from Yale, and an MPA from Harvard, and led me through a deanship and a vice presidency at Boston University, political appointments at the U.S. Department of Health, Education and Welfare and Congress, and two university presidencies. In short, almost my entire career has been immersed in the joys and challenges of American education.

I have been lucky; in fact, fortunate. There has been a lot for a person like me to do in my chosen field, and over the years I have received generous reviews for what I have been able to accomplish, especially as president of the University of Hartford and as president of GW. Of course, I have also had some brickbats hurled at me now and again.

GW is a sound and thoughtful institution—in many ways a great one—and will be fine without me as its president. I predicted that the opening created by my departure would get applications from many sitting presidents, provosts, and deans who have been in their positions from five to six years, ages fifty to fifty-eight, along with a random cabinet member or two. My expectation was pretty accurate; the new president, Steven Knapp, was chosen from an impressive group of more than one hundred highly qualified people. After all, the position is one of the top academic jobs in America, and upon my departure, the university had no major problems and enjoyed a strong foundation on which to support the next leap forward. All the important things—students' test scores, outside rankings, the endowment, and the building program—were at the highest point in our history, and our location in Washington, D.C., was a huge draw for students, faculty, and staff. In short, I feel good about the shape in which I left the institution when I departed the president's office.

WHEN I was a senior in college, I took a test that was supposed to help me figure out what to do with the rest of my life. After analyzing the results, the Counseling Center told me I ought to become executive director of the YMCA. The test may have lacked subtlety and imagination, but the conclusion was close to the mark. In a way, the skills required for such a job are like those of the post I have been in all these years. Somehow the paper-and-pencil test I took actually revealed my personality, my ability to work with people, and my interest in and curiosity about managing an organization—but not just any organization. The YMCA is a social services organization, and universities are similar in many ways. And another job I was interested in—that of hospital administrator—is also not far from the mark. There was a striking commonality in what the test concluded and what I ultimately did for a living.

It is hard to say how one's early experiences have shaped a career or a set of skills, but I know that I have been sort of "the president" since I was a kid. I was a leader at P.S. 254, president of the Student Government Organization at James Madison High School, and an officer in student government in college. I always felt that I was headed into public service without specifically knowing what I was going to do. Over the years people have said to me, "You should have gone into politics." Well, I have! Anybody who thinks a university president is merely an academic pretty face is wrong. It's a political business. Just ask Lawrence Summers.

Could it be that somehow my status as a first-generation only child was a factor in deciding my career path? Did I value my own education all the more given my parents' modest formal schooling? Did an early sense of being an outsider fuel my strong desire to earn degrees at three of the best universities in the nation? Did the extraordinary teachers and mentors I encountered along the way influence my career choices more than anything else? I am guessing *yes* to all these questions. Stories of my childhood keep playing themselves out in my head when

I look back at my education and my career. Perhaps a bit of personal memoir can provide some perspective on all these matters.

WHEN I was a boy, I went up to the roof of our six-story apartment building with some friends. This was an activity that was specifically prohibited, but we spent quite a bit of time up there that day. Our play soon began to evolve into daredevil acts, and we all started leaning out over the edge, trying to see how far we could go without falling off. This game soon lost its luster, and we thought of an even more exciting stunt; we decided to hang the smallest of our group out over the street. I had him by the ankles as he dangled upside down. Soon, however, the boy became frightened and began wriggling and crying. It was clear that I couldn't hold him much longer, and my friends quickly helped me drag him back safely onto the roof. Nothing happened. But that is not the story. The real story is that, many years later, I had a terrible nightmare in which I dreamed that I had dropped Joey. I woke up in a sweat and wondered, terrified, What if I had let him slip? What would the balance of my life have been like? And what of the lives of his parents and mine?

That story scares me. If a tragedy had happened, it would have been a never-ending moment; beyond redemption. I am a big believer in redemption and think America is all about second chances. It is a country where the ethos allows invention and reinvention. People in this country change their names and professions, get face lifts, have orthodontia and Lasik eye surgery, and move from coast to coast. But when I think of that incident, I cannot think how I could have ever been able to forgive myself. I don't think I would ever have been whole if it had ended badly. How could I have lived with such an act? I cannot imagine.

I GREW up in a small apartment in Brooklyn. It had one bedroom. My parents took that space, and I slept on a pullout sofa in the living room. My bed was folded up each morning so that the room could serve as a family room by day. I studied at the kitchen table from grade school until my freshman year in high school, when my father had a particularly

successful year. He had a little extra money, which he planned to use
to get a new car. My mother managed to snatch the money for a down
payment on a house just before he spent it. She had been collecting
pin money in a Swee-Touch-Nee tea canister and had about $1,000.
My father had about $1,000. He believed that customers trusted suc-
cessful salesmen; a new car was a symbol of success. But this time, my
mother got out ahead of General Motors, and with their $2,000 and an-
other $1,000 she borrowed from a friend and a mortgage, they bought a
private single-family row house for $8,000. This was where I spent my
high school years. And where I first had a room of my own.

Before we moved, when I was preparing for my Bar Mitzvah, my
mother told me that she would have a party for me after the ceremony.
I was elated. She told me that, since our apartment was so small, I
couldn't host my entire class; I would have to limit the number of
friends who attended. As it turned out, I invited everyone, leaving out
only one classmate—a girl. The party was a great success in spite of the
modest size of my family's dwelling, and all was well. But on the Monday when I returned to school, the uninvited girl came up to me and
said, "How was your Bar Mitzvah?" I told her it was great. She asked,
"Why didn't you invite me to your party?" I told her that my mother
had limited the number of guests and that I had been forced to leave
out some classmates. She said, "Oh, who else did you not invite?" After
a long pause, I had to tell her she was the only one. She looked me in
the eye and said, "You hurt my feelings." Then she walked away. Years
have gone by, but I have always had that sad moment someplace in my
head. In fact, it has been a useful memory and has helped inform my
behavior. Because of this incident, I have tried especially hard not to
hurt anyone accidentally.

Now that they have retired, many people my age use their spare
time to google names from their past on the Internet. One of these is
a friend of mine from P.S. 254. Recently he was trying to locate all of
our classmates for a reunion. This is quite an undertaking because a
gathering for the class of 1951 would involve people who are about
seventy years old—if they are alive—and, presumably, scattered geo-
graphically; and surely most of the women classmates have different

last names. Nevertheless, Myron has been tracking them down. When he called me to try to find the location of someone who I was close to, I asked him if he knew the phone number of the girl I had not invited to my Bar Mitzvah—Myrna Schwartz. He had it! She was living in California. So I called her. When I told Myrna who I was, she brightened up. "You're a celebrity!" she said. "Well, no, not really," I said. She continued, "I know you are a celebrity, because I saw you a few years ago in a Dewar's scotch whiskey advertisement." I said, "Well, yes, I was in one, but that was published over a quarter of a century ago." She said, "But you live in Saint Louis now—you're the president of Washington University." I said, "No, I live in D.C. and I'm president of The George Washington University—the other school is a Washington pretender." We had a nice talk, and we told each other all about life since P.S. 254. I finally got up my nerve and said, "I believe I owe you an apology." And I reminded her of the story of my Bar Mitzvah. She was swell about it and said she didn't remember the incident at all; hearing that made me feel like a character in a Guy de Maupassant story but happy and relieved at the same time.

I am convinced that Myrna had psychologically blocked the event and that I overplayed it. Maybe it hurt her so much that she buried it deep inside her psyche. Or maybe it was just a passing thing and she forgot about it when she became an adult. But I myself remember most of what happened in the eighth grade, and I definitely remember any slights taken or given.

As in the case of Myrna and my Bar Mitzvah, I do think about the things I am not proud of in my life. Some of the things I am not proud of have to do with the way I related to women when I was a younger man. Not that I did anything unusual for the time, but this is the twenty-first century, and as we look back at the way we comported ourselves back in the twentieth century, we see that young men like me were not as empathetic as they probably should have been with all the women they knew or dated. So now I have expanded my Myrna Schwartz list! There are a few women who cared for me once, and not only did I not fully reciprocate their affection, I wasn't very gracious about how I manifested that. I could have been nicer. Of course, I can hardly go about asking them all for forgiveness now! However, I will say that this realization has been useful to me and I have generalized it as a mature adult to try to be more thoughtful with people I work and live with. I still don't always get it right.

THERE WERE times in school when I was restless because I was bored. At one of these times, my mother was sent for and arrived at an interesting compromise with the teacher. The two of them agreed that during certain segments of the curriculum, I could be seated at the back of the class with a copy of *The New York Times* to read until the class was dismissed!

One of my elementary teachers, Miss Levine, thought I had promise as a writer. For a year, she gave me special assignments in addition to what the other students were required to do. First she gave me a daily three-hundred-word essay. Next she gave me a five-hundred-word essay to write, and so forth. Through it all, I thought she was punishing me for some unexplained misdemeanor. Of course, she was trying to help me learn how to write—but how could I have known that then? I was just a kid. As I later learned, she *was* singling me out, but not for punitive reasons. The project represented extra work for her, too; she reviewed my efforts every night, critiqued them, and then gave them back to me with her comments written on them in red ink. I celebrate her here. I wonder if she had a first name.

I was blessed with wonderful instructors in both grade school and high school; many of them were the last of the Depression-era teachers. These were people who had professional degrees and maybe even a PhD or a law degree. They had graduated during the 1930s, couldn't find work, and had latched onto teaching jobs in the public schools. In the case of the women, the situation was also complicated by their already limited career alternatives. By the time World War II ended, these people were sufficiently senior that it made sense to stay in until retirement. I got there just in time to experience some of these wonderful people.

Bernard Jaffee was a chemistry teacher at James Madison High School. He was the author of the textbook we used in school, and he was over-the-top brilliant. He was also a memorable instructor. His clothing looked as if it had been handmade on Bond Street in London; he wore three-piece tweed suits and sported a gold watch chain.

I also particularly remember Philip Rodman, an English teacher at James Madison. One day he gave a lecture on Dadaism, and I thought he had to be fooling around because the name sounded so absurd. Of course, when I got to Columbia and discovered that other people knew about Dadaism, I thought, My god, Mr. Rodman wasn't just making that stuff up!

Elizabeth Whitlock was also an English teacher and advised the school newspaper, of which I was editor in chief. Elizabeth Horne was an assistant principal. At the time of my inauguration at the University of Hartford, the two colleagues were retired and living in a senior community in a small Massachusetts town. They drove down together and attended the ceremony. It was a special joy at such an important event in my life to see them and their pride in me.

At an early age, these faculty and many others inspired in me a love and respect for teachers and education. At Columbia, I took courses from some extraordinary faculty members who set the bar high for teaching excellence and scholarship. These teachers were never far from my mind as I grew professionally.

MY FATHER, Oscar Trachtenberg, was a classic American immigrant who was born in Europe and came to this country as a young man. He had a heavy Russian accent. He wasn't the sort of dad who would take me out to ball games or anything conventional. I knew he was there for me, but it was never something he could say much about. He held me to an almost impossible standard. If I came home and said I had received a 99 on an exam, he would ask, "Who got the other point?" When I told him that I had been elected president of the Student Government Organization, he asked, "How much does the job pay?" He found a way to keep my eyes continually on the receding horizon. That probably helps to explain my own behavior in certain instances—although, as a father, I tried to learn from his behavior to be more forthcoming with my own children. I have always told them, uninvited, that I love them. I also regularly try to praise them, although I don't want to cheapen the words by celebrating insignificant things. Not everyone who runs a race ought to win a prize; but I don't think it is right to make the goal impossibly high the way Oscar Trachtenberg regularly did.

About a week after I had been admitted to the New York bar, my father, while driving home, got a moving violation and was upset that it would cost him ten points against his driver's license. He said, "I have to get a lawyer to challenge the ticket." I offered to be his lawyer. He declined the offer saying, "No, no, I have to get a *real* lawyer." My mother persuaded him to give me the ticket so that I could represent him. The charge was driving with his lights out after dusk. It turns out that dusk is not solely a poetic word; it is an actual term meaning a specific time of the day, and the time changes each day depending on the movement of the sun. I learned that dusk is established each day by the U.S. Meteorological Service. Dusk on the day of my father's violation was 6:07 P.M. The time recorded on the ticket was 6:06 P.M. My father had had a full sixty seconds before he was required to turn on his lights! I went to traffic court with this argument. When it was my turn, I stood before the judge and showed him the ticket and the meteorological report. I then said, "I submit that my client is not guilty." The judge noticed that Oscar's and my last names were the same and asked what our relationship was. I told him, and he smiled and said, "Tell your father you did a good job. Dismissed." I went home that night very pleased with myself. My father said, "So, Clarence Darrow, how'd you do?" I said, "I won!" He said, "How'd you do that?" I told him and he replied, "So what's the big deal? The cop screwed up!" In other words, anyone could have won this case because the officer had erred. I suppose my father would have been impressed only if the ticket had been written at 6:08 P.M. and I was still was able to get him off!

When I was raising my own sons, I sometimes had to overcome an instinct to behave as my father might have done with me. I had to avoid reacting critically when something went wrong. In such moments, I consciously took a deep breath and searched for a better way—my own way—to handle problems. When my older son, Adam, was small and we were living in Hartford, we had a cellar and a pretty good collection of wine in it. One evening, my wife, Francine, sent me to pick out an especially fine bottle to go with a wonderful dinner she was serving. Adam came down to the cellar with me. I chose an expensive wine, and Adam asked if he might carry it upstairs. I handed it to him saying, "Be careful, Adam, this is a very good bottle. We don't want to break it."

Almost immediately, it slipped out of his little hands and shattered on the floor. My first instinct was to do or say something testy—as my own father might have. But I looked at Adam's face and saw that his lips were quivering and he was starting to cry. I paused. Then I picked him up, gave him a hug and a kiss, and he put his head on my shoulder. I said, "How many bottles of wine are in this room, Adam?" He answered in a small, thin voice, "A lot." Then I said, "How many Adams are in this room?" He said, starting to perk up a bit, "Just one." I said, "That's right. We have a lot of wine and only one Adam. So let's not worry about this. Let's just choose another bottle of wine and you can take that upstairs." Then I handed him another bottle of wine and said, "Be careful, Adam, this is a very good bottle. We don't want to break it." He carried it upstairs without incident. It was an important moment for me; I saw that my solutions could be better than the ones I might have borrowed from my own father. I am happy to say that this is an event that my grown son Adam remembers to this day—and remarks on now and again in a positive way.

My father was short on compliments of any sort. Nevertheless, he did have a sense of humor, and, after many years of not understanding this, I now believe that some of his sterner comments might have been intended to be funny. Of course, I never found them much to laugh about and wouldn't have minded a big embrace and some congratulations instead. But as a son, you take what you can get.

When my father died, I told the rabbi that I would do the eulogy. I recalled a number of sentimental things about him, but one of the things I said was that he had infrequently said anything complimentary to me. After the funeral, several people who had worked for him over many years came up singly and in groups to tell me reproachfully that

my father had been obsessive about telling others about his son's accomplishments. One man told me he had once seen my father stop a
total stranger in the street and tell him about "my son, the dean." Who
knew? He never shared any of this with me! It was shocking to hear that
he had been proud to the point of being boastful! He often said when
I was rushing out of the house and didn't have time to talk to him,
"Someday you'll want to talk to me and I won't be around." This was
one of those times I would have loved a chance to hear from him why
he was so reluctant to praise me.

My parents had a testy relationship, and on two separate occasions
they separated. Even now, I remember these as semitraumatic events
and they have stayed with me. My mother used to say about my father:
"Divorce? Never. Murder? Maybe." I believe she may have thought
about killing him from time to time. He wasn't easy. The first time
my parents split up was when I was quite young—about five—and my
mother took me out to California, where we stayed with some of her
childhood friends. My mother had known the woman when they were
schoolgirls in Palestine before emigrating to the United States. We took
the Twentieth Century Limited out of Grand Central Station to Chicago, where we stayed overnight. The next day we went on to Los Angeles, where she quickly found work with a famous designer and I went
to a local school. We were in California for about a year. One day, my
father showed up at the door and gave me a present—a wooden truck.
As best I could make out, he told my mother that he had learned that
he was a man who could not live alone, he had met another woman,
and although he would much prefer having my mother come back to
him, if she wouldn't return, he would ask her for a divorce so he could
marry the other woman. The exact words may have been a bit more
engaging, but this is my understanding of what transpired. My mother
did return, and they stayed together until my junior year of college,
when she went off to Israel and lived with cousins for six months. Once
again, my father pursued her, asked her to reconcile, and convinced
her to come back.

Everyone in the family remembers my father as a man of very strong
personality who generally knew what he wanted. He came from the

Ukraine and considered himself Russian. He spoke Russian, Hebrew, Yiddish, a little Moldovan, and English. My parents both sounded as though they were from elsewhere and spoke mostly Yiddish when they didn't want me to understand. Either that or they spelled words, but Yiddish was more frequent. My father started out in America as a floor boy in a doll factory, where his principal duty was to sweep up. He went to high school at night, but I don't think he ever graduated. He had to make a living.

My father got into insurance sales and became very good at it. He saw opportunity knocking everywhere. Once he left his car parked in neutral and it rolled onto a neighbor's newly sodded front lawn. The owner of the lawn was furious and came to confront my father. During the ensuing conversation, my father sold him a life insurance policy! In hard times—even in the Depression—he always made a living. He sold insurance mostly to Jews, but in 1939, New York State passed a law that made it illegal to use race as a criterion in setting rates on insurance. There are a number of reasonable factors used to establish rates: age, gender, health, and so on. But when they used race as a criterion in New York State, if you had two forty-five-year-old brain surgeons and one was black and one was white, they would charge the black person a higher premium for the same coverage. This was because it was said that black people had shorter lives—or perhaps it was simply another case of outright bias.

Oscar Trachtenberg saw a door open when New York State eliminated race as a criterion, and he made a sale to an African-American doctor. The man was so pleased with the service my father provided and what he took to be my father's integrity and demeanor that he referred him to a black dentist. Subsequently, my father built up a practice serving African-American professionals in Brooklyn and, later, Manhattan. His business flourished as they did. He was the first white person elected to the Bedford-Stuyvesant Real Estate Board. He also became very involved in the Urban League and became an officer. He took me to meetings of both groups. Out of a sense of family tradition, I later joined the Urban League in Hartford, Connecticut, and ultimately in Washington as well. Because of my early exposure, I had good feelings toward African Americans that the average white kids of that era didn't because they did not know anyone from that community.

One day my father said that my mother and he had been invited to dinner at the home of one of his black clients. They both got dressed up and went to the Cambridges' house. In response to this evening, my father invited his hosts, along with several of his other clients and their spouses, to a meal at our house. My mother was very nervous about this event and asked, "What will they want to eat?" She wanted to be hospitable but didn't feel confident about what to serve. My father said, "Just prepare whatever you make best." She made a big turkey and some of her own special dishes like kasha, a form of groats (the hulled and crushed grains of various cereals) that is terrific with gravy. Having solved the menu problem, they worried, What will the people next door think when black people start showing up at our threshold? So I was dispatched to assure a neighbor that we were not selling the house; we were having a party for my dad's business associates. In other words, we were not blockbusting!

As I got older, I started going to social events at the homes of some of these clients more frequently. Most of them were of a higher social and economic status than we were and lived in much grander residences. Once we were invited to spend a weekend at someone's summer house on Long Island. We went, and I was nervous because I was going to sleep under a black person's roof. I wondered what would happen and expected that somehow the experience would be different than what I was accustomed to.

The Bedford-Stuyvesant Real Estate Board once held a Christmas party on the roof of a major New York hotel. My mother couldn't go, so my father took me in her place. The elevator operator, who was black, looked at my father when he named the floor we wanted and said, "Are you sure?" Obviously, knowing that this was an African-American event, he didn't think we had been invited. My father disappeared into the crowd quickly, leaving me alone. It seemed that, aside from my dad, I was the only white person there, and I felt nervous. People were dancing and having fun, but there were very few young people. The drinking age was eighteen at that time; I must have been about nineteen. I ordered a scotch and water and was standing, looking at the crowd, when I saw a blond woman about my age and asked her to dance. While we were dancing, I said, "I'm really pleased to see you here." When she wondered why I was so pleased, I told her that I felt uneasy being the only white person there until I saw her. She said, "Well, you still are." She was a fair-skinned African American. It was a very important experience and a good lesson about the silliness of race stereotyping.

After I was inaugurated as president at the University of Hartford in 1977, my father came up to me and said, "To tell you the truth, you did better than I thought you would." Of course, one could take this remark on its face and assume he was talking about my performance at the inauguration, or you could extrapolate to my career in general. To this day, I cannot say which interpretation is the correct one. He was a tough personality, my father.

MY MOTHER was Shoshana Weinstock Trachtenberg. She thought of herself as a Jewish pioneer, having spent her life from age ten to twenty-one growing up in what was then Palestine, and for some of those years having lived in a settler's tent. When she and her family emigrated from Odessa in Russia to Palestine in 1918, the local economy was terrible, and her father, Israel Weinstock, found it very difficult to find work. He ultimately came to the United States, leaving his family behind until he could send for them. He opened a hand laundry in the Bronx and slept in the back of the store. Meanwhile, the family in Tel Aviv lived very modestly. There were three siblings: my Aunt Esther, my Uncle Ralph, and my mother. When local doctors couldn't do much for Esther after a bout with polio, my grandmother took her to Vienna, where she worked as a domestic while Esther received treatment. Ultimately, the effects of the disease were arrested, but Aunt Esther always had a game leg. They were in Austria for a year or so. My mother and uncle stayed behind in Tel Aviv, looking after themselves.

My mother was much more cultured than my father. She loved music and literature, took me to concerts and museums, and made sure that I had an unending supply of books. As a result, as a very young boy,

I read way above my age level. Since I was an only child, she poured her love of the arts on me and, to some extent, compensated for her difficult relationship with my father by overindulging me. Her values became important to me. Also, I knew that I was loved. I believe that having this knowledge as a child gives a person confidence for a lifetime.

My mother also died when she was seventy-one, but three years after my father. As an adult, I used to call her a couple of times a week. One day I called her and got no answer. I called again before I went to bed. Then, in the middle of the night, I woke up, thinking that I had heard her voice calling out, so I got out of bed and telephoned her again; still no answer. By then I was worried and couldn't sleep, so I sat up watching TV all night. At about 10 A.M. the next day, I got word that she had died. Her best friend had noticed that my mother had not picked up the newspapers and let herself into the house, where she found my mother dead. I didn't sleep very much for a year after that. On the anniversary of her passing, we had a ceremony at the unveiling of her memorial. That night, I went home and slept like a baby. As I look back, it is clear to me that for months I had been grieving and was unable to allow myself to rest. But after the unveiling, I was able to permit myself to move on with my life.

THE VOICES of my late parents are in my head, and I converse with them on a regular basis. What bothers me is not that my parents are with me—notwithstanding that they have both been gone for many years—but that I keep losing arguments! One would think that by now I would have figured out how to win. They show up when I am on the cusp of some daunting decision—when there is a knife-edge moment. They don't care about questions like whether to wear the red tie or the blue tie. But if it's how to address an issue of equity or justice or how to respond to something important, they step in. They are an unending resource for me—a super superego.

My parents are big stones in my mosaic, but there are other stones, too—voices that advise me. These voices belong to the late Harold Howe, formerly U.S. commissioner of education; John Brademas, president emeritus of New York University; and John Silber, president emeritus of Boston University. All of them, plus all the other things that have happened in my life, are what make me who I am.

After I finished my law degree, I worked as an assistant to John Brademas when he was a congressman. One day I got a call from Harvard. I had applied earlier for a master's degree in public administration there, but I hadn't been given any financial aid, so I had gone to work. The person on the phone was Gertrude Manly, the registrar of what is now called the John F. Kennedy School of Government. She said that they had given a two-year fellowship to someone else in the class, but he had dropped out after the first year. As a result, they had the second year of the fellowship available and realized that since I had a Yale law degree, they could give me a year's credit toward the master's and I could come to Harvard and take the second year of the master's program with the fellowship. I told this to Brademas and said I would turn it down and stay on for the term I had promised. He said, "You can always work. You'll be working the rest of your life. So go get the master's at Harvard." And I did.

While I was in that MPA program, I was a teaching assistant to Theodore Sizer, the dean of the Harvard Graduate School of Education, who was giving a seminar on the Politics of Education. At the end of the semester, he asked me about my plans. I didn't have plans other than knowing that I needed to go find work. He said, "Why don't you stay here as my assistant dean? You can get a doctorate concurrently. That will give you all the background you could possibly want for a career in education." And so I applied and was admitted to the Harvard Graduate School of Education and was assistant dean—for about a week! I received a phone call, and the voice on the other end said, "Would you please hold for the U.S. commissioner of education, Mr. Harold Howe?" I knew that Howe had been named commissioner, but I didn't know him. All I knew was that the previous commissioner, Francis Keppel, had been invited to leave by President Lyndon Johnson.

Howe came on the line and said he wanted to meet me. He had been looking for an assistant, and Brademas had told him that I was the man for the opening. I said, "I am honored, but I am not sure I am free to take a job—I just took one." He said to come anyway and have lunch with him. After our lunch, he made me an offer. I told him that I knew if I stopped now, I would never finish a doctorate. He said, "I only have a master's, and I am the U.S. commissioner of education. You have earned degrees from Columbia and Yale and now Harvard. Even though you are Jewish, that should be enough! One could certainly argue it is sufficient for most. And I am offering something very special. President Johnson is really committed to education and has made it clear to me that he expects something transformational. This is a unique opportunity." I said, "But there is a question of honor. What do I say to Dean Sizer?" He said, "Leave that to me." So Howe called Sizer, who agreed to let me back off my commitment to him. I left the job at Harvard before I even moved into the office! Nevertheless, Ted Sizer and I have remained friends ever since.

Harold Howe II was a definitive Yankee. Among other things, he was on the Yale Corporation. He was an authentic American, someone so establishment that he could follow a North Star of his own without worrying much about what other people might think. What I mean by that is that he could say no to Lyndon Johnson and LBJ would take that answer almost without objection. When Howe was commissioner of education and President Johnson asked him to go easy on something, he would argue with the president and persuade him not to ask what he was asking him to do. This was important because Johnson was under a lot of political pressure from Mayor Richard Daley of Chicago not to be as rigorous in the enforcement of certain civil rights laws in the Chicago public schools as Howe wanted to be. LBJ had political debts to Daley but agreed, nevertheless, to give Howe a lot of room. Clearly he had respect for Howe, just as I did. I miss him to this day.

I often drafted correspondence for Howe. He received mail from a lot of his friends who were also part of the eastern establishment; people like the Bundy brothers, Elliot Richardson, and John Lindsay. I would be writing to John Smith, for instance, and would go to the Rolodex and see that Smith's wife's name was Betty. When I wrote the return letter for Howe, I would draw from the substance of the letter and then would add a personal note from Howe, like "Give my best to Betty." One day he called me in and said, "Damn! I almost signed this letter. I went to Betty's funeral a year ago. You have to watch that!"

When I worked for Howe, my title was special assistant. I carried the bag, drafted speeches and correspondence, represented him at meetings; it was an extraordinary opportunity. It was so special that I would frequently say to myself, I hope someday my children will have a chance to do something like this. And I had no children then! Harold Howe was a great American. The country is richer for his courageous public service. I have always had him as an ego ideal.

When Richard Nixon came into office, he replaced all of LBJ's political appointees, including Howe. At that time, a colleague of mine named Calvin Lee was going to become dean of arts and sciences at Boston University. He offered me the job of associate dean. I asked, "What does an associate dean do?" He said, "Don't worry, you'll figure it out." That was the beginning of my career in university administration.

I learned an awful lot of what I know about university work at Boston University. It was there I had the good fortune of working for John Silber. He is a remarkable mentor and the dearest of friends. I know of specific cases where he has helped people out who are in dire need or in tragic circumstances but gave his support on the condition that the recipient kept his involvement a secret. And sometimes he would insist that in return for his support, the recipient would have to finish a degree. In other words, he was moving them to the next level of their own success while pretending that doing so was an obligation to him.

If you are ever besieged, you want John Silber covering your back. Lyndon Johnson used a Texas phrase when talking about someone he considered a stalwart. He would say, "That is a man you can go to the well with." The story had to do with the danger back in Indian days of going to the well to get water. Someone had to leave the fort and get water, bringing it back up the hill to the fort. It was necessary to have protection during this task, as it was slow going on the return because of the heavy buckets of water. The man chosen to be the protector had to be brave and willing to stick with the water carrier if there was an attack. John Silber is a man you can go to the well with. The worse the circumstances get, the more he will defend you and stick with you.

Nevertheless, being human, John is a man with shortcomings to complement his virtues. Sometimes he is more human than most. In watching him, I learned as much from his errors as from his successes. I learned to do some things and not to do other things. I generally avoid provoking a fight for its own sake, whereas John takes some joy in com-bat and will invite controversy just for the hell of it. He tries to surround you with argumentation. There is always scorched earth after a dispute with John. He trained as a Kantian philosopher, so he tends to be very certain and he is always more absolute than I am about everything. In addition to having my fair share of self-doubt normally, I generally see several sides to an issue and try to work my way to a compromise. To complicate the process, I frequently argue with myself against my own arguments.

John Silber usually clears the field with his arguments. You have to be really good if you take him on because he can be impatient and annoyed with people who contradict him—unless their arguments are better than his, in which case they earn his respect. If you are merely opposed but can't stand toe-to-toe with him, eventually he has no time for you. If you can go one-on-one, you are okay. But you don't want to be in an arena where it's you against John with other people watching. The audience serves as a catalyst for him. He becomes the athlete in a spectator sport. If you get him alone, your chances of persuading him are better because there is no chance for embarrassment. Sometimes I think he would cede me an argument just to indulge me. Or he would simply conclude that I had a set of skills that he didn't have and maybe he should accede to my judgment.

I care a lot about what John Silber and John Brademas think of me, and I care about what Harold Howe thought of me when he was alive. These three men have been very consequential in my life. I don't want to get psychoanalytical, but you could ask if I compensated for the shortcomings in my relationship with my father by investing so much in my attachments to these three role models. Sure, there is probably some of that in there. Also, they were in a position to teach me things my father could not.

3.

BELIEVE IN THE UNPROVEN

I am an accidental president—in other words, not someone who was the first in his class, got a PhD in philosophy, and then went on to become a university president by moving up through the ranks. I started life in academia as an associate dean and associate professor; most university people begin as assistant professors. And I became president of the University of Hartford at thirty-nine, an age more likely for a dean. Because of that unusual career path, I am somewhat less committed to the protocols and habits of academic life, with all the gravitas that implies. After almost four decades in the university, I am clearly a member, but mine is an outsider-insider perspective and I am still not completely socialized. This is a source of occasional friction, and I am aware that there are times when I seem too lighthearted and unreconstructed for some of my colleagues.

In my career, opportunities have come my way that seemed important and interesting and I have followed my instincts, but not as a feather in the wind of circumstance. I was purposeful and stepped from stone to stone to get from place to place. However, some of my decisions were counter–career moves. To have a fully articulated career as a university administrator, a person has to keep one eye on the clock, and I did not always do that.

My first six years at the University of Hartford would have been sufficient to prepare for my next move. But at the end of those six years, the calls coming my way did not justify leaving. I was having a wonderful time, and my family was happy. I loved the university. I loved the community. My administration was making a difference and putting up buildings and changing the standing of the institution—it was pretty heady stuff. My colleagues and I had taken a regional university and raised its level in a number of important ways. For instance, we developed programs abroad, brought in serious new resources, acquired property for playing fields, and raised the academic benchmarks for faculty and students. Because this was good, honest, exciting work, I willingly stayed there for eleven of the happiest years of my life. That made me almost fifty when I got to GW for the next nineteen of the happiest years of my life. Because of that timing, I was sixty-nine when I stepped down; an awkward age for going the next step. Should I have relocated after ten years at GW and six years at Hartford? From a careerist's perspective, the answer is *yes*. But as I have said earlier, the GW position is one of the best jobs in American higher education, and it was hard for me to even consider leaving work undone.

GW has wonderful students and professors, an excellent location, an endowment that has grown by a billion dollars during my term, an active building program, and very high ratings for both its undergraduate programs and its professional schools. In short, its profile is very appealing to presidential candidates of the highest quality, and my chosen successor validates that statement. Unlike me, he is a bona fide academic with a PhD in English, has been provost and senior vice president for academic affairs of the Johns Hopkins University, and was chosen for his thirty years of higher education experience and his impressive record of academic, fund-raising, and leadership accomplishments.

When Benno Schmidt stepped down as president of Yale, a friend of mine was on the search committee for the next president. He inquired if I would be interested in being a candidate for the job. I asked my wife, Francine, "What do you think?" She is very smart about these things and said, "We spent eleven years in Hartford. We loved Hartford.

But now that we're here in Washington, you have to admit, this is an exciting venue. New Haven is probably less rewarding and is probably not as good for me or the kids. So let's ask if it's sufficiently better for you. Will you add value there as you do here? No. Are they going to pay you better? No. Are you going to do different kinds of work? No. Are you going to be more respected by the faculty? No. Are the students going to be nicer to you? No. In the end, how is it distinguishable? You get an arguably better first paragraph in your obituary! 'Stephen Trachtenberg, the former president of Yale University' is going to get better placement in *The New York Times* when you die and more space—and maybe even in GW's hometown paper, *The Washington Post*—than 'Stephen Trachtenberg, the former president of George Washington University.' But is that sufficient compensation for pulling up your life and moving your family?" When she put it that way, I called up my friend and said, "I'm going to pass."

THE QUALITIES that define a president have changed from those of a less complicated past. As a result, the broader the thinking of those searching for a new leader, the greater the pool of talent they will explore. Based on the expectations I have encountered along the way, it seems to me that a university president must have these important qualities:

The iron endurance of Cal Ripken
The intellect of Gottfried Wilhelm Leibniz, the last man to know everything
The money sense of J. Pierpont Morgan
The inventiveness of Thomas Alva Edison
The spontaneous rhetorical ability of Winston Churchill
The diplomacy of Dag Hammarskjöld or maybe Bismarck
The ability of Harry Houdini to get out of tight situations
The conciliatory powers of Abraham Lincoln
The storytelling talent of Stephen King
The loving kindness of Mother Teresa
The virtue above suspicion of Caesar's wife

The luck of the Irish
The patience of Job

Having all of these qualities is—*maybe*—enough to get a candidate called back for a second interview. I am aware that most of the people I cited—except for Stephen King, Cal Ripken, and the lucky Irish—are dead. This is not to say that I think these qualities—virtues, even—have also died. Far from it! But it is no small undertaking to find them all in one person who can also deal with today's students, with alumni, with those who see themselves as constructive critics of the university, with poets and magical thinkers, as well as with those solid citizens who sit on the Board of Trustees. It's a lot of water to carry, and most candidates have only two shoulders.

TALK ABOUT how much one loves the job is generally not the norm in academia. For instance, if you ask a couple of former faculty members how they happened to become deans, they will often give an answer of the following kind: "I was walking across the campus one day and someone threw a net over my head and when I got free, I discovered I was the dean; woe is me!" They are not telling the truth. Everything they knew, every trick, every bit of their energy went into being selected as dean. There is something inherent in the culture of academia that makes people feel obliged to deny ambition and to publicly reject any desire to be an administrator. For some, it is imperative even to apologize for moving up. But make no mistake about this: anyone who gets to be a college president or a dean made it happen! They tried hard to get to that place. No one is shanghaied in academe. In my case, I am not embarrassed to say I was delighted—thrilled—to have the job. Ninety-eight percent of the time I had a great time; 2 percent of the time, well, too bad for me. If everyone were as happy as I was in my work, it might be a better world.

I was outer-directed when I was younger and cared about how I compared to other people and how I was seen by other people. These things mean less to me nowadays. In fact, in recent years I have almost transcended the envy that comes with ambition. While president, my envious thoughts turned to what I wished for my institution. What could I do for my faculty? My students? I would think of what I could do to make GW a better university if only I had Harvard's endowment. After all, if Harvard wanted to, it could stop charging tuition. But at GW—like hundreds of other universities—I had to work with more limited resources. While I marveled at what we were accomplishing at GW, I could always dream of doing more.

That kind of envy is not the same as wishing for a new car. On a personal level, I was minimizing and downsizing my material life. While my personal needs grew smaller, my official self would think, Wouldn't it be great if we could get that new science building right now rather than in five years? Also, I became a bit wistful about things I would like to revisit. I sometimes remembered behaving in a way that no longer meets with my approval and I thought I would like to go back, live those moments again, and get it right. There were times when I came out of conversations and thought to myself, What I should have said is . . .

One such occasion came when I was thirty-four and was being considered for a college presidency. The search had been narrowed to two people, and the chairman of the search committee asked me, "Mr. Trachtenberg, don't you think you are a little young to be a university president?" I suppose I could have given him a list of five outstanding people who had risen to the position at my age or younger. I could have said something like "Robert Maynard Hutchins was a very distinguished president of the University of Chicago who achieved the post when he was thirty years old. He had previously been dean of the Yale Law School at the age of twenty-eight while he was an associate professor without tenure and then went on to Chicago where he did brilliantly." But I didn't say that! Instead, I made a flip remark that could have been construed as mildly sacrilegious by someone who didn't know me. It was meant to be a funny line, but I knew immediately that it was totally inappropriate. The chairman of the search committee certainly didn't think it was humorous; I saw his jaw drop. Not surprisingly, I didn't get the post.

One would hope I was informed by that experience and became

more thoughtful as a result. On the other hand, it has always been very hard for me to suppress what I think is a really great funny line. I suppose another interpretation of that situation might be that I knew even before I said it that the comment was the wrong thing to say and I wanted to test the knife edge. Or, maybe a psychoanalyst would say it was my way of rejecting the job before the committee rejected me.

As president, when I sat in GW Faculty Senate meetings, I thought of many things I *could* say, but refrained. If I had said them all, I probably would have had a no confidence vote years ago. Fortunately, the faculty members usually understood and generously laughed at my humorous remarks. As much as they enjoyed fencing with the administration, I think most of them knew that I was devoted to them and to their best interests. It's just that they couldn't resist being faculty and I could hardly ever resist being me.

Humor—ethnic and otherwise—comes as part of my New York background. The city is a lippy place, and it was always useful for me to have some defense to use in schoolyards and classrooms, where tough kids and funny kids had to coexist. There are rewards for the occasional funny remark, and humor becomes part of who you are, along with your ethnicity and background. I am no different. It's probably not an accident that comedians are often outsiders peering in—a good position from which to see the absurdity of life.

Looking back, I will have to say that one of my favorite unscripted comic moments occurred when President Bill Clinton came to campus to make a major address. As President Clinton and I walked onstage, the behind-the-curtain voice of an announcer filled the room with stentorian tones and said, "Ladies and gentlemen, the president of the United States and Stephen Joel Trachtenberg." It was my job to introduce the president, so I walked up to the podium while President Clinton stood nearby. I waited for a second, pointed to myself, and began, "Good morning. *I'm* Stephen Joel Trachtenberg." The audience immediately saw the joke and roared. The president paused, then understood and laughed heartily, patting me on the back. But for a split second, I worried that I had gone too far.

• • •

THERE IS always a tendency to see things in patterns. I don't know if that is a good idea, but at a minimum, one can perceive a copycat tendency. For instance, if there is some excitement such as the Harvard dustup regarding President Lawrence Summers, suddenly everyone is watching the American campus. Faculty members at small community colleges start to think, Well, if Harvard's faculty can do something like that, so can we. In other words, people start feeling empowered. The impermissible thus becomes permissible, and we suddenly witness a rash of boldness within university faculties. When something like this happens, some presidents don't know what to do and resign rather than saying something like "This is a teaching moment, not an occasion for a beheading. Let's talk." Such resignations often have less to do with the actions themselves than with trustees who are unsure about how to behave under such circumstances.

In the Summers case, I can only speculate about what would have happened if the Harvard Corporation had talked with the faculty leadership of Arts and Sciences (which was the source of most of the arguments against President Summers) and said, "We understand you have issues with Larry Summers, but he is the president, his tenure in the job is our responsibility, and, although we have heard your concerns, it is time for you to stop this. You have become dysfunctional. If he fails, Harvard fails." The faculty might then have had the sense to seek less traumatic ways to articulate their concerns.

I have been told that the faculty of the Harvard Law School, Medical School, and Business School—unlike the School of Arts and Sciences—were *not* particularly critical of President Summers. I am left to wonder, what would happen if the corporation had asked, "What do the professional schools think?" They might have answered, "We think he's fine." The corporation fellows could then have said, "We polled all the schools and found that Arts and Sciences have issues; the Law School, Medical School, and Business School think he's fine; and so on. Our judgment is that several 'fines' are better than one 'not-so-fine.' We think we should all just carry on. Arts and Sciences faculty, you need self-restraint." Wouldn't the faculty have been obliged to be more graceful? I think the whole thing was a failure of leadership on the part of the board. We hear that the board settled generously with President Summers and rightly made him a university professor. I think its members were properly embarrassed at their failure and felt obliged to find some way to assuage their guilt.

The problem of voluntary boards is that there has been very little downside for getting it wrong. Even in a major scandal like the one at American University in Washington, D.C., where the board overlooked excesses by the president, no one remembers the names of board members, in spite of the fact that the story was reported in *The Washington Post* for weeks. The fact is that university board members aren't obliged to wear a scarlet letter when they make bad mistakes. Most university trustees work diligently and give substantial time, effort, and money to the institution. But some people join a university board, never show up for meetings, and don't give financial help to the university either. For those people, board membership appears to be an honor to wear on their lapel rather than an operative responsibility for them to shoulder.

A lot of the situation with boards is currently in transition. This is probably because Enron has made the world a different place. Today, if you are on the audit committee of a public company board and aren't paying close attention, you are some kind of fool. In the case of an upset, if you can't explain how and why you voted, you can be fined or otherwise sanctioned. Board members now feel they are under scrutiny as never before. Of course, this hasn't completely translated to the not-for-profit world. But increasingly, the Sarbanes-Oxley sentiment is creeping into that world and, done properly, this can be a good thing. Sarbanes-Oxley is the act that established new or enhanced standards for accounting and reporting practices for all U.S. boards and management of public companies and public accounting firms. It will also be a good thing for universities *if* it doesn't make administrators and trustees excessively risk-averse.

•   •   •

YOU CAN'T drive an institution without a leap of faith—sort of like what you have in religions. In other words, you have to believe in the unproven. Things that in normal discourse we would find implausible without evidence, we are prepared to believe in other circumstances. Why do people feel great pride in their city if the Washington Redskins win at football or the Boston Red Sox win at baseball? They get fanatic about it; they wear hats and scarves with the team logo; men wear funny faces and women's dresses and act crazy. Before the team began to win in recent years, people bemoaned the Boston Red Sox World Series experiences and attributed them to a curse by Babe Ruth. Is it just Americans who act this way? Not at all. It's all very interesting. I admit that I am a participant and often actively root for a basketball team. But why?

Presidents have to believe in the institutions they head. If you manufacture, say, slippers, you see how you add value and how society is better for your product and why you are receiving money for it. But if you are educating people, assessing your results is far less easy. How can we really know if, after four years as a student, someone is enhanced by the experience? Or is he simply four years older? Has she developed sufficiently beyond where she began to justify the time and expense of those four years, as contrasted to four years of doing something else? To a certain extent, we accept on faith the value of an education.

People from all over the world make immense sacrifices to get higher education. Each year, 20,000 people apply to come to GW as undergraduates and only 2,300 become freshmen. Why do people accept the myth of collegiate rankings and make important choices based on them rather than on personal perception? Why do young people let their parents drop out of the country club and give up family vacations so they can pay college tuitions? Why are their parents willing to accommodate them?

My own father urged me to go to Brooklyn College. It was, and still is, an excellent municipal university. But I wanted to go to Columbia, an Ivy League University. For me, the choice was due to a quite real yet somewhat irrational belief that I would "do better" for having gone there. My mother sided with me, and we induced my father to accede.

I would have been just fine if I had gone to Brooklyn College. But I believe I would have been a different person if I had. Something happened to me at Columbia that allowed me to see myself differently than if I had gone elsewhere. Perhaps the difference for me was a different threshold of aspiration.

Scott Cowen is the president of Tulane, who was at the university's helm when Hurricane Katrina hit New Orleans and devastated it. The Tulane Web site says this about Scott:

> *In August of 2005, Hurricane Katrina devastated the city of New Orleans, flooded two-thirds of Tulane's campus and dispersed its students, faculty and staff around the country. Despite incurring more than $400 million in losses and damages, Tulane, under Cowen's leadership, was repaired and a remarkable 87 percent of its full-time students returned for classes in January of 2006 . . .*
>
> *In the aftermath of Katrina, Cowen . . . re-opened Tulane, the city's largest employer, took the lead in re-opening the city's first post-Katrina public school and helped other New Orleans institutions such as Xavier and Dillard universities recover. Cowen also chaired the education subcommittee of Mayor C. Ray Nagin's Bring New Orleans Back Commission, [which] developed and presented a plan to city and state leaders designed to rebuild and transform the city's public schools into a model system.*

The Katrina tragedy provided a launching pad to greatness for Cowen that might be far beyond what most people could have reasonably anticipated. He is now the savior of an important American institution and, as such, will go down as a hero in history. I'd like to think he learned much at GW, where he got an MBA and a PhD.

I wonder if it is possible for Scott Cowen ever to do anything greater than what he did at Tulane. Clearly Tulane is depending on him to continue leading it out of its very substantial challenges. I wonder if he could ever be comfortable leaving Tulane for another presidency; it seems that he has become too important to that institution to even contemplate that—at least for some time.

One obligation of a university president is to help seed the future with tomorrow's college and university presidents by encouraging them in their careers and helping prepare them for the job. In the coming decade, there will be an immense turnover in university leadership as the baby-boom generation retires. I worry that college and university presidencies are seen as daunting. The kind of people with the necessary vision, courage, confidence, and dedication for the work might be dissuaded from taking these jobs because of the unattractive and overly demanding aspects that have become part of the assignment.

Alas, that statement might also be true of our national political leaders. Over the years I have had the good fortune to sit in on discussions with people who were plausible candidates for president of the United States as they worked through a decision on whether or not they wanted to be candidates, and after examining the issue, decided not to do it. One of these was Colin Powell. I was at a dinner party at the embassy of Uruguay seated next to General Powell and said to him, "General, there is talk that you might run for president, and I surely hope you will do it. If you do, I'll take a year's leave from the university and, because I used to be a reasonably good speech writer, I think I could make a contribution to your campaign." He said, "I thought you were a Democrat." And I said, "Well, I am, but I am an American first and a patriot and I think you would be a wonderful president and I'm willing to do what I can to help you." Long after that evening, Colin Powell telephoned me at home. He said, "I am calling to give you a heads-up. Tomorrow I am announcing that I will *not* be running for president. I remember our conversation, and I didn't want you to read about my decision in the papers." I told him, "You make me doubly sad. Somebody with the political grace to give someone like me a call at a time like this ought to be president."

4.

TO GET THINGS DONE,
RISK BEING WRONG

Many nonuniversity people view universities through a lens conditioned by a variety of perceptions. Many images of the university come from American literature, TV, and film. I suspect that, to many people, the picture of a university president is somewhere between Dr. William Todhunter Hall, the scholarly and witty president of Ivy College in the famous radio series *The Halls of Ivy*, and the authoritarian and humorless Dean Wormer of Faber College in the classic movie comedy *Animal House*. Another is the image imbedded in the history of the university; it comes from church institutions. For instance, the word "dean" is closely associated with the word "deacon," a clerical ranking in the Christian Church. The ceremonial caps and gowns that academics wear derive from clerical garments worn in medieval churches and then in universities. I think that because of their clerical roots, higher education institutions are uncomfortable talking publicly about money. That is, unless they are asking for it.

Americans seem inured to the enormous sums great athletes or hedge fund managers receive. But they become troubled when a university employee—whether a professor of medicine, a prominent law dean, or a president—is paid a salary considered too robust for the university setting; a salary that would be seen as quite modest in a corporate, entertainment, or sports environment. I wonder why people accede to someone in a corporation being paid millions of dollars and someone in a university—with an equally challenging portfolio and commensurate responsibilities—being paid far less. Perhaps they believe—in some subliminal sense—that university presidents are descended from those clerics I mentioned and should have taken vows of poverty when they entered the profession! There is an implicit assumption that in deciding they were going to be professors and college administrators, they also agreed that they were going to be compensated dramatically less than what they would be if they were to become lawyers, physicians, or executives in corporate America.

Even the best-paid American university presidents would hardly be noticed on any kind of chart of high executive compensation in America. This includes even those at the biggest, most complex universities with billions of dollars in operating budgets and the need to constantly make important economic decisions affecting a sizable resource. If university presidents were paid on a par with corporate people, I believe they would be excoriated. Having said this, I must add that because of competition for talent, university salaries have recently become somewhat more competitive and more generous than they once were.

A LOT of people believe they are stakeholders in our business and are both empowered and entitled to tell you what they think about what you are doing, how you are doing it wrong, and how you could do it better. A former president of Columbia University once said that the first thing he did each morning was read the student newspaper editorial to find out what he had done wrong the previous day!

It is a good thing for people to have a proprietary interest in the university, but it is also important that stakeholders understand that there must be a limit to their participation. For instance, I had an exchange of letters with a very caring alumnus of our Law School who argued that the law school alumni should have been consulted before the school took a position on the very controversial topic of whether or not to allow military recruiters into the Law School. In our case, the GW law faculty believed that the military's discriminatory policy "Don't ask, don't tell," regarding gays and lesbians, justified banning the military from the law school. Our alumnus was irked that the Law School faculty had voted on a national subject without consulting the entire Law School alumni body. I understood his perspective, but the thought that we should have a plebiscite of all our graduates before the Law School can decide on a controversial subject is implausible as well as impossible. We certainly did not want to lose his patronage or his affection, so I took a lot of time to discuss with him why the university is not like a law firm, where all the partners could conceivably gather in a room and come to an agreement. It's just not practical or possible to get thousands of graduates who are scattered all over the world to have an educated discourse on a controversial subject.

Very few issues in a university are uncomplicated, and I had my own trouble with that faculty vote. Specifically, Congress was concerned that universities that were receiving a great deal of taxpayer money were preventing military recruiters from visiting to seek talent because they objected to the discriminatory military policy against gays and lesbians. By law, federal funds were denied to any university blocking access to the federal government. Our Law School and others thought that was unconstitutional. A number of law schools then decided to test the law. Our law faculty participated in the litigation, which ultimately went to the Supreme Court of the United States for resolution. I said to the dean of the Law School, "I cannot let the Law School faculty, by its actions, imperil the federal funding for research and financial aid of the entire university. If the law permitted us to carve out the Law School as separate from the whole, I could agree to have you go ahead because the amount of money the Law School gets from the federal government is so much less than, for instance, the Medical School. It's one thing to be the dean of a law school in a matter like this; it's another matter altogether to be the president, who has the welfare of the entire university to worry about. All of GW's federal money could be cut off!" I told the dean that the university would comply with the law. Testing issues like this is more comfortably the role of institutions that have huge endowments and can suffer the economic loss better than a university like ours. I suspect that most university presidents—out of responsibility to the larger community—do not like having to take a position that they might not take as individuals. But that is the nature of the presidency and the responsibility that goes with it. The case went to the Supreme Court, and it was unanimously decided that the U.S. government *could* cut off the funding in such a case.

As a president, I think that deciding when you need to listen to others and when you need to go your own way is a real art form. People want you to acknowledge that they are stakeholders in the institution and they have a role in determining its direction. But sometimes, because you are thinking about the university all the time in a very intense way, you have to believe that your vision is more informed and thus the one to follow. It also matters that you are ultimately responsible.

When I came to GW, the campus didn't look much like a university to me. People used to say, "I didn't know when I got on the campus, and I didn't know when I got off." Where was the center of the campus? Where was a place to sit down and read in the shade of a tree? Where could a professor take a small seminar group when the spring weather suggested an outdoor class? Where were the ceremonial gates? Where were the statues? What said "campus" to visitors? Over time, the many new buildings, along with public art and new green spaces, all came together in a greatly enhanced physical place more worthy of our academic ambition and our prime location in Washington, D.C.

I like to think that the best scholarship and the best learning take place in an environment that is stimulating and attractive. We have changed the rather drab aspect of the old GW with the placement of attractive university flags and signs, with art, and with new or enhanced existing architecture. GW has built more than $500 million worth of new buildings, with more to come. At each corner of the campus is a bust of George Washington; they mark the boundaries of the campus. We have put up outdoor sculptures on lawns in front of buildings, in the yard, and in the plaza. For the first time, sculptures on the GW campus are being included in a book on outdoor art in Washington,

D.C. Some pages of this book will be dedicated solely to works on our campus.

I believe it is also helpful for a university to show a sense of humor and overcome the tendency to take itself too seriously. For instance, I always think fondly of the wonderful stone gargoyles that embellish the facade of the Yale Law School. They are delightful spoofs of judges, lawyers, masked criminals, and more. The alumni of the school are constantly reminded of them through detail photographs in the annual report, the alumni magazine, and various fund-raising materials. A hippopotamus statue I gave to the university as a faux mascot is a tongue-in-cheek inside joke. Although an "official" plaque claims that there were hippos in the Potomac River, of course people know this is not true and that our hippo is kind of a gag. But I find that some people who come on campus actually begin to wonder if there were hippos in North America! In any case, people appreciate the statue and it does make the campus a bit more user-friendly. Many students and visitors actually rub its nose for luck—as the plaque suggests. Like the Yale gargoyles, the hippo often shows up in photos in school publications.

I don't think there are many people today who would criticize the ornamental gates we added to the campus a few years ago. But when we started to put them up, there were those who asked, "Why are you spending money on those gates and not on my priority?" We had raised the money specifically for the gates because it seemed that they—along with many other touches aimed at improving pride of place—were important to the university. Today, the gates are a visual symbol that signals the university's sense of self. They have an aesthetic quality, and when prospective GW students and parents come to look at the university, they actually remember later that the university looks like a campus and not just a collection of faceless buildings in an urban neighborhood. We could not pay for all the work associated with the gates at once, so we did so over a three-year period. People saw the tempietto, the sculptures, the landscaping, and the gates coming together slowly, little by little. In other words, they didn't have the advantage of the full vision that we had in our mind's eye. So for three years there were questions and criticism until the project was done. In the end, the comments stopped, but no one ever got up and said, "You know, on second thought, what a terrific idea!"

If you are a university president and what you do for a living is think about the university, you are going to have ideas about what the place can be and do that are not as apparent to people who are teaching chemistry, working in the hospital, or simply living in the neighborhood. As president, when I wanted to do something I could see clearly in my mind, I tried to do my best to bring as many people into the picture as possible. But I did not always succeed. I couldn't wait for uniformity of judgment, so I just went ahead and suffered the criticism of those who thought that what I was doing was wrong, irrelevant, or too expensive. I just had to have faith that if I was right, the passage of time would heal the divide. Or not. If you want to get things done, you have to risk being wrong.

WE OFTEN have unrealistic expectations for our institutions and our fellow human beings. A new children's park near my house has a bouncy surface—something built in so that when children fall down, they don't get hurt. A question comes to mind: How did those of us from earlier generations ever survive, having spent our youth using playgrounds with asphalt or cement surfaces where kids actually got hurt? Obviously, no one has a yearning to go back to those days of hard, uncompromising park surfaces. It makes sense to use our twenty-first-century technology to make a more forgiving, child-friendly surface. But the effort to make all of life safe from any kind of bruise or hurt is very troubling to me, especially when institutions like universities are held to an ever higher benchmark. For example, we often find ourselves at the cutting edge of the development of standards in human relations. Universities are basically very pious and want to do the right thing with their students; but sometimes "the correct thing" has not been resolved and we find ourselves groping in real life toward a definition of what the best practice should be. To complicate things, we often end up in a catch-22 situation and can be held liable no matter what course we take.

A specific example of this is trying to decide what to do with a student who some believe may be a danger to him- or herself or others and has attempted or threatened suicide; or a student whose roommate has committed suicide and who, in a time of melancholy, indicates the type of thinking that makes another person wonder if he or she is going to hurt himself or herself as well. The question for the university becomes: How can we best serve such a student and, moreover, the other students on campus? We ask ourselves if we should keep a troubled student like that in the university and try as best we can to provide a therapeutic environment—or, being humble about our ability to actually be effective, find a way as gracefully as possible to have the student relocated to where he or she can receive necessary professional help. I think universities are groping in the dark trying to figure out how to get it right in such circumstances.

There are external groups with many different positions on the suicide issue, for instance. Some advocates argue for what they think is best for students and others argue for another view. Parents say they will sue a university because it didn't take an action. Other parents say they will sue because the university *did* take action. There have been cases of this sort at other colleges and universities, and also in a private boarding school. One institution put the student out on the basis that it couldn't be sure the student would not commit suicide. Others have not put students out and they have committed suicide. The parents of two such students sued, saying that the university in question should have known their child was in trouble. They took the position that the resident counselor should have been more alert and the institution should have protected the student from committing suicide. In the case of the student who was dismissed, the suit claimed that the university overreacted to a student's remarks and prematurely declared its inability to oversee the student.

Even more recently, we have the tragic consequences of a murderous rampage by a mentally ill student at Virginia Polytechnic Institute. How could his strange, menacing behavior on campus among his increasingly concerned peers and professors have been properly interpreted and the student removed to a therapeutic environment before thirty-two people—professors and students—died needlessly and many others were grievously wounded? In this case, the student who committed the atrocities had previously been found to be a danger to himself—presumably, that would mean suicidal.

In such matters, to what standard can we hold our people? How comprehensive is the responsibility of a university for the welfare of a student who is living in its residence halls and attending its classes? Are there different standards for a small rural liberal arts college that has 1,000 students than for a large urban university that has 10,000 or up to 40,000 students?

I don't know the answers; I do know that we are never going to be able to make the world incident-proof. Much of the reason for lawsuits is tied to plaintiffs' lawyers, who see an opportunity to turn a tragic and troubling moment into litigation and a controversy over money. Even without the threat of litigation, universities are, by nature, inclined to do the right thing and will almost always try to be as empathetic as possible and to accommodate to changing definitions of "best practices" as they evolve. I certainly don't think that situations like these are enhanced in any way by someone winning a lawsuit against the university and collecting money.

A CAMPUS is a place to embrace diversity, to witness passions, to delve into history. Alas, now and again, grown-ups intrude. We worked diligently on the dark days after 9/11 to persuade our government not to keep international students out of our universities and thereby create further bad feelings all over the world when young people were seeking visas to study here. Of course, one can't be a fool about this issue. Terrorists do have the ability to masquerade as students, and universities should exercise caution. But we don't want to keep international young people from meeting our young people and learning about us. When I have traveled around the world, I have met graduates of GW who are inordinately proud of their time at the university, and they boast of it. Why would we want to cut this off?

While still president, I struck up a conversation with a young man on our Mount Vernon campus, asking, "Where are you from?" He answered, "Riyadh." I asked, "The one in Saudi Arabia?" He asked, "Is there another one?" We both laughed, and I asked him if he is facing any issues. He said that not a single harsh word had been directed at him and that he was very happy at GW. I thought, What a wonderful thing. People worry about the ability of groups like Israelis and Palestinians to get along, but somehow, on a campus, students go about their lives and work together, study together without difficulties. The truth is, undergraduates generally set a very good example for grownups throughout the world.

5.

Don't Make Everybody
Mad at You at the Same Time

Some of the things I have learned came the hard way: I made a mistake and the result made me wiser. I can only assume this is true not only of university presidents but of all those who manage institutions and people. In the spirit of fellowship with the presidents yet to come into office or, in fact, yet to be born, I offer the following list of rules in no particular order.

> **ONE:** *You shouldn't make everybody mad*
> *at you at the same time.*

ONE PRESIDENT of a small college had a very brief presidency—in fact, less than two years. When he came to the college, he became concerned that the student body was consuming too much alcohol and that the faculty wasn't being sufficiently rigorous. Who would not want to reduce alcohol consumption and enhance academic standards? I think his mistake was in trying to take on both issues at the same time. If one chooses to go down this road, it is better to address only one constituency at a time. He provoked the students by seeming to suggest they were a bunch of drunken louts, and he provoked the faculty by seeming to suggest that they were lazy or not living up to expectations.

Then the college's student newspaper published a very critical editorial saying that if he was truly as unhappy with the students and the faculty as he seemed, maybe he was in the wrong place. That was picked up by the local papers, and the question began circulating in the wider community. This underscored a great truth: the media plays an extraordinary catalytic—as well as observatory—role in the life of institutions. At this point, the issue reached the attention of the board of trustees, who perceived that the faculty and students were unhappy with their president. That provoked the board members, and they became the third angry constituency. The president had not been at that college long enough to build up enough goodwill to sustain the levees when this hurricane hit. It wasn't his first presidency, so he should have known this rule.

TWO: *Your message should be uplifting rather than blatantly critical.*

A PRESIDENT of a university made a speech in which he referred to "mush" when talking about the minds of the student body. Essentially he said that the students' heads were full of mush coming in when they matriculated and full of mush going out when they graduated. In one phrase, he provoked the student body, the faculty, and the alumni— and all of them turned on him at once!

Obviously, a college president should be concerned if he or she feels that the academic experience provided by the university has not sufficiently served the students. It would be appalling for a president not to care if students are underwhelmed by their undergraduate studies. But a better way to handle this disappointment would be to say, "What a tragedy it is that, given the special quality of the students we admit, we are not honing them into the best they can be. We should commit ourselves to making them even more accomplished. This is a nonthreatening statement; generally, people can all agree that there is always room for improvement. Even Mother Teresa might well have believed that she could do better, and more! How you suggest "We could all be better and live up to our potential" is the critical ingredient in a president's success in delivering the message.

THREE: *You should avoid introducing more than one idea at a time.*

I HAVE long realized that if you are writing to someone, you shouldn't ask two questions in one letter. In fact, I have been known to write to the same person twice or more in one day, asking one question in one letter and another question in the next. My reasoning is that the two questions could actually be going to two different departments to be researched. It is much cleaner for the addressee to refer letter A to person one and letter B to person two, if more than one person will be providing information for the answers.

This principle also applies in a more important scenario. For instance, if you go to the faculty and want to propose some innovation, you don't want to give them many issues to fight with you about. You want to narrow the debate to the specific matter you have on your agenda. So if you say to the faculty, "We should go from offering five three-credit courses to offering four four-credit courses per semester as a normal curriculum, or, to put it another way, we should go from a forty-course BA degree to a thirty-two-course BA degree, as they do at many other first-rate colleges," that is a sufficient change for the institution and should be considered by itself.

That was one of the issues I myself raised in a letter. Alas, I then added a second idea. I wrote that since the city had put a cap on enrollment at the university, we needed to find a way to use our facilities more efficiently. If we were to go from a two-semester to a three-semester curriculum, we could actually increase our enrollment and still comply with the mandates that the city had imposed to limit enrollment. We would expand our universe by spreading it over three semesters rather than two. That would mean that we would use our facilities a lot more with not much greater cost and we would earn additional tuition money to support faculty and student interests. It seemed clear that the efficiencies achieved by those two changes would probably give the university ten years of budget breathing room, during which time we could run a capital campaign. We could invest the capital that was raised during that decade and be stronger by a billion dollars beyond our current endowment. Presumably, this would ultimately allow us to improve the quality of the institution, pay the faculty appropriately and competitively, and continue to enhance the facilities; all good things.

Unfortunately, in my passion to get the job done and my belief in the obvious added value of these changes to the institution, I made the blunder of proposing these two innovations at once. The faculty rejected both of those ideas outright and further refused to even talk about them. In doing so, they ignored the very high risk that without such a new departure, our ability to stay as academically aggressive as we have been during our revitalization period would be diminished and the resulting capital campaign would be less successful. To my great regret, I was forced to conclude that a different spokesperson might have more traction. And so I left this happy assignment to my successor. Perhaps if I had introduced each idea separately, the result would have been different.

FOUR: *Try to build a community constituency.*

AT THE beginning of my presidency, I visited every corporate leader in town, the mayor of Washington, *The Washington Post* editorial board, and more. I really urged the outside community to support the university and the changes that were ahead. For instance, I went to many churches every Sunday for months. Benjamin Mays, the late former president of Morehouse College, once said that the way to get to know the black community was to go to the black churches, and I followed his wise advice. So in the beginning of my presidency in a city that was predominantly black, I would call a church and ask the pastor if I could come on Sunday. When services began, I would join the congregation. Frequently, I would be asked to stand and say a few words, and I would often be asked to remain and eat lunch with them. This was just one of the many outside constituencies I knew would be important to the future of the university. I tried to cover as many groups as I could, and in the long run, I think it helped me advance some of what the university needed and served the city well.

FIVE: *Improving the overall image of a place is important.*

WHEN I arrived at GW, the university was a much grayer place and its self-perception was very different from what it is now. So was the perception of the people on the outside. I believe that a lot of life is optics; how you are seen is how you are in the minds of many people. Therefore, I devoted a lot of time not only to having the school become better but also to having observers *see* it as better.

The principle works in the following way: If you don't get into Princeton and come to GW and spend four years feeling that you came to your second choice, the slightest inconvenience confirms your feeling that you are at your second-choice school. On the other hand, if you are at your first choice, you will put up with a great deal because you believe you are at a great place. When I was at the University of Hartford, friends of mine would stop to visit or they would be dropping off their children at places like Wesleyan or Yale and would tell me about the experience. They didn't know what was going on in the philosophy or geology departments and could only comment on what they saw in the brief time they were there. So, of course, they would tell me about the horrible, small, or dirty room their freshman son or daughter was assigned to live in and would complain that it was a lower-quality facility than the cells felons are kept in. But the kids were at their first-choice schools and were so happy to be there that they ignored their poor accommodations and lived with them cheerfully!

On the other hand, if students came to the old GW feeling that they had "settled" for it after being denied by their first-choice schools, even if you gave them Four Seasons Hotel–like accommodations, they would still be discontented. Anything that went wrong would simply be a confirmation of their unhappy status. If you go somewhere you believe is first-rate, you may complain that the registrar is screwing up, but you probably won't use that as evidence of the inadequacy of the entire school. But if you are at a place you consider a second choice, you probably will see it as a justification of your view.

Soon after I arrived, we started advertising my office hours and inviting people to come and talk to the president. At first, students would come to me with a litany of complaints. They would tell me what was wrong with the residence halls, the faculty, and so on. We had set about visibly improving things immediately and making them better. So after five years, although all was still not perfect, I began to notice that the people coming to my office hours were saying things like "I'm having a wonderful time here!" Or they would say, "No complaints, I am just stopping to meet the president." Of course, there were still complaints, but I could see that we had turned the corner. Some of the problems students came with were quite natural: things like, "My father died and I won't be able to come back next semester unless I get more financial support." We would look into the specific issues and fix them if they were fixable. Over time, our efforts had enhanced the place in the minds of the students. Along with the reality, the perceptions had also turned around. Of course, we had also been working very hard on the academic condition of the university to make it a first choice.

It also doesn't hurt to pay attention to the way things are named when you want to improve perceptions. When I came to GW, the Law School was called The National Law Center. Who would ever know by that name that it was a university law school—and a good one, too? One day the Law School dean and I took a walk around the neighborhood near campus to do some rough research on the name. We stopped one person and I asked, "Can you tell us how to get to the National Law Center?" The man hesitated for a long time and then pointed in the direction of Union Station on Capitol Hill. We asked several others and got more answers as off target as the first. No one indicated that something with that name was a block away on a nearby university campus. The dean and I decided that calling it The George Washington University Law School would help give the Law School the kind of recognition it deserved. Today, in a world in which institutions are competitive and all of them like to say they dominate the rankings, I can truthfully say that GW is one of the thirty law schools that claim to be in the top twenty.

SIX: *Maintaining perspective can be difficult.*

I WONDER if all university presidents spend a portion of their time with very small problems, as I often did. In my case, when a department felt ill-treated I would try to help it get over that. By the time the negotiations and soothing were over, I might have spent so much time thinking about the specific mission or curriculum or petty cash budget of that department that all the other departments had momentarily vanished from my sight. The same is often true of many other burning issues—such as whether three additional security cameras are worth more or less than one additional officer. It boils down to a problem of focus and perspective. You can't see all of America when you're in the depths of Death Valley or even at the heights of Mount Rainier. Thus, when I tried to focus on the future of higher education in America, I sometimes experienced a panicky vertigo and a desire to say something like "Can't we just solve this problem by growing our budget?"

SEVEN: *Every faculty needs a few crackpots.*

NOBODY WANTS a university where every faculty member is a crackpot, but I think every university should have some of these; very likely, many do. It adds a certain frisson to conversation, and it helps to define the nature of academic institutions. After all, they are places where the strangest things can be said without censure and where people are allowed to be innovative, and even—I dare say—revolutionary in their thinking. Certainly, one doesn't seek revolutionary thinking in most normal endeavors. But a university is not ordinary because it thrives on competing ideas and styles.

Often university professors are in the profession because they are the kind of people who want the freedom to be more outspoken and less conventional. Some trade higher incomes for this freedom and live more modest lives because of it. If the university is working well, we explain this to people even when they are undergraduates. I have sometimes written to critics of the university and said to them, "Look, I'm disappointed; apparently we let you down when you were a student here because we failed to make you understand the nature of the institution and why we are not a branch of the Republican or Democratic Party, or why we can have in our midst somebody whom we might not want to invite home to dinner but who is, nevertheless, a useful participant in the larger university conversation."

When I think of this subject, I think about pearls. The beauty of a pearl is achieved by layers of a coating that an oyster generates to surround a bit of grit that has gotten into its shell. If you think about a law school faculty, for instance, having a few annoying voices among sixty is not the worst thing in the world. If there are 1,000 faculty members in a university and one of them is saying something a person doesn't like, there are 999 others that person can listen to whose views probably won't disappoint or offend them. Those seem like good odds to me.

EIGHT: *Computers can perpetuate myths and complicate communication.*

WHEN THE media use Google to find their background information, the same files come up again and again—for years. Even if the stuff isn't right, the Googler rewrites it, using the old inaccurate stories, and the myths are perpetuated through more search engines. For instance, when I was leaving the University of Hartford to take the job at GW, I had not seen the GW president's house. The then-current president had resided in the university's house for twenty-something years. I said to the chairman of the Board of Trustees, "My wife has expressed a desire to see the president's house. She is trying to plan where the children's rooms will be, where the furniture will fit, et cetera." Also, the board had said it wanted the new president to be "social" and reach out to the community, and my wife and I were certainly agreeable to that, but we wanted to see how the house would accommodate our style of entertaining. He said, "You know, I don't recall seeing it in a long time. The president is a very private man, who considers his home a personal place."

So the three of us visited the GW house. Though it was a very nice house, it was difficult to envision institutional entertaining of students, faculty, alumni, and friends of the institution because of the way it was laid out. The rooms were small, and traffic flow was constricted. The house had a kitchen that did not have enough space for a table and chairs, and none of the house was air-conditioned. So the board decided to seek another house; the vice president for finance found one. It was a $2 million house. The board chairman did some research to find out how much the sale of the existing house would bring. The answer was about $1.5 million. In view of the difference, and anticipating critical comments, I offered to get a mortgage, buy the remaining $500,000 share of the house with my own money, and resell it to the university at the fair market price when I left office. The chairman said, "No, the university can afford to buy a house. If we think the school needs a bigger house, it is up to us to find one. We don't need you as a partner in the ownership of a house."

So the university bought the house. The media immediately fixated on the fact that we were buying a house for $2 million. They did not take the trouble to discover that GW was also selling the first house for $1.5 million. A story appeared in the student newspaper that was subsequently picked up by *The Washington Post* and *The Washington Times*. It was about how the new president wouldn't accept the job unless the university bought a $2 million house. All of this was pure fiction. This whole story had evolved from an unsupported speculation by the student newspaper, and it had become part of someone's file.

Five or six years later, a story about university presidents' houses appeared in a national magazine, which repeated that inaccurate story about the GW president's house. I invited the magazine editor to lunch and told him the facts just the way I have related them here. He said, "Well, my reporter checked the file." The file the reporter had checked was the information from an old newspaper! It was the story that had had no truth to it from the outset. I said, "The article was wrong then, and it's wrong now. Your reporter never called me to check the story contemporaneously." The editor said he felt bad, but obviously he couldn't run around and pick up all the outstanding copies of his magazine before they could be sold.

When something gets into computers, there often is no extricating it. It just keeps coming back and coming back in a recurring cycle. Earlier, I mentioned the issue of student suicide. The Google principle exists there, too. Every time reporters write a story about a suicide at another school, they add a line that says something like "And at GW, there was a lawsuit about a suicide." This information is repeated in hundreds of newspapers all over America!

Here is a variation on what I have just described. A university employee in charge of the study abroad program at GW was worried about the welfare of GW students when she saw that the State Department was issuing travel advisories about travel to certain places abroad. She began urging students not to go to specific "dangerous" places, where terrorist bombers were active. A bomb had been set off at Hebrew University, and it was characterized as one of those dangerous places. Over the years, we had successfully sent many of our students—without incident—to that university. A student came to meet with the director of study abroad. She told him that in order to discourage him from going to Hebrew University, GW would not give him academic credit for work done there. Clearly, she knew that would be a major disincentive to attending. The student left that meeting and immediately e-mailed news of the no-credit decision to a friend of his who was at Hebrew University and asked if he was aware of this situation. That student e-mailed it to twenty other friends and also gave the information to the president of Hebrew University. We now had a metastasis of communication.

Soon my desk was littered with little pink slips reporting urgent telephone calls. One was from the Israeli ambassador and one was from the president of Hebrew University. I called them back and found that they were very troubled about the GW decision. I knew nothing about it! First I had to figure out where the decision had been made. That wasn't difficult; our study abroad director had made a perfectly reasonable "low-visibility decision" (an expression I learned in law school, which means that a police officer can make what appears to be a reasonable decision at his or her level that eventually rises up and bites the mayor!). I said to her, "We shouldn't do that. I grant you the students are young, but they are young *adults*. I can imagine that while there is a State Department alert, you might ask them to sign a release indicating that they understand the danger of going to a particular place. But we give credit for going to a university based on the academic merits. If the courses and faculty are good, and if a student wants to go there, we should give credit for it and not say that a course is not acceptable to us on the basis of a State Department travel alert." She suggested that someone could still sue us notwithstanding our requiring a signed release. In my opinion, that risk was just the price of doing business.

Here was an instance in which GW found itself in the middle of an international situation. These things happen to us as an institution—alas, more frequently than not. Again, it is a case of wanting to do the right thing, having your heart in the right place, and maybe overreacting a little bit. And, of course, there is the frequent assumption by those on the outside that everything done in a university has first been discussed in every quarter and blessed at the highest levels. It is often assumed that the president is on a first-name basis with every sparrow that flies over the campus and has personally participated in all decisions.

That incident also points out the way information spreads these days. Years ago, the student would have left the adviser's office and might have written a letter to someone about the issue. But there wouldn't have been instantaneous delivery of the information to hundreds—perhaps thousands—of people, many of whom feel affected or offended by the decision. We operate now in a far faster, more fragile, and more transparent environment than most people can imagine. There are no secrets anymore.

6.

No Tired Bureaucrats Need Apply

The course of a university president's day is never the same twice in a row; no tired bureaucrats need apply. The problems are frequently unique and call for an agile mind and a responsive personality. To do the job, I used everything I have ever read, witnessed, or experienced, and I used this information in ways I would never have anticipated. In the end, I would say that to be effective, a president has to love the university, like people, and want to solve problems and clear obstacles out of the paths of students, parents, professors, neighbors, and other stakeholders who perceive an issue. In addition, the president has to figure out ways to add value to the conversation and be willing to expend more energy than the average bear by just keeping up with events. The president must also be physically present and visible whenever and wherever possible.

One of the reasons college presidents find the job so rewarding and challenging, while at the same time physically demanding, is that the working day often starts at 8 A.M. or earlier and regularly runs full bore until eleven at night or later six days a week. Seven, even. While it is physically taxing, a president's schedule is filled with substantive content mixed liberally with ceremonial and procedural duties, the total of which, it seems to me, calls on all the usable areas of the brain.

In England, the government is divided between a ceremonial head of state, the queen, and a political head of state, the prime minister. The queen travels the country and engages in activities designed to spread goodwill among her subjects, other countries, and Commonwealth nations. She cuts ribbons, dedicates buildings, lays cornerstones for orphanages, and performs a myriad of other niceties. Meanwhile, the prime minister runs the government. In an American university, the president is the queen *and* the prime minister, expected to show up at countless events including ceremonies for visiting dignitaries, memorial services for deceased members of the university community, events honoring outstanding professors and scholars or celebrating the publication of a book or the winning of a prize, the digging of the first shovelful of dirt for a new building, and a range of other ceremonies, the most notable of which is the commencement ceremony. People involved with these activities notice if the president is there; and they *really* care. They are crushed if the president is absent, and they let him know how they feel about the slight.

The president must also attend countless meetings. The list starts with dates that are reserved on the calendar a year in advance. For instance, the president must attend all of the trustees' meetings, which usually occur four times a year for several days, and then there are the regular weekly and monthly meetings with the vice presidents, the deans, and the Faculty Senate.

As president, you cannot sulk at Balmoral Castle and take long walks in the woods. You have to show up at Buckingham Palace *and* No. 10 Downing Street, and while you are there, you have to do the work needed to run the university. For instance, in a time-consuming process, the president must sign countless documents for transactions like buying real estate and submitting reports required by the government for affirmative action and research.

The president is running an institution with thousands of people in it who are engaged in countless activities that are important to its mission. These activities are as varied as going to a meeting with deans, attending a basketball game, joining a meeting with city officials, talking to a benefactor with ideas for a donation, meeting with a student group, or using presidential persuasive powers to get a person to lend a hand or invite a celebrity to speak at commencement.

WHEN I was president of the prelaw society in college, I wrote to ask Dean George W. Hibbitt to come to an event we were hosting two weeks later. His office contacted me right away and said that he couldn't make it because he was prebooked for that date. I remember thinking, What sort of a person is so busy that with an entire two weeks' notice he can't show up at something? Over the years I have learned the answer to this question. As a university president I was usually committed two *months* in advance. People would say to me, "You are impossible to get hold of!" I would reply, "No, quite the contrary, I am possible to get hold of, which is why we have to wait two months. Other people got hold of me before you did!" It is not inaccessibility but *accessibility* that causes the delay.

The president's day is relentless, so much so that I used to worry that after I was out of office, it would be hard to regain my powers of concentration. Over the years I mastered the ability to multitask amid the frenetic activity around me. And then, when I got home, I would still have mail and messages to deal with, and, as I always made it a practice to have my phone number listed in the D.C. telephone book, there might have been a phone call from a parent or a student with a problem he or she thought only the president could solve and couldn't wait until tomorrow. This phone listing was, I think, a small price to pay for demonstrating that I was available.

As president, I had office support staff. They worked in shifts because I worked longer hours and more days each week than they were expected to. One of these staff members was in charge of keeping my appointment book. I am not a twenty-first-century man comfortable with high-tech tools. My appointment book was made of paper, written in with a pencil, and frequently revised with a large eraser. When I had been traveling or had a particularly busy week, the worst thing that could happen was that my Monday morning—or whatever morning came after my return to Washington—was filled with too many meetings and activities. After thirty years with me, my secretary knew my preferences, but still there were times when I would see a packed early schedule after being away and I would not be happy. In addition, I was often vexed at the number of meetings planned around a snack, a cup of coffee, a meal, or drinks. Not only was my time scheduled by others, but to my mind, my dining preferences were being controlled by others. Sometimes the mere sight of that appointment book filled me with apprehension. How would I get to all these events, give all the talks, shake all the hands, eat all the meals and drink all the drinks, have all the meetings, and still have time to concentrate on the larger issues that needed my attention? Somehow it would all work out, but often at a physical price. Here is a sampling from one forty-eight-hour period during my presidency:

Sunday:

12:15 A.M.: Return from Denver, Colorado, alumni events

1:00 P.M.: Omni Shoreham Hotel—JCPA-Hillel Plenum (keynote address)

2:30 P.M.: Attend GW women's basketball team game versus Charlotte

7:00 P.M.: 10th Annual Hippo Dinner (give informal remarks)

Monday:

7:30 A.M.: Racquetball at GW Health and Wellness Center

9:00 A.M.: Meet/greet entering student Saudi princesses

9:45 A.M.: Meeting with professors' committee re: salaries

10:45 A.M.: Conference call with board re: budget

12:30 P.M.: Lunch with president and senior staff of Bahcesehir University, Istanbul

2:00 P.M.: Memorial service for Professor Smith (prepare to give remarks)

3:30 P.M.: Interview by students for class project

4:30 P.M.: Meet with Law School dean re: fund-raising

6:30 P.M.: President's Night dinner/reception (make welcoming remarks)

8:00 P.M.: President's Night performance (make introductory
remarks)

The calendar alone doesn't give a complete picture of the life of
a president. For instance, it doesn't mention the twenty phone calls I
made in between meetings, the thirty letters and memos and e-mails
I read and wrote answers to each day, or the many outside obligations
that took up my time. It doesn't mention the endless letters of con-
gratulation and well-wishing to students and faculty who won honors,
letters to visiting dignitaries, meetings with the president of the Student Association, unplanned walk-in meetings with staff and outsiders, and phone calls from reporters wanting a quote on an issue with
significance to the university or to academe in general. It doesn't show
the time I spent on the many substantive memoranda I received from
the university's general counsel and the various vice presidents that
required my attention and ultimately my signature.

Instead, the calendar shows only the bare outline of a Christmas
tree. By the end of the week, that little tree—so neat and unencum-
bered at the beginning of the week—is loaded with bells and whistles
and tinsel and ornaments representing all the other things I did that
weren't in the plan. Of course, lurking in every corner is the dreaded
but inevitable unanticipated crisis. On an urban campus, this could
be anything, including the horrifying events of 9/11, which—because
of our proximity to the White House, the State Department, and the
Pentagon—was a particularly dramatic and frightening episode for my
university and the worried parents who heard news of the event in the
media and tried desperately to contact their sons and daughters on
campus. When an unanticipated crisis, such as the unspeakable events
at Virginia Tech, comes to pass, it instantly thrusts aside any other plans
the university president might have had.

A HOST of other commitments and responsibilities were constantly
calling for my time. For instance, as a university president I had to keep
reading all the time. Each day I plowed through *The New York Times*,
The Wall Street Journal, *The Washington Post*, and *The Washington*

Times. These newspapers simply formed a platform for other required reading. A president has to read *The Chronicle of Higher Education* or *Inside Higher Education* and *The Chronicle of Philanthropy*—important sources for learning what is going on in academe—and other periodicals such as the neighborhood newspaper, from which it is possible to learn the local sentiment toward the university's projects and activities. I also went online each day to scan *The Harvard Crimson, Yale Daily News,* and *Columbia Daily Spectator* to see if there was anything going on that I ought to know about. For example, the events swirling around Harvard and the criticism of its president, Lawrence Summers, were very important to everyone in academia, and it was essential to keep on top of those events as they unfolded. During that episode, in addition to scanning the Harvard newspaper, I would also look at *The Boston Globe* to help me think and speak about the issue. Otherwise, I might have appeared uninformed if asked for a comment. If a president knows what is happening at other universities—for instance, students becoming concerned about the working conditions of people in Asia who are making logo items sold in the university stores—he or she can spot ahead of time the issues with national significance in the university world.

It is important for a president to keep in tune with the zeitgeist. It will not do if you don't know who Bono is, for instance. You at least have to know the contemporary musicians that students listen to, what's hot at the movies, and what books are being read on campus. If the president doesn't know what's going on, he will seem dusty and worn to students. I felt I needed to be able to engage on the issues of the day, certainly the wars in Afghanistan and Iraq. Even if I was planning to be discreet when reporters asked me about an issue, I felt it necessary to do so with knowledge of what was going on.

And then there are books! I had to read everything from current academic books—some by my own faculty—to blockbusters and, frankly, books I simply wanted to read for my personal pleasure. Then as now, I always had at least two books next to my bed, and every night I would try to read until I couldn't keep my eyes open. About journals, magazines, and other professional publications I will demur.

As a college president, you have to keep educating yourself. On two occasions I tried to learn a new language. In the case of Arabic, I found I just couldn't find the time to study—and Arabic is a language you can't learn without diligence. Then I took Spanish at an off-campus location. I thought it was less embarrassing to take a course off campus than be on view in a class where everyone knew me. I had to stop the Spanish classes during the transition period before I left office, but in my last class I had a ten-minute conversation with my Spanish teacher. At the end of that conversation she asked, "Do you realize that you have been talking on and on and haven't used a single verb?" Well, I did notice that, because I have developed a way of speaking that serves in foreign countries and allows me to be understood without having to conjugate verbs, which is a weakness I have; regular, irregular, or radical.

UNSCHEDULED EVENTS occur all of the time in a university president's life. Often these involve helping people who expect the services of the university to be up and running at all times of the day and night and find it surprising—even shocking—that they are not. Three examples from my last year in office come to mind.

The first incident occurred at about four on a Saturday afternoon outside my office building. I had been catching up on my correspondence, and my secretary had gone home. Outside my building, I stopped to talk to the registrar, who was also working that day. A young man came up the stairs and tried to open the door. I told him I could let him into the building but everything inside was closed. I asked what he had in mind. He said, "I need to go in and cash a check at the Treasurer's Office." I said, "It's like a bank, they are closed on Saturday afternoon and won't open until Monday." He told me he didn't have any money and wasn't sure how he could go two days without it. He looked at me, as if for the first time, and asked, "You seem familiar, who are you?" I told him my name, but it didn't seem to mean a thing to him. I found that amusing; since he said he was a GW student but didn't recognize the name of the university president, I asked to see his ID card. Then I gave him $20 from my pocket. He seemed startled that a complete stranger would give him $20. But he took it and started to walk away. I said, "Hold on, how about giving me a check for the $20?" He returned, wrote out a check to me, and started walking away again. I said, "How about signing the check?" I guess he was a bit rattled. Anyway, that is not the point of the story. The point is that there is no end to the responsibilities of a university president. You can't leave a student without enough money to get through a weekend!

One Sunday morning I received a phone call at home from a woman who was quite upset. She told me she had been calling various university offices all morning and couldn't get anyone to answer the phone. She wanted to let me know how distressed she was with the lack of response from the university on a Sunday morning. When she was finally able to articulate her concerns, the story was a not uncommon one in student life, but it wasn't the kind of issue that was usually brought to the president's attention. Her daughter was a freshman with several roommates. Apparently, some of the roommates got along well, but her daughter was not one of them. So she told her mother that the roommates were ganging up on her. The mother wanted her daughter moved out of her downtown dormitory to our Mount Vernon campus immediately. After asking her some questions, I determined that the situation was not life-threatening and asked the mother if the daughter actually wanted to move out of the downtown dorm and to the other campus, several miles away. It was a long and emotionally fraught conversation—the child was an only child—but I was able to get the mother to agree to let me contact the university personnel who regularly handle such issues, and I also got her to agree to allow her daughter to decide how to solve the problem herself using the help of our professionals.

Before we hung up, I also persuaded the mother to promise that she would not—as she had been planning to do—immediately get on a plane from her faraway home and come to campus to solve a problem that thousands of freshmen all over the country in countless universities handle on their own at the beginning of their first year. She agreed to hold off until we had met with her daughter and worked out a mutually agreeable solution. I was happy to help solve this problem. But I couldn't help wondering if the mother had hesitated at all before calling the university president's home on a Sunday morning!

In a third incident, a member of the board called me during the workweek. He was very concerned because he had just been diagnosed with cancer. He told me his doctors believed that the leading practitioner in his type of cancer was at Memorial Sloan-Kettering Cancer Center. The personnel there had made an appointment for him to be seen a month later. He asked me to help him by getting him an earlier appointment. I told him I didn't have any contacts at Sloan-Kettering. He said, "You've never let me down, please try!"

I love that man like a brother, and I certainly did not want to disappoint him. I worried that I would be unsuccessful, but I asked my secretary to call the doctor at Sloan-Kettering and tell him that I would like to talk to him. She called with the phone on speaker mode and said, "President Trachtenberg of GW would like to talk to Dr. Brown." A woman answered, and when she heard my name she said, "Oh my god, Steve Trachtenberg? I just graduated from GW last May!" I said to my secretary, "Forget about Dr. Brown, I want to speak to *her*!" So I got on the phone and told her the problem. In the background I could hear pages turning as she searched for an appointment with the doctor. Soon she said, "How is tomorrow at four o'clock?" The entire transaction took fifteen minutes!

THERE IS another element attached to scheduling and time management in the presidency. People forget that you have a family life. You have a spouse, children, parents, a mother- and father-in-law, and friends to whom you need to pay attention because otherwise they think you have died. In the midst of all the professional action, you have to be available to all those important people who care about you. As the time came for my departure from the presidency, my wife, Francine, mentioned that we should get season tickets to the symphony, something that we had never done in the presidency because if we ever had the rare night off, I would—with great relish—prefer to stay home. I once got a call from someone who asked, "What are you doing for New Year's Eve?" I blurted out, "I am a professional partygoer!

So all I want to do on New Year's Eve is curl up with a good book, a glass of wine, and a cigar!"

Speaking of going out, it has always seemed strange to me that people actually care if the president shows up at their event. But they do. I could never understand how my presence brought added value to an occasion. But the fact is, the being-there factor counts. Knowing this immutable law, if I went to women's sports, for instance, I made sure I also showed up at men's sports. If I went to a musical event, I took pains to also go to theater events. When an undergraduate died in an accident and the students had a memorial service, it was particularly important for me to show up. I once attended such a service, and the students seemed surprised that I was there. Seeing me, they asked me to say a few words, which I did. Several years later, I still had graduates coming up to me and saying that they remembered what I had said at that service! It is the aura of the office.

When I made all these appearances, I realized that they can steal your life away from you. Oddly enough, when I saw the movie *The Remains of the Day*, I found myself identifying strongly with the main character, Mr. Stevens, a butler who sacrificed body and soul to domestic service. The need to get the job done for other people squeezed out his own private life. In his case, he had this realization too late for salvation. In my case, Francine has always kept an eye on what went on and resisted my tendency to become totally absorbed in the service of the university to the detriment of our family.

7.

THE BEST FOUR YEARS OF YOUR LIFE ARE THE NEXT FOUR YEARS OF YOUR LIFE, FOREVER

As president, I felt that meeting with students was one of the most important and enjoyable things I did. Surely this is part of the legacy of the wonderful teachers I had myself over the years; they took time to talk to me and to listen. Scheduled office hours were one way I got to sit down with students, but there were many other instances in which I could get face time with a couple of students or a roomful. It didn't matter to me how many there were. For instance, every year I addressed 2,300 incoming freshmen and their parents during the summer before they moved to campus for the fall semester. The event is called Colonial Inauguration (CI). I came prepared but spoke informally, without a text. I tried to cover many topics I thought were important as well as a few marginal subjects. The event gave me a chance to give the students advice, share various truths I have learned over the years, and make them feel welcome. I think stories are the best way to get ideas across to a captive audience like this. Over the years I received much positive feedback about the CI talks. Here follows an extract from what I said to the CI audience on June 2006.

I GO to Martha's Vineyard for two weeks every summer. Being there has given me a great respect for what it means to be president of a university and the extraordinary effect it can have on one's life. For example, a few years ago my wife and I were at a house we rent. Also in attendance were my two sons and their respective ladies, and my mother- and father-in-law—eight people in all. At about ten-thirty one day, my wife said to me, "The toilet won't flush." "Okay," I said, "what do you want me to do about it?" She said, "I want you to fix it." I said, "I can't even make the television clock stop blinking twelve all the time!" She said, "Well, we can't make it through the weekend. My father's eighty-four. He won't hold out for two days. So you have to get the plumbing fixed. I'm going to take everybody into town for lunch. That will clarify the opportunity for you." So she rounded the family up, took them out to The Bite for fried clams, and left me with the toilet. Understand, the only thing I know about toilets is that you push the handle and the water goes down.

The owner of the rental house has a corkboard in the kitchen with the business cards of craftsmen, tradesmen, and vendors pinned to it. Sure enough, there was one for a plumber. So I called that number and got the plumber's receptionist/concierge. After hearing my problem, she explained that it was the July Fourth weekend. Actually, I knew the date; that wasn't the information I was seeking. She continued, "The plumber's really booked from sunup to sundown, but he can come on Monday." I said, "In two days, we'll all be dead." She was talking about how she would put me on the waiting list, and I was thinking, I'm going to have to fly a plumber in from GW. I said, "All right, all right, please put me on the waiting list and call me when the plumber's available. In the meantime I'll try to make other accommodations, and if I work it out I'll get back to you." She said, "Great, what is your name?" I said, "Trachtenberg" and started to spell it, "T-R-A" and she said, "No, I know exactly how to spell Trachtenberg, it's T-R-A-C-H-T-E-N-B-E-R-G, right?" I said, "Remarkable! All my life I've had to spell my name for people. Hardly anybody can spell it." She said, "Well, I have a son. He's a student at a university in Washington, D.C. The president there has the same name." I asked, "What's your son's name?" She answered, "Randy." I said, "Listen, I *am* the president of George Washington University." I paused and added, "I can't guarantee that Randy will graduate . . ."

She got the plumber out there in fifteen minutes. He pulled a Bic pen out of the toilet and threw it away. An hour later, when my wife and all the family showed up, I was a hero. It's extraordinary; being the president of GW is actually a position of power—off campus! . . .

There are GW people everywhere; I mean *everywhere*. My wife and I were recently in Barcelona and our rental car tire was punctured. The person who came to help us was part of a gang responsible for puncturing the tire; when we pulled over and got out to look, he stole my wife's purse from the car. It was a Friday. By the time we realized what had happened and got to the police station, reported the theft, returned back to the hotel, and called the consulate because we desperately needed a passport so my wife could travel on Sunday, we discovered that the consulate closed at four o'clock. It was a fiesta, and they wouldn't be back until Monday. So my wife said, "Okay, hero of Martha's Vineyard, let's see you do it in Spanish."

I then remembered that the American ambassador to Spain was a GW dad. He's got a daughter matriculated here. I thought, Well, this works with plumbers, and I called the embassy in Madrid. A woman answered the phone, and I said to her, "My name is Stephen Trachtenberg, I'm the president of The George Washington University, and I'd like to speak to the ambassador." Of course when you do that, parents immediately feel a cold fist on their hearts, so I quickly added, "There's nothing wrong with his daughter." Relieved, she put me through, and when the ambassador picked up, he immediately said, "What's wrong with my daughter?" I said, "She's probably in the library studying. But Mr. Ambassador, *I* am the one with a problem." I told him about not being able to get a replacement passport. And he said, "We can take care of that." Sure enough, in ten minutes he called me and said, "Get in a taxicab, go over to the consulate, tell the marine your name, and you'll be all right." Sure enough, the guard let me in and we went upstairs. There was one man there, and he introduced himself by saying, "Hello, are you Steve Trachtenberg?" Then he said, "Are you related to the president of George Washington University?" I said, "As a matter of fact, I am—very closely." It turned out that he had a BA and an MA from our Elliott School of International Affairs, he was in the Foreign

Service, and he had a drawer full of passports. In spite of our close relationship and long-standing friendship, he still charged me ninety-seven dollars for the passport. But now we had a passport and made it to Madrid on schedule. . . .

In my freshman year at Columbia University, I had a dean who said to us, "Someplace in this room there sits a future Nobel Prize winner," and I thought, Maybe he's talking about me. I worried for a long time and thought, Gee, am I doing everything I'm supposed to do to win this Nobel Prize? As I got older and nobody called, I decided that perhaps I had messed up. And so I redoubled my efforts; I was starting to become slightly obsessive. Then one day I came down for breakfast, opened *The New York Times*, and saw an article about Roald Hoffmann, a chemist in my class at Columbia; he had just won the Nobel Prize in Chemistry. I was so relieved. It was Roald all the time! I wrote him a letter and thanked him for taking the burden off my shoulders. And I got him to accept an honorary degree and give a commencement address. . . .

I would like to dispel some urban myths about GW.

Myth 1: Regarding the faux mascot (GW's *real* mascot is a Colonial). Hippopotamuses are mean beasts. I say this on the basis of information and belief, not personal knowledge. They are apparently very territorial if you're going past them on a river in a raft. They may try to knock you over, and if they get you in the water, they may bite you. But the one on the campus—the bronze one—that one's okay. People ask me all the time, "Why do we have a hippopotamus as a faux mascot?" Here's the story.

My wife and I were sailing in Newport. At the time, she was the vice president of WETA, the educational television station in Washington. It called her back with an emergency. She had to fly home and left me in Newport "unattended," as she likes to say. I had a day to kill, so I was wandering around looking at old houses and boats. But I could take only so much of that . . .

Then I stumbled onto a place that sells remnants. These are pieces of buildings that have come down but have some architectural interest—finials and mantelpieces, the stuff loved by decorators. In the middle of this yard full of tchotchkes was a bronze hippopotamus. The man who runs the place came out while I was looking around. It was a hot day, and he asked, "Would you like a beer?" I said, "Sure." So I had a beer. We spent the afternoon together this way. At the end, nobody else had come into his place! I was about to leave so I could pick up my wife at the airport and was feeling a little bad that my new best friend hadn't made a sale all day. So I bought the hippo, arranged for it to be shipped back as a surprise for my wife, and promptly forgot about the whole thing.

A couple of months passed. Then a truck showed up at our house in Washington and the driver knocked on the door. My wife came out and saw something on the truck that looked like a coffin. The driver pointed to it and asked, "Should I bring it in?" She asked, "What's in it?" He pried open the box, revealing the hippo. She took one look at it and said, "Oh no, no . . . no." He said "Lady, either I can take it back to Rhode Island or I can put it down in the street." She then called me at the office. I could tell that my wife was really surprised by the arrival of this hippo. She told me, "You've got to get it out of here."

Then I had a great idea; I arranged to have the hippo dropped off at the delivery dock at the university with instructions to place it in front of Lisner Auditorium. It was there for about a week. People started asking questions like "Why do you have a hippopotamus in the front of Lisner?" As if you need a reason!

When someone asks you a question, no answer is also an answer. We tried that for a while. Then we crafted a plaque to address the questions. It says something like "This hippopotamus is symbolic of the hippopotamuses that used to swim in the Potomac once upon a time, back in the days when George and Martha Washington sat on the plantation. The little children used to like to go down and swim with them and pat them on the noses for good luck. Students can pat this one on the nose for good luck before exams or whatever it is they're doing." Next thing you know, people believed the plaque and believed in the power of the hippo to get them an A in an exam. I see tourists and university students—who ought to know better—patting the hippo on the nose and putting little children on its back and taking photographs. That's the story of the hippopotamus, our faux mascot. One caveat; even if you like me, don't buy me hippopotamuses. I'm all stocked up on hippos. People have been bringing me hippopotamuses for a long while now, and I've got shoe boxes full of them!

Myth 2. Regarding Colonial Parking. There are parking lots called Colonial Parking all over the city, and inevitably people tell the freshmen and their parents that GW owns the company because we are known as the Colonials and they think we named the lots after ourselves. Alas, it's not true; we don't own Colonial Parking. However, the company *was* named after GW. It was founded by two graduates of the university who worked their way through school by parking cars. They majored in English, and when they graduated, one looked at the other and asked, "Okay, where can we go with *Beowulf?*" Then they got an idea: "Parking lots, we know about parking lots!" So they opened a little parking lot, watered it, and it grew. Parking lot number one led to parking lot number two, and, lo and behold, one day they looked about and saw they were a success. Out of respect for the university that had prepared them for their profession, they named their parking lot company "Colonial Parking." Which goes to prove to any concerned parents—your kids *can* make a living with a degree in English if they own a parking lot or two on the side.

Myth 3. Regarding the Smith Center. People think that the reason GW doesn't have football is that Charles E. Smith, after whom an athletic center on campus—the Smith Center—is named, had a son who was injured in a football game and as a precondition to making the gift that made the Smith Center possible, he insisted that GW give up football. There's no truth to that. We gave up football because we didn't think anybody would notice. Nobody came to the games, sometimes not even a team! There was a period way back where we did have a serious football team and were part of the Southern Conference. I read a novel set in 1937 where there's a reference to a football player named Tuffy Leemans—he played at GW and went on to enter the Pro Football Hall of Fame after a career with the New York Giants. Only someone who has studied the history of the institution would today spot the reference to him. . . .

• • •

I NEED to tell some stories by way of saving people from making the same mistakes I have made in my life. For example, when I was nineteen, I was selected by Columbia University to go on a mission to Cuba. This was when Fidel Castro and the United States were still talking to each other. Castro had recently seized Havana and taken control of the government. After he did that, he invited universities around the world to send student delegates to a ceremony for the reopening of the University of Havana, which had been closed during the revolution against the prior dictator, Fulgencio Batista. I was to represent the student body of my college. The hosts put me up at the Hotel Nacional, a grand facility. I was a little nervous, woke up very early the first day, and went down to the lobby, where there was a pitcher of fresh orange juice. I took a glass and went out on the deck. I was sitting enjoying the quiet and the sunshine when I saw a woman in a big swimming pool doing laps. Eventually, she emerged, and, to my astonishment, I recognized her. She was a famous movie star of the time, Ava Gardner. For those of you who don't recall Ava Gardner, she was very tight with Frank Sinatra, whom you will all remember.

Ava started walking in my direction. As she got near, I looked at her and she looked at me. I looked at her again and she looked at me again, and then she said, "Hello, young man." And I said, "Hello, Miss Gardner." She replied, "Oh, you know who I am." And I said, "Yes, you're a famous movie star." And she said, "May I join you?" I said, "Sure." She pulled up a chair and said, "May I have a little of that juice?" I said, "Please do." She took my glass of orange juice, which was only half done, and proceeded to ask me my name and why I was in Havana. It was a nice conversation. Eventually she said, "You'll have to excuse me, I'm sitting here in this wet bathing suit, and I want to go upstairs and change into something more comfortable. Awfully nice to meet you; I hope to see you again soon, have a wonderful time." I said, "Thank you," and she left. No sooner was she gone that I realized she'd left her room key next to the now-empty orange juice glass. I was uncertain about what I was supposed to do about that.

This is where the education part comes in. I picked up the key and took it into the lobby, where I gave it to the manager of the hotel. From that day to this, I have had continuing angst. I feel I have unfinished business with Ava Gardner. My advice to the entering students is this: *Under similar circumstances, give the key back to Miss Gardner in Room 703 directly; it's a chance to meet Frank Sinatra. . . .*

Part of the reward for being president is the benefit of free tuition for your children at the institution. So naturally *my* two sons went elsewhere! They thought it was important to go away to school. I said to their mother, "What do you think that says about us?" She said, "About *us*? About us, nothing; about you, *everything*." Ben, my younger son, who's now the lawyer in the family, articulated it best. He said, "I don't want to be any place where people will know I'm related to you." I said, "How are they going to know you're my son?" He said, "*Trachtenberg*. You know, it's not that common a name. If I come in and register as Ben Trachtenberg, people are going to say unrelentingly for four years, 'Are you related to the president?' " Then I suggested, "For the price of four years' tuition you could change your name and have something left over." But no, he insisted on going away. He enrolled at Yale University. For anyone here who has any doubt there is a god, I will now demonstrate beyond any possibility of contradiction that there *is* a god. *The name of the Dean of Students at Yale was Betty Trachtenberg!* (She is no relation to me.)

Columbia University was an all-male school when I was an undergraduate there. The drinking age in New York City was eighteen, and the dean of students used to hold a beer party—free, all you can drink—during freshmen week just to see how sick he could make the entering class. He wanted to teach us a lesson in limits and capacity. I take the subject of drinking dead seriously, and I put the emphasis on the word "dead." If it were up to me, I'd make eighteen the legal drinking age, as it once was. And I'd see to it that students who wanted to drink would do so on campus, where I could keep an eye on them and walk them back to their residence halls rather than have them going through the city streets, coming back from Georgetown or someplace else where, with the aid of a fake Florida driver's license, students have persuaded a guileless bartender to give them a drink, or two, or three. I'm not asking students to be teetotalers; I'll leave that to their parents and the authorities. What I am asking students to do is demonstrate to the world and to themselves that they are as smart as their SAT scores say they are. *Students have got to be intelligent enough to look after themselves and to look after their classmates and friends and roommates.* I want all our freshman to graduate four years from now. I don't want our dean of students—or me—to have to call a parent and say, "We've got bad news." But we need students' help to make that happen.

Classmates of mine in college who drank to excess kept on drinking that way after college. Many of them died young, frequently as the result of alcohol-related diseases. I realize, in its place, drinking is a social thing. Out of its place, it's like a fire. Fire in a fireplace is a friendly fire. Fire on the carpet really makes my wife unhappy, so we have a grate that we put over the fireplace when we start a fire in it. I want students to put a grate in place if they ever drink someplace. Life is contingent. It can be dangerous. Students need to be responsible and look both ways before crossing. . . .

CHANGING THE subject, this is a terrific time to study Arabic. It's also a terrific time to study Chinese and Japanese. I don't want to discourage anyone from studying Spanish, but students could probably teach themselves Spanish. They are not going to be able to easily teach themselves Arabic or Chinese or Japanese or Russian. These are extraordinarily important languages in the world today and, therefore, extraordinarily important languages for Americans. People can buy in English. They will sell better in the language of their customers.

A few years ago I noticed that only twenty-two bachelor's degrees in Arabic had been granted in the United States in the previous year. So we offered Arabic courses for free to honors students during the summer. Their folks had to feed them, but we gave them tuition with the hope that we would inspire more of our undergraduates to study Arabic. And it worked. The language is learnable, even if it doesn't look like it at first. I sat through the first ten weeks, and I was at the point where I could make a sentence, although that sentence was mostly asking for directions to the market. I also learned how to say "My name is" and "I'm the president of The George Washington University." Even that little bit came in extraordinarily handy on trips to the Middle East. Once, appearing on a television show being beamed live to the Middle East, I was actually able to introduce myself and give my title in Arabic. This absolutely amazed the host and made him think that I could speak Arabic, albeit with a very, very bad accent. Of course, when he started speaking to me in Arabic, I could reply only by asking for directions to the market. . . .

DURING MY undergraduate years, I worked my way through college with a variety of jobs. For example, I was *The New York Times* representative at Columbia. This was a far less glamorous job than one might think. I didn't write anything; I was the person who distributed the newspapers in the morning. I would get up at 6 A.M. and drop the paper in subscribers' doorways. They would pay me at the end of the month, and I would give some of the money to *The New York Times* and keep the rest for myself. That made it possible to go out on Saturday nights, way back in the day when men paid for dates.

One summer I decided to get a summer job as a waiter at a Catskill Mountain resort hotel. I went to an agency where they hired people for such positions. I had invested twelve dollars in a pair of old but still serviceable black tuxedo trousers with a satin stripe down the side, a pair of black shoes, and a pair of white socks. I don't know why white socks seemed important, but I noticed that all the waiters seemed to wear them. I've never worn white socks since—well, maybe when I'm playing racquetball. But white socks and a white shirt with a clip-on bow tie with only one clip left on it and the collar open was, you know, jaunty. So I went to this employment agency, and at the door they had a machine of the sort you see at bakeries; you take a number and wait to be called. When my number came up, I went to meet one of the hotel representatives—or maître ds—who were sitting in little booths along the periphery of the room. I walked up to a man from the Raleigh Hotel who asked, "What's your name, and what do you do?" I replied, "I'm a sophomore at Columbia." He seemed unimpressed and asked, "What kind of background do you have?" I said, "I used to deliver pharmaceuticals for Hoffman's Drugs. And I was a *New York*

Times representative." He said, "No, no, I want to know how much experience you have as a *waiter*; we only hire experienced help." I didn't have any experience as a waiter, but I said, "My experience as a waiter is sitting down for dinner and watching. But I know how you do it; you take the plate here, you put the plate there. I can do this." He replied, "We only hire experienced help." I said, "Where does this experienced help come from? There's no waiter school; experienced means you get on-the-job training." He said, "I'm sorry, that's your problem, not mine. N-e-e-x-t."

I was very disappointed that I had to get up and leave. After all, I had an investment in these trousers and couldn't imagine where I'd ever wear them again. So I took another number and sat down again. This time, I went to a different booth; the man there was from Brown's Hotel. He asked, "What's your name, and where have you worked before as a waiter?" And I said, "The Raleigh Hotel." And he replied, "Sol Hotchkiss from the Raleigh Hotel is here today; I was just talking to him. Why don't you go see about getting your old job back?" I said, "Well, I did the Raleigh. Now I want to try Brown's." He said, "Come with me." He took me down the hall, opened the door, stuck in his head, and said, "Sol, what can you tell me about this kid, Trachtenberg? He says he knows you." Sol looked up and said, "He's a fast learner!"

LET ME explain my father's reaction to my various philosophies of life. He called me when I was a young dean at Boston University and said, "I've got some free time, so I'd like to visit you." So he came and we had dinner, and that was nice. I was ready for him to go home, but he was prepared to stay for the weekend. On Saturday morning, he woke me up at 6 A.M. and said, "Let's go get pancakes." There was an International House of Pancakes near where I lived. On the way out, I collected all my dirty shirts from the past week and put them in a pillowcase to drop off at the laundry on our way. My father and I ordered pancakes, and while we were waiting for them to come, I noticed that he was brooding. So I drew him out a little and said, "Hey, Dad, there's this dark cloud over your head, what's up?" He said, "Well, I couldn't help noticing, you didn't count the shirts before you gave them to the laundry. That's not a sound practice." I replied, "To tell you the truth, Dad, I've got a philosophy of life about this." He said, "So share it with me."

I said, "Look, if you count the shirts going into the laundry, it follows that you have to count the shirts coming out. Otherwise you wasted your time counting them going in. If you count the shirts coming out, there are three possible outcomes: (1) Exactly the same number of shirts both times, in which case you wasted your counting time in and out. (2) More shirts. Not likely, but more shirts nonetheless. Let's say you gave ten, you got eleven—one shirt more than you should have, but it's the wrong size or a color you don't like or you're an honorable person and give the worst shirt back. So why'd you have to bother counting in and out? You've wasted your time. (3) Fewer shirts; you gave ten, you got nine back. You have to do something with this data, because otherwise you've wasted your time counting in and out. Now you know you gave ten, you got nine, you're one shirt shy. You go back to the laundry and say to the man who's running the laundry, 'Listen, I gave you ten, you gave me nine.' The first thing that happens is the man no longer speaks English. Second, he points to a sign in a language you can't read, which translated means, 'We're not responsible for lost shirts. But if we lose a shirt, we're going to give you ten dollars.' Your thinking is, 'Wait, I paid twenty dollars for that shirt; I know it was a long time ago, so now I'm losing ten dollars.' Now you are unhappy because he lost the shirt and you feel obliged to take your business to another laundry! That new laundry is four blocks away, and it's more expensive and not as good. It's very annoying, and you're sorry you ever got into this in the first place."

I said all this to my father and then I added, "Look, during the course of a lifetime, how many shirts can a person lose, ten? And if it's twenty dollars a shirt you're losing twenty dollars a shirt, so that's two hundred dollars. You can amortize the two hundred dollars over a lifetime and won't have to count the shirts going in and the shirts going out." After all this, my father said, "That's your philosophy of life? I have a philosophy of life about this, too." I said, "What is that, Dad?" And he said with some irony, "It's nice to have a rich papa." In other words, because he had supported me, I had become more cavalier about keeping track of my shirts than he was brought up to be. To him, the loss of a shirt was consequential. That's my father's wisdom passed on to me; I give it to freshmen at no tuition charge. . . .

Speaking of my father, when I was president of the University of Hartford, my father was in a nursing home in White Plains, New York. I was driving back to Hartford from New York City, where I had been doing fund-raising all day. When I came to the White Plains exit, I suddenly decided to try to see him although it was well past visiting hours. When I got to the home, I tapped on the glass and a nurse came to the door. In spite of the hour, she let me in. When I went into his room, my father looked up and said, "Oh, I'm glad to see you! I couldn't sleep." So we sat and talked awhile.

Then my father said, "I am going to die soon." I said, "No, Dad." He said, "I am; don't bullshit a bullshitter. I *am* going to die soon. And when I do, your mother isn't going to be up to taking care of the funeral arrangements. You are going to have to do it." He continued, "When your grandmother died, I was responsible for the funeral. And it is one of the great embarrassments of my life. I was so filled with emotion about all the things I didn't do for my mother while she was alive that I permitted the undertaker to exploit me. He talked me into buying a $30,000 coffin. Later, I was at the cemetery while they were lowering the coffin. Instead of thinking about my mother, all I could think about was that I was about to bury a lot of hard-earned dollars. We cannot allow the undertaker to do this to our family again! So when I die, you are to ask to see the most expensive coffin the undertaker has; it will probably cost plus or minus $30,000. Then have him show you the Orthodox Jewish coffin. This will be a plain pine box with no nails or ornamentation and some holes drilled in the bottom to allow for earth-to-earth. This coffin will probably be about $300. I want you to buy the inexpensive box and bury me in it. After the funeral, I want you to give to charity in my memory the difference between the cheapest and the most expensive coffins."

I said, "Dad, that's a very moving idea. What charity should I give it to?" He said, "I don't know. It always seemed to me that the Red Cross had more money than I did. And it seemed counterintuitive that

I should give them my money. So I will leave that decision to you; it's your line of work."

And so it came to pass that my father died. I went to my mother and told her the story of the conversation with my father. She said, "Do what he wanted. Give the money to charity." I said, "What charity should I give it to?" She said, "You know about charity, you decide." I agreed to do it.

I called in the vice president for development at the University of Hartford, gave him a check for $30,000 from my father's estate, and said, "Do something for the university in my father's memory." Eventually, he came back and said, "I added the money to funding for the new theater. And we're going to put up a plaque in the lobby in your father's memory." I said, "Lovely."

A year went by, and we wanted to mark the anniversary of my father's death. Since he was buried in New Jersey, the conventional thing would have been to gather in New Jersey at the cemetery to unveil his headstone. I decided instead to have a ceremony in Hartford at the university. During that ceremony, we unveiled the plaque that had been mounted in the theater. It was next to the box office; you couldn't buy a ticket without seeing it. We gathered people and unveiled the marker, and I made some remarks and my mother made some remarks. Afterward, we all walked back to the house for some coffee and cake. At this point, my aunt said to my mother, "Shoshana, I never knew that Oscar was so fond of the theater." And my mother said, "The theater? No, no, it wasn't the theater. It was box offices. He loved box offices!" So what's the lesson? *Do your philanthropic giving while you are alive so you can make the choices you want and see the good works come to pass!*

I ALWAYS gave the freshmen some goals I hoped they would pursue while they were undergraduates. This included advising them that they should actually learn some things in school with which they could support themselves. In particular, I reminded them that they should try very diligently to learn to write. I find it astounding how many people come to college from very good secondary schools with excellent transcripts but who cannot, in fact, write at an acceptable level. A student who graduates from college actually knowing how to write well is ahead of most of the other college graduates in the country. If a person can write and speak, she'll be able to find work and pay back those college loans!

Another goal was that I wanted the freshmen to leave college with people skills. A lot of people who come to college have never had a roommate. They've lived in their own bedrooms, they haven't had siblings, or they had siblings but the siblings had separate rooms and they've never been obliged to know how to compromise and how to live life with other people's interests and concerns in mind. College is a good place to learn to do those things. If a student and his roommates can't get along, chances are that he will also find it hard to get along with a partner or spouse or potential new friends and business associates.

I THINK it's nice when universities have bell towers and at noon and six o'clock, they play the university fight song on the bells. When I became president, I looked into the possibility of building a bell tower, but I ran into problems. One was that land is very dear in the District of Columbia and a bell tower would be ornamental rather than absolutely central to education. Nobody liked the idea of taking some of our limited land and building a tower with bells that played the fight song. Another problem was that a bell tower is very expensive—a few million dollars! Yet another problem was that we would have to find somebody to play the bells, and that can be hard to do these days. Still, I wanted to hear the university fight song at noon and in the evening. So I got a tape recording of bells playing the fight song. We put a speaker and a timer up on the roof of one of our buildings. At noon and six o'clock it plays the GW fight song. I got this whole project done for a few hundred dollars! Now, walking on campus, I see people listening to the bells and looking around for our bell tower! . . .

I encouraged students to come talk to me, and so I explained to the freshman that they would see a notice in the student newspaper from time to time saying, "President Trachtenberg will have office hours Thursday from four to seven." Students showed up for these and felt free to tell me what's good and bad about the university. I also explained where I have lunch frequently on campus and that I walk the campus so that people can tell me their stories and make requests or just say hello.

One year, two people wearing identical blue blazers came to my office to see me. They were the captain and the cocaptain of the GW Sailing Team. They started telling me about the sailing team and I said, "Let me interrupt you for a second. I didn't know we had a sailing team." As it turned out, sailing is a very low visibility sport at GW. The reason it's a low-visibility sport is that they never sailed at GW! They had no boats. But sailing teams participate in regattas hosted by universities. The host university supplies boats for the home team *and* the visiting team because it is too difficult to move boats around from place to place. Our team specialized in being a visiting team! They would go to the University of Pennsylvania, for instance, and they'd be loaned the boats to use in the competition.

I said to them, "How do you practice?" They said, "Well, we don't practice." I said, "Then you can't be very good." They replied, "That's why we're popular as a visiting team!" So I said, "You've got to have boats—I'll buy you boats." When I bought them, the team gave me a T-shirt that said "GW Sailing Team" on it.

Soon the word went out that I had bought boats for the GW Sailing Team. A couple of weeks later I was visited by a couple of students from the GW Equestrian Team. A pattern was developing here. The nice thing about boats is, they don't eat. Horses do. I said to the equestrian team, "I'll help you with the rental fees, but you're on your own with the horses. I'm not buying any horses."

One thing I always warned the freshmen about was the way people tell new students they are about to start the best four years of their lives; I tell them I hope this is not the case. It would make me very sad if I thought these were going to be the best four years of such young lives. I think the best four years of a person's life ought to be the next four years, forever. It's a rolling concept; get through the first year, and then it becomes the next four years—including a year after graduation, then two years out, and so on. I told them to just keep extending four years out. I wanted them to go out of the university with a bundle of skills, a point of view, attitudes that would keep them curious, engaged, committed for the rest of their lives, and energized. Every four years is the start of the best four years of anyone's life.

I told them to keep trying new things, to keep looking for new opportunities after college. I told them about my son Ben. He was a senior in college when I said to him, "Why don't you try for one of the fellowships that let you study abroad? The Rhodes Scholarship, the Marshall Scholarship, the Fulbright Scholarship, the Mitchell Scholarship, the Goldwater Scholarship. There are lots of fellowships and honors and opportunities, and *they*—not your loving parents—will pay for you to travel." Well, Ben applied for fifteen different scholarships of various sorts. Then the rejection slips started coming in and he was getting discouraged. Number eight, *No, thank you.* Number nine, *No, thank you.* And I said, "Listen, don't worry about it, Ben, it's our secret, I won't tell anybody except thousands of GW families." When the tenth rejection slip came in, I said, "You see, we don't mention it until you win one." By God, he won the last one. They named him a Mitchell Scholar. He went to Ireland, had the time of his life, and learned a lot.

I told those new students to apply for everything they were interested in and promised to send out a press release on the ones they actually get. I did a little cheerleading and told them that this beginning represented a moment studded with opportunity. I encouraged them to consider themselves on the first step of the Nobel Prize walk. I told them that maybe, just maybe, there were two Nobel Prize winners in the room. I told them they might just be the other one. Hello, future.

I belong to a synagogue in Washington, but I haven't been there for the High Holy Days in a number of years. On the High Holy Days, I go to services on campus with the students. I always thought it important that the kids on campus see that their president, who happens to be Jewish, showed up at the services to pray with them. In my last year at GW, I addressed the students attending services on Yom Kippur. The following is a summary of what I said to them.

For Jews, this is a solemn time of the year, time to think about the oaths we've made, time to empty our pockets of sin and to atone. This is not a moment for frivolity or for being cute. Yet I want to begin by telling a story that I can only describe as cute, even—another word I do not like—adorable. The events took place in the wake of the tsunami of December 2004.

It concerns a hippopotamus—not GW's Potomac River horse but a live baby hippo that had been washed down a river into the Indian Ocean, then washed back ashore on a beach in Kenya. Rescuers found the little hippo—weighing about 600 pounds—and took him to a game park. It was there that the hippo decided that a male tortoise, about a hundred years old, would be his mother. He followed the tortoise around as he would a real mother. The two swam, ate, and slept together. The article had photographs of the hippo and the tortoise sleeping with their heads next to each other, the hippo lying on one of the tortoise's legs, and the two of them nuzzling each other. As I said, cute; even adorable.

But one of the rangers at the park made an observation that—if not solemn—is surely profound. "Life," he said, "is not measured by the breaths we take but by the moments that take our breath away. The real story shows that our differences don't matter much when we need the comfort of another. We could all learn a lesson from these two; look beyond the differences and find a way to walk the path together."

I think that is very good advice. Isaiah 11:6 foretold a time when the wolf would lie down with the lamb, though we usually say lion instead of wolf. Both wolf and lamb are mammals, while the tortoise is a reptile and the hippo is a mammal. Their differences are truly immense, yet they have learned to live in peace.

The world does not have much peace today. We are living in perilous times, and what can make these times even more perilous is our forgetting history or not knowing it in the first place. Harry Truman was quoted in Merle Miller's oral history called *Plain Speaking* as saying, "The only new thing is the history you don't know." A keen insight. For example, we will understand ourselves better—and, perhaps, those who do not wish us well—if we embrace Jewish traditions and holidays but also understand other traditions and histories. Let me explain. This year's entering class has no living memory of the Soviet Union. Yet not to know about the Soviet Union is to be incapable of understanding the history of the twentieth century—and incapable of seeing the roots of the tensions that continue today in the Balkans.

Thus, to know history is also to know the story of Passover and of the whole of Exodus and the Books of Moses, and more significantly the lessons they teach. God will punish our enemies, but he also holds us to a very high standard. Moses died across the river from the Promised Land. This, I hope, is history that you know and take to heart.

I say this hopefully but not altogether confidently. There is a statue on campus of Alexander Pushkin. Every once in a while, I stand near the statue and stop students to ask them if they know who it is. They dutifully go up to the statue, and there, on the pedestal, they read the name and report to me that it's Alexander Pushkin. Well, I tell them, I read that, too, but who was he? Hardly anyone has been able to tell me that he was a nineteenth-century Russian poet and story writer. I find this discouraging. If a high school or GW has not taught students about Pushkin, then shame on us. But shame on the person if he can walk by a statue of someone unfamiliar and not have the curiosity to look up that unknown person; what could be easier than googling Pushkin? Forgive me if I seem to be scolding. But I feel like an escapee from a J-Walking segment of *The Tonight Show* with Jay Leno when I stand by that statue. I want young students to be better than that. The study of history is important.

Not very long ago, a man in India opened a restaurant called Hitler's Cross. The place was decorated with swastikas and photographs of prominent Nazis. I'm not making this up. It's a relief to report that the place did not do well and closed down. But what is most alarming about this episode is that the restaurateur seemingly had no idea what the fuss was all about. He seemed confused by the storm of bad press he got. I have a strong hunch that he actually did not know who Adolf Hitler was, had no idea that Hitler started a war that cost, by some estimates, thirty million lives, six million of them Jewish. He probably never heard of the concentration and death camps. It hadn't occurred to him that the most hateful man who ever lived should not grace the awning of his restaurant.

This leads me to a more solemn question, more fitting for the day, I think: What is our responsibility at GW to our students? I know that the consequential historical events of my lifetime so far are rather mysterious to many students, even remote. But the Korean and Vietnam Wars, the Soviet Sputnik satellite and the first landing on the moon in 1969, a National Hockey League with only six teams, and baseball where pitchers were always in the lineup are all still bright and living events for me. I can't fairly expect the same from people about a quarter of my age, some of whom were born after I became president of GW. But I do think it is the university's responsibility to do at least two things for its students. The first is to see that they are as well informed as we can possibly make them. This includes the possibility of requiring a few essential courses. The second thought I have is that we must find ways to make history and its many lessons relevant to all students. For example, how do we teach the Holocaust so that it touches us? It is one thing to say, "Never again," but should that be a phrase only on the lips of Jews? I think not.

The idea we must embrace is that everyone, no matter the faith, must say "Never again" to genocide, to ethnic cleansing, to religious hatred. That's a tall order when we think of the fighting between Israel and Hizbollah, between Shia and Sunnis in Iraq, and Arab Muslims and black Christians in Darfur.

There is a very simple model for mutual respect or even affection. Its author was George Washington. It comes from a letter he wrote in 1790 to the Hebrew Congregation of Newport, Rhode Island. Here's an excerpt:

> *It is now no more that toleration is spoken of as if it were the indulgence of one class of people that another enjoyed the exercise of their inherent natural rights, for, happily, the Government of the United States, which gives* to bigotry no sanction, to persecution no assistance, *requires only that they who live under its protection should [comport*] themselves as good citizens in giving it on all occasions their effectual support.*

---

* The original uses the word "demean," which might be confusing.

Natural rights belong to all of us equally. They may, as Thomas Jefferson put it, be at the disposal of the Creator, but they are not to be parceled out by any one person or class as a gift. It is a melancholy reality that what was settled belief more than two centuries ago now in many parts of the world would be greeted as a radical—not to say dangerous and unwelcome—notion.

There is, of course, an even older expression of Washington's idea. It is one of the most famous sayings of Rabbi Hillel as recorded in Pirkei Avot: "If I am not for myself, then who will be for me? And if I am only for myself, then what am I? And if not now, when?" The saying is so familiar that perhaps it no longer has the freshness it deserves to have. So let me take it a phrase at a time.

"If I am not for myself, then who will be for me?" We must all stand up for ourselves, as individuals and as a group. It is also implicit that if I do not stand up for myself, what reason would anyone else have for standing up for me? None, it seems.

"And if I am only for myself, then what am I?" The answer is probably a lone wolf who will never lie down with a lamb or any other creature. We are a gregarious species by nature, and, besides, we live in an ever more crowded world.

"And if not now, when?" The smarty-pants answer is "Whenever," I suppose. But the question is real. If we want to seek justice, there is no putting off the search until tomorrow or the day after. As the old saying goes, "Tomorrow is the day that never comes." We do not have that luxury.

What can we do to get our arms around this idea, whether we take Hillel's, Washington's, or our own formulation? We are not powerless in the face of history. It is not a driverless freight train that will run us over. Here are a couple of ideas. First, something we did a couple of weeks ago. Scholars from the GW Elliott School of International Affairs and other scholars and diplomats from Americans for Informed Democracy and the Brookings Institution invited three hundred young leaders from Muslim countries to a conference, the idea being to promote better understanding in American-Muslim relations. As we know, levels of distrust in our respective populations are very high. We are hopeful that these young leaders will return to their homes and host meetings at the grass roots to help build trust among our peoples. It's ambitious, but it is worth trying. Soft power—that is, personal and peaceful diplomacy—will always trump angry rhetoric intended for public consumption at home for political gain and bombs and rockets.

Second, there is something students can do later this fall. For several years now, GW Muslim and Jewish students have been jointly hosting an *iftar*, the breaking of the fast during Ramadan. An *iftar* is, I suppose, the functional equivalent of the break-fast at the end of Yom Kippur. Although this has been going on for several years, this year I thought of canceling it. The obvious and proximate reason was the awful hostilities between Israel and Hizbollah: I thought the situation might be too delicate, even explosive. Then I thought, "If not now, when?" What could be a better time than a time of tension and mistrust to break bread together? What more important time to speak directly to the "Other"? What more pressing time to recall Martin Buber's concept of I and Thou, not just as the relationship between man and God but between two earthbound humans? We must see the Other as Thou, not It, as a human mirror image, not as a lesser, distorted creature. So the *iftar* will go on.

I like to think that students can teach a lesson to their elders in the world, that the young children of Abraham can transcend the issues of the moment, with all their hearts and passions, and contemplate a higher vision of the human condition. And I like to think that there is more to us than there is in a hippo and a tortoise, that we can walk the path together and find a moment that will take our breath away. That could be a solemn oath for the new year, one we renew year after year after year. *Chag someiach!*

8.

FACULTY ENGAGEMENTS

I have a very high standard for faculty. Perhaps this is a direct reflection of the example set by two of the best of my Columbia professors, Professor Walter P. Metzger and Professor James Patrick Shenton. I thought about them—often wistfully—when I was troubled by some of the difficulties I encountered with faculty while president. And so, before I discuss faculty encounters, it seems only fair that I touch briefly on those qualities that made Metzger and Shenton the models for whom I yearned.

Professor Walter Metzger was a great scholar and lecturer with the aura and demeanor to match his reputation. Athletics were a required part of the curriculum when I was an undergraduate, and I had gym class right before Professor Metzger's class. We played basketball and other games in an antiquated facility on the distant other side of campus from his classroom. I would play the required sport for an hour, take a quick shower, and go into the steamy and fetid locker room to towel off with the thin, well-worn washcloths generously referred to as towels. They would not absorb or dry. The best you could do with them was to smear the wet feeling around on your body. I was always in a hurry to set off to Metzger's class and had to pull my clothes on while still moist, and in the process my underwear and shirt would go soggy. In this condition, I would come up from the basement locker room into the cold afternoon fall and winter air and run across campus to Hamilton Hall. After this run, I would be perspiring profusely. Metzger's class was on the top floor of the building. The elevator was reserved for faculty, so I had to run up the stairs. I generally came into the classroom huffing and puffing—and tardy. Invariably, Metzger was already lecturing. Several times he gently suggested that I try to come to class earlier; but I was doing the best I could!

One day, Metzger instructed a student to lock the classroom door when he began to lecture. So, after my usual race from the gym to class, I was greeted with a locked classroom door. Peering through the pane of smoky glass, I could just make out that the class was in session and Metzger was at the blackboard. I thought to myself, Hell, I'm paying tuition for this class, and I'm not going to miss it! So I tapped on the glass. Metzger ignored me, and I tapped again. This continued until, finally, I tapped on the glass so loudly that the noise disrupted the class and Metzger told someone to open the door for me. As I entered, he commented, "Mr. Trachtenberg, this is not a continuous performance." Brilliant! I was forced to explain my predicament and petition for clemency, which he granted.

Years later, when I was a dean at Boston University, I was attending a conference of college administrators at Colorado College when someone came up and said, "Our speaker for this evening has canceled. Could I impose on you to give some remarks tonight?" I said, "About what?" He said, "Anything you want." He then added generously, "It's only noon; you won't have to speak until seven P.M." So I skipped the rest of that day's agenda and went to the library to prepare a text. I was with my people—a collection of deans—so I decided to do a humorous commentary on the shortcomings of tenure.

But when I got up to speak, I spotted Walter Metzger seated in the audience and fear clutched my heart. He was a leading member of the American Association of University Professors and had been particularly active on Committee A. I knew that he, along with the committee, was the great paladin of tenure. It was too late for me to back out of the talk, so I forged ahead. I ignored Metzger during the Q-and-A session as long as I could and answered all the other questions. Finally, I had no choice and had to call on him. He said, "Mr. Trachtenberg, that was the best defense of the indefensible I have ever heard!" And he proceeded to excoriate me, refuting all my arguments with great skill and finesse. Walter Metzger was as wonderful as ever.

James Patrick Shenton, who was my undergraduate adviser and a gifted professor of history, is a legend among Columbia graduates. Shenton was the most caring—if gruff—classroom teacher I have ever seen. Some of his famous lectures on American history were so popular that there was standing room only in the largest lecture hall on campus. People who were not studying history attended them for fun. In his class on the Roaring Twenties, he wore a raccoon coat, played period records on a wind-up Victrola, and recruited women from Barnard College to wear antique clothes and dance the Charleston as part of his presentation. His Civil War seminar was the stuff of legend. A description by Henry Ebel of the Shenton learning experience reads:

> Here the placid facade of American historiography is torn away, and one is brought face to face with the naked ferocity of human motive and ambition; here the piercing light of analysis is turned on text and footnote alike; here the great are leveled and the humble raised from the dust; here the ultimate questions of human morality are unflinchingly confronted. It is not an experience for the weak, the pulpy, or the intellectually flabby. From September to May a Darwinian selection is at work—laggards fall by the wayside, dilettantes are ruthlessly crushed. Beneath pleasant banter and the civilities of gentlemen lies the cold, passionate fire of the search for Truth.

Of the thirteen of us who took Shenton's Civil War seminar, many came from the Bronx and Brooklyn and were first-generation college students. Shenton was himself of Irish background and knew the limitations of our upbringing, which is to say that when we ate at our houses, we did not use a butter knife, a fish knife, a salad fork, or any of the other implements arrayed in more articulated surroundings. To help us become accustomed to the finer points of table etiquette, Professor Shenton often brought homemade cookies to the seminar and arranged for tea to be served. He even took us to the Faculty House, where, at his own expense, he hosted dinners during which he taught us about red wines with red meat, white wines with fish and chicken, and which of the knives and forks and spoons were to be used with what and when. His thoughtful coaching helped us overcome our apprehension about challenging social situations. He thought that this was an area in which we might need finishing and that he was the only one likely to give it to us.

After I graduated, I returned to campus to pick up my things and pay my final bills. I ran into Jim Shenton crossing College Walk. He said, "You know, Trachtenberg, I have a feeling about you. I predict that in the years to come, you are going to become a felon, a congressman, or a university administrator!"

Years after I received my BA, I was dining at high table at Pembroke College, Oxford, and noticed that there was a yard-long lineup of silverware. There were so many pieces it seemed to me that some were just there merely for decoration. But Shenton's etiquette lessons served me well. I thought fondly, Jim, thank you!

One of the great joys in my professional life came when I received a John Jay Award from Columbia in 1995. This is an honor given to selected graduates whom Columbia deems to have succeeded in their chosen calling. The night I received the award, Professor Shenton was also honored for his teaching and scholarship. The John Jay award meant a great deal to me, but the fact that I received it standing next to him made it all the more meaningful.

BEING A professor has always seemed to me to be one of the most wonderful, extraordinary, protected, and privileged positions in our society. But at times, like other people, professors complain and appear not to like their jobs. Once they have tenure, their quality of economic security is at a level equal to that of federal judges. Professors in some disciplines are paid better than U.S. Supreme Court justices, who are, of course, paid much too little. In any case, both professions provide a lot of ego nutriment in exchange for a degree of material wealth. I suppose the ideal would be to earn some money and *then* become a professor or a judge. Three professors who earned money by writing successful books are Paul Samuelson, the author of an enormously popular economics text, H. W. Jansen, the author of a definitive art history book, and Stephen Carter, a Yale law professor *and* the author of a best-selling novel, *The Emperor of Ocean Park*.

Groups like the military, the police, and firemen see outsiders as civilians; in other words, people not in their subgroup of the universe. It is likewise with university professors. However, professors are a little different because they are a bit more judgmental in their view of others. The other groups see themselves as part of a team or brotherhood. But university professors constitute a collection of determinedly individual people; self-contained units who have been rewarded for being solo players, not team members. As a result, trying to get them to rally around a single university-related cause is very difficult. They don't like to think that they report to anyone, and they perceive themselves as independent professionals who happen to receive a check regularly from an organization with which they are loosely affiliated—the university!

Once professors have received tenure, they know the organization they are engaged by has little or no capacity to censure them. This knowledge liberates them to think freely and to say and write things without fear of material consequence. But it also takes away from bonding and larger accountability to the institution. An untenured professor might be anxious, conflicted, and worried about what student surveys will indicate about his performance or what senior faculty will think of him. But as soon as he has tenure—a lifetime contract unless he does something like assaulting the dean's wife in public and with witnesses—he knows that he can do the most bizarre things and the institution will tolerate the behavior. I once went to a retirement dinner for a faculty member who had always been viewed as a bit strange and even offensive in his demeanor and off-putting in his relationships with other people. Clearly he knew this about himself because in his farewell remarks he said, "I want to give my thanks to tenure, without which I would not have been able to stay here all these happy years." I thought, He's probably right! God bless him; the system worked for him, and he knew it.

I think that the hardest part of being a professor must be the loneliness of scholarship. Professors are very smart and are accustomed to being the brightest in their school and college classes. They were probably told they were special and were encouraged to follow academic careers. But then they get to be fifty and still haven't received the Bancroft Prize or the Fields Medal and haven't written the great American novel, or the job becomes a little repetitive and they learn that the dentist down the street makes a lot more money than they do. We all have midprofession crises, but I suspect that professors might have these to a greater degree, possibly because they are constantly surrounded by the potential they see in the young people around them.

A president is always thinking of new ideas and initiatives and is always trying to make things happen. With the passage of time, people don't necessarily remember where ideas came from. Too often it is the president and staff who initiated them. The faculty initiates change infrequently. If you want to introduce a new idea, the faculty and other campus groups often have to hear it again and again before they really begin to pay attention. Or they may not listen to the whole idea and instead listen to gossip or disinformation, which gets in the way of instituting the change. Universities are devilishly difficult places to govern because there is very little actual corporate power and the administrators are shepherds; not of sheep, but of cats! Issues can be defined by a faculty attitude of "What's in it for me?"

Look at the example of a professor in Washington, D.C., who ran successfully for public office. Those who did not want to see him elected argued, "He is a GW professor and will be in the pocket of the university and will not have free will if elected." To refute their argument, he pointed out that he is tenured, there is nothing the university can ever do to sanction him, and he owes the university nothing. Of course, there is some accuracy in that representation. But if you overstate it, it becomes offensive. I wonder, at some point, don't we all have some obligation to the institution whose name is on our paychecks?

Others opposed to this professor's candidacy said that being a professor is a full-time job and might be too much for an officeholder. His answer was, in effect, "Don't worry about it! Being a professor doesn't require any time! There's nothing to it. It's almost like being unemployed. I'll be able to devote all my time to elective office." I may be overstating this a bit for dramatic effect, but not by much. Hearing such a pronouncement, I mentioned it to him. When I did, he pointed out quite accurately that his teaching load was only two and one. In other words, in the fall semester, he is obliged to be in class six hours a week and in the spring he is obliged to be in class only three hours a week. Depending on how you view it, that could be pretty close to having a hobby rather than a real full-time job! Our faculty is paid well. Of course, in addition to teaching, professors also have responsibilities to scholarship and service that call for some time. But a critic of their workload surely could conceive of ways to run schools more efficiently.

My father once telephoned me during the Vietnam era. While watching TV, he had seen an antiwar demonstration going on in Boston. Some people there were said to be Boston University faculty. He thought it was noble of them to give up a day's pay to advocate their political views. I said, "No, Dad, these are professors, they are not going to lose a day's pay!" He said, "So they unilaterally declared it was a holiday?" I said, "Well, sort of." He was upset. Everyone he knew, if they gave up a day's work, they gave up a day's pay.

But in the faculty, my father concluded, it seems there is no equal understanding of the value of time. Of course, if the president raises such an argument, the faculty would assure him that they work constantly, that their subject is always on their minds, that even as they drive their cars they are doing higher-level calculations, and that on the weekends they are endlessly working and thinking. I feel that way about the presidency, so I am somewhat sympathetic to the perspective. I know that when you have a responsible job, it never completely leaves your consciousness. But one might ask: What does all this mean as we try to be the best university? What does it mean for the students?

Students are always striving to go to the "best" university. But the "best" is not the one where the teaching is the best or the undergraduate life experience is the best; it is the place with the best reputation, as defined by research scholars. So it may be that a student goes to a brand-name university but doesn't have any access to those Nobel Prize winners until, maybe, she becomes a post-PhD student. In fact, until that point, her classes might be enormous sections taught by graduate students. We have made significant trade-offs in order to give faculty lighter teaching loads so they can dedicate more of their time to scholarship and publication. We have reduced teaching obligations, but in order to fill in we have added adjunct faculty. Often, this is followed by complaints from students, who object to being taught by part-time professors and teaching assistants.

Luckily for my university, the Washington, D.C., metropolitan area is blessed by a very rich adjunct faculty environment. But many universities around the country are not; they have to draw from a much smaller talent pool. We have to ask, Have we diluted the quality of education for undergraduates in order to make universities more scholar-friendly for faculty? What does that mean for the value of a BA degree, a graduate degree, or the whole educational experience? Is all this scholarship necessary and useful, or would it be better to surrender what is in some cases marginal scholarship generated merely so that someone can be promoted and instead dedicate that person to teaching full-time or to devoting more time to students?

Research falls into several categories. Some of it stretches the boundaries of what we know and propels the human race forward—for instance, discovering germ theory, splitting the atom, or finding a cure for polio. Other research delves inward: understanding consciousness, passion, or motivation or celebrating beauty and the Divine. But, alas, some research is undertaken solely to add a line on the researcher's résumé. Some research on campuses can be a study of trivial, marginal information that is quicker to join the pantheon of footnotes in an obscure journal than a bad Hollywood film is released on DVD. Research needed solely for credentialing not only diminishes serious scholarship, it is also unfair to faculty who are required to produce it and on the students who are obliged to read it.

I don't want to be misunderstood on this issue. I am not saying that those who can, do, and those who can't, teach. The issue is much more complicated. What I would like to see is a healthier balance between excellent teaching and important research, along with public recognition that not everyone excels at all things, nor should the academy expect them to do so. If we muddy the waters of advancement, we should not be surprised at the consequences.

Teachers struggling to publish just one more article before tenure review might be tempted to neglect other matters. Faculty members pushing to write just one more book might reduce the time they spend with students. Simply giving lectures each week is certainly not mentoring. The truth is, the students' favorite faculty members are not usually the Nobel Prize winners. They are often the ones who invite their seminar groups to meet a visiting scholar, occasionally lead a walk through the city's historic district, or are willing to critique first and second drafts of student papers before getting the final one. They are the ones who, by giving of themselves, awaken the spirit of learning and discovery in their pupils.

What I have just outlined seems like an ideal when compared to the reality on both sides of the teaching-versus-research equation. When I was president of the University of Hartford, we had a department that consisted of only three faculty members. They worked very diligently and had a lot of courses to teach. Consequently, they were not very productive from a scholarly point of view and didn't publish. Then I hired a fourth faculty member of great academic promise and reduced everyone's teaching load accordingly. A couple of years went by, during which the new fourth member was quite productive. He taught and wrote a book and some articles, but the other three were no more productive than before, even with the reduced teaching load. Nevertheless, they complained about their salaries. When the fourth faculty member got an offer from somewhere else and left, I said to the original three, "Let's return to the original teaching load and I will divide among the three of you the salary that went to the fourth faculty member." They wouldn't do it! It was more important to them to have the reduced teaching load, even though they weren't doing any scholarship. They already knew they could handle the heavier load because they had been doing it for years. But the reduced load had become a status thing for them; it was now imperative to them to teach three rather than four courses even if they were paid less than they had been offered to teach the previous number of courses. In the end, we didn't replace the departed faculty member and didn't increase departmental pay either. It was sad on all sides.

One university that I hear about is very pleased with itself because it recruited some Nobel Prize winners to its ranks. These people arrived long after they won the prize and at a point in their careers beyond which they could be expected to start very many new fires. Their arrival gave the university a chance to talk about its distinguished faculty. But those Nobel Prize winners are not getting engaged with very many students. It is an instance in which the halo effect drives campus decisions. The question for a president should be: Are you better off recruiting someone late in his or her professional life and spending what it takes to get one of them, or are you better off hiring three junior faculty with promise? These are not just symbolic issues; nevertheless, they are not being asked nationally.

It's a big mistake to underestimate the strength of the status quo in universities. The culture is entrenched. And it is not a culture that asks, "What can we do to be more student-oriented?" Too often, the first constituency is the faculty. I don't think the university is well served by this. Other aspects of society take technology into account and are seeking ways to be more and more productive. Universities say, "No, no, no, what we will do is have our faculty teach less! Even if we have fewer students and fewer classes, salaries must go up." There is a limit to where you can take tuition. There is also a limit to where you can take an institution—unless you find ways to be more efficient.

The challenge to the president is to persuade senior faculty to be allies of the university, partners in the university's well-being, and collaborators in crafting its future. Informed faculty need to be more broadly and positively engaged with the university agenda and responsible—even accountable—for where it goes. Their contribution will be critical to sustaining higher education in the days to come.

• • •

IN ANY discussion of the future of higher education, a few topics always make their way rudely to the head of the queue. The endowment— that is, increasing the endowment and annual giving—is frequently first in line. Then the discussion moves on to matters academic: competing with your market-basket schools; improving the involvement of the Board of Trustees; and deciding how to rationalize intercollegiate athletics as part of the educational mission. The combined topic of institutional governance and the faculty is usually not even in the line.

It is said that when Ronald Reagan was governor of California he remarked that you would not be able to get a majority of faculty at the University of California to come out to vote "no" on an initiative reading, "RESOLVED, next Friday we will line up the faculty and shoot them." Apocryphal or not, this story points to a very troubling situation that was a problem throughout my presidency: the faculty assumes that there will always be a university. They felt less urgency than I did when looking at the problems facing higher education and the university. It may be true that the university will always be here, but what that university will look like and be like is far less clear.

For example, I think it is fair to ask, "What do we know about learning?" We know that people learn in different ways; by seeing, by hearing, and by doing. But think about lectures. They are an artifact from medieval times and preceded movable type. Students in those days sat in their seats and the professor delivered a set of lectures, which made up his book. He got in front of the class and read out the text while the students took notes. By the end of the course, the students had transcribed his book for their own use. With the invention of movable type, it became possible to print books—at first for a very high price, so students didn't own them—but students could go where the book was chained to a desk in the library. Today everyone in the class can have a personal copy of a book, which, ironically, is itself being overtaken by digital technology. One would think that by now the use of the lecture would be substantially diminished. But no, we continue to build classroom buildings where students are obliged to come and hear (perhaps even listen to) lectures and take notes. Does that make sense in the twenty-first century? Probably not, but professors are very reluctant to move beyond the lecture as their primary medium.

Today there is increasing talk about measuring what we get for our investment in education. Margaret Spellings, the secretary of education under George W. Bush, appointed a task force that tried to get its hands around this question and faced a very difficult time. What its members don't want to say, for instance, is that it is an indulgence for faculty members to have the kinds of teaching schedules many now enjoy. But the nature of university governance is that the administration doesn't get to decide. It can't change things without the concurrence of the faculty. Under the contemporary model, if you want to actually manage an institution, you must do so with the agreement of the faculty. You can persuade, cajole, and induce, but you cannot order people to change. Therefore, the university is a unique culture in which there is little management and only some administration. The mission of administrators is often to carry out the will of the professoriate. Of course, this is not always in their best interest—professors, like the rest of us, don't always know what is best for them. This is radical talk, I realize.

There are those who say the place-based university is obsolete and will ultimately disappear. We now see the increasing development of distance learning, offering courses that are available to students all over the planet. Someone sitting in Anchorage, Alaska, can listen to a professor teaching in Foggy Bottom, and because we have the technology, the session can even be interactive. That class no longer consists of thirty or forty people gathered on the campus but is distributed all over the country—or the world. Certainly this is likely to have a growing impact on universities.

I don't think that the university campus will disappear, because education is more than schooling, more than what goes on in the classroom. It also has to do with the interactions of people, the development of a certain sociology and courtship patterns, and the process of passing from child to independent adult, working on the school newspaper, and playing on a team. There will always be a role, especially at the undergraduate level, for universities where people come to be with their age group and go through the initiation from high school student to university student and then out into a larger world. Different cultures have different ways of initiating their youth into maturity, but a university education is one of the ways we in the Western world, and increasingly in the rest of the world as well, transform people into full-fledged adults. We give them a diploma as a symbol of that metamorphosis. However, in the days to come many graduate courses will be increasingly taught via distance technology. This will be truer of some fields than others. There are disciplines where it will always be necessary to come to a particular place because it hosts a critical mass of scholars or has laboratories and other facilities that are necessary for teaching and learning the subject matter and skills.

While universities will not disappear, I think that, going forward, they will experience change on almost every level. Unhappily, we are inadequately prepared for such change. In their desire to keep things as they are, faculty continue to deny the need for or the inevitability of what lies ahead. Ironically, these are people who, in their scholarship, often study and advocate innovation. Is it odd, therefore, that they are in denial when innovation and change confront their university? Possibly this reflects human nature.

Faculty Senate agendas at GW over the years indicate that it has addressed issues the administration proposed. If the administration went silent for any length of time, the Senate would cancel meetings for lack of an agenda. Faculty generally do not see themselves as responsible for proposing new institutional departures. Rather, they see themselves as guardians of tradition. They have a faculty code, and that defines the rules of university engagement. They are more committed to process and less committed to outcome. For instance, the nature of their tenure review is one in which they defer to the discipline department. Tenure—a life contract for a professor—is a multimillion-dollar commitment on the part of a university! It can take the income on $3 million to pay for one professor for a year. But the Faculty Senate will never say that a person's record as a biologist or a sociologist is completely mediocre. They defer evaluation to the sovereignty of the

Biology or Sociology Department and, instead, expend their energies in making sure that a defined process was observed in the review proceedings, however obvious the shortcomings of the final outcome.

I think that when tenure is about to be given to a faculty member, there should first be a demonstration that it is being given to a really first-class biologist, sociologist, or whatever—and that there is proof of accomplishment as a scholar and teacher and a potential for future excellent work that will help move knowledge forward. Faculty senators are not against these things; they just see their role as the narrowly defined one of the process itself, not the larger, critical one of anticipating the candidate's performance in the next thirty years.

If the administration comes forward with a proposal for change, the faculty wants to see if the proposal observes all the protocols for change. Did everybody agree? Was there any dissent? But if the faculty doesn't carry its part of the load, any forward movement breaks down. And that is where I have issues with the faculty. Universities are properly much more collegial, consensual, and almost Quaker-like in the way they govern themselves than armies or businesses are, for instance. Universities are not fashionable institutions, interested in the mode of the day. But if they are not fashionable, I would like to think they could at least be a bit stylish. They could add value to society by being an anchor against the thoughtlessly novel. But, like any virtue, resistance to things new can be overdone. Faculty shouldn't be feathers in the wind of circumstance, but they should be amenable to the novel and acknowledge when the world around them, which supports them, calls for them to adapt to doing new things in different ways.

There is a general confusion about how the president of the university ought to behave. But even if I had been a typical faculty member before I became president, I know that once I assumed the presidency, the faculty would not have wanted me to speak too forcefully on any scholarly issues involving them. This is a great internal contradiction. In some ways, I have violated the rules by addressing many of these matters. It could be even more frustrating for a president who, unlike me, has a PhD and is, therefore, a bona fide member of their club to be told, "We, the faculty, want you to be our paladin. When you are facing out from the university, be a lion, but when you are facing in, be a lamb."

I have noticed that faculty members are always a little embarrassed at being caught doing their work. They want to do it in private and certainly do not want the president to see them doing it. And so there are protocols within the university that limit administrators. I think professors are normal human beings, and I understand that they do not want to be exposed to the usual kinds of checks and balances that other professionals endure. Doctors, like many other professionals, can be expected to occasionally err in the course of performing their jobs. This is why they carry malpractice insurance. And it is why there are internal peer reviews of hospital proceedings. But universities offer tenure for faculty, and the latter are protected by it like almost no other professional group. Posttenure review, for instance, is very unpopular and infrequent.

As far as I know, if at GW we were to dismiss a tenured professor, it might be the first time since the university was founded in 1821. We have had a few faculty resignations under difficult circumstances, but for ten years we attempted to separate a particular professor for cause. We went through warnings, stern conversations, hearings, and faculty reviews with no final outcome to date. In this we are no different from most other universities; the number of fired tenured faculty in the country as a whole is *de minimus*. Can it be that professors are exempt from the failings and shortcomings that exist in all other human beings? Surely not! Tenure is doing its job—protecting faculty from arbitrary firings—but it seems reasonable to ask: Is tenure overdoing its job? Is tenure unfair to universities because of the demand on resources involved in trying to get incompetent, unproductive, or irresponsible members out of the faculty? Is it unjust to students that because of the daunting effort of taking on such a task, administrations tend to just let them sit? Is it reasonably a cost of doing business to keep on the faculty and invent busywork for a member who is unproductive or incapable and cannot be put into a classroom under any circumstances?

We no longer have a legal mandatory retirement age. As a result, people can stay on the faculty beyond their ability to contribute. Universities just tolerate the situation. Frankly, this is a wise, if unsound, business decision because the process of getting rid of someone is so time-consuming and resource-intensive that it just doesn't pay to go through all the processes and appellate steps it would take.

I certainly don't think a collection of professors is more virtuous than a group of doctors, clergy, accountants, or lawyers, or—dare I say it?—even congressmen. They have feet of clay like other people, but they often seem to feel that they have been elected as judges of society. For instance, what are we to think when, before the facts were known, and before the accused were able to present their case, eighty-eight Duke professors placed a notice in *The Chronicle of Higher Education* referring to the circumstances surrounding the allegations of rape against members of the Duke lacrosse team in 2006? Part of their provocative public statement follows:

> *We are listening to our students. We're also listening to the Durham community, to Duke staff, and to each other. Regardless of the results of the police investigation, what is apparent every day now is the anger and fear of many students who know themselves to be objects of racism and sexism, who see illuminated in this moment's extraordinary spotlight what they live with every day. They know that it isn't just Duke, it isn't everybody, and it isn't just individuals making this disaster. But it is a disaster nonetheless. These students are shouting and whispering about what happened to this young woman and to themselves. The students know that the disaster didn't begin on March 13th and won't end with what the police say or the court decides. Like all disasters, this one has a history.*

I have noticed that there is sometimes an extraordinary temptation on the part of university faculty to rush to judgment. Athletes can be a good target; administration is also tempting. These two groups might be accused of motives that neither group ever even dreamed of. The case can become theoretical instead of actual. When they speak about things, faculty might be thinking something like: "Even if the Duke athletes were not guilty of the specific crime they were accused of, they were somehow guilty generically for being loutish, over-privileged kids."

When people are thus willing to pass judgment on the administration, the students, their parents, the society, it seems it is usually an attack on some larger issue or collateral agenda. For instance, acts of racism on campus are a terrible thing and should be condemned. But not every stupid kid who says something racist is representative of institutional racism or some generalized flaw in society. That youngster might be just an eighteen-year old who talks without thinking.

There are instances of group mentality and ideological focus that, ironically, seem almost anti-intellectual. I have seen professors who are highly trained in their disciplines and are engaged in excellent scholarship but are nonetheless prepared to vote on questions, issue judgments, sign petitions, and act out of a commitment to some larger cause while abandoning all the standard habits and caution that they would bring to their own scholarship. It is interesting to note the disciplines of the people who were so quick to condemn in the Duke case, for instance, and the people who were not. The lawyers and the engineers held back. But some of the humanists were willing to rush to judgment. This is not something unique to the Duke faculty. It is a phenomenon fairly endemic in the academy and has been for the almost forty years that I have been involved. I assume it existed even before I became involved in academic life. During the Vietnam years, the engineers and the lawyers I witnessed were more cautious, while the social scientists and the people in the humanities were more apt to pass resolutions and push for action on issues they felt strongly about. Basically, this can be seen as endorsing political correctness—the side to which they are committed. In the case of the Duke professors, although one could rightly assume that they should feel committed to all the young people they teach, no matter what, I can only assume they think they are protecting a larger group of young people when they focus on a specific group of young people within the university whom they think of as rogue, racist, and antifeminist.

We certainly do need people who can speak truth to power, and we encourage philosophers and others in universities to serve a distinguishable role. Of course, there are others—people who write editorials, for instance—who lecture us and try to direct us to our better selves. But even *The New York Times* can be wrong from time to time. So I have never felt it was obligatory to agree with it any more than I have felt it obligatory to agree with the president of the United States or the Congress.

ONE STORY stands out in my career that might shed some light on what I have been saying about certain types of engagements with the faculty. It is the case of Ronald Radosh.

One day, I received a call from an acquaintance of mine, Michael Horowitz, a political activist in Washington who was once a thinker on the left but, in the course of his personal evolution, found himself firmly on the right. Michael is a robustly intellectual writer and theorist with a very interesting, aggressive mind. I always enjoy talking to him because he never lacks a strong point of view and he articulates it very forcefully and provocatively.

Michael asked me if I knew the historian Ronald Radosh. I did not. He explained that, in his world, Radosh is a bit controversial. Radosh himself was a man of the left who had drifted with the passage of time over to the right. One of his books had caused his former colleagues on the left to view him as an apostate.

Michael told me that Radosh had a grant from a foundation known to be very conservative. The grant would support him as a visiting professor at a university for three years. He had already been at one university for almost two years, but there was much excitement going on at that university and Radosh found it was distracting him from his work. But he still had money for another year, and it was completely portable. Michael asked me if Radosh could come to GW. I told him I didn't make faculty appointments, but if he would send me the man's résumé I would inquire. I got the résumé, and it seemed perfectly plausible to me; he had earned a good PhD and had a list of serious publications. He had spent a year as a speechwriter for Albert Shanker, president of the American Federation of Teachers. I knew Al and called him. He told me that Radosh was intellectually sound.

I called the then chairman of the History Department and asked him to review the résumé and, if he thought it worthwhile, to call Radosh and take him to lunch. I told him to see if Radosh would add to the department. I reminded him that Radosh would be free to the university and that we would not have to make any funding commitments to him at all. I told him that since Radosh was not of the same ideological stripe as the rest of the department, it might be interesting to have him around, and perhaps he could teach courses not otherwise available. The chair of the History Department agreed to meet Radosh and share the opportunity with the rest of his department. For reasons that are probably predictable in academia—although a little crazy—the department faculty concluded that I was trying to force the man upon them. They perceived this opportunity as an imposition and a violation of their right to recruit whomever they wanted. They seemed confused; they thought the money Radosh would bring with him was available to them to hire whomever they wished! They did not understand that Radosh was like a man coming to a picnic and bringing his own sandwiches!

They started making inquiries about Radosh. In the process they talked to someone at Columbia, a contemporary of Radosh who had known him since they were young children. But the two had fallen out. That person had been given the impression by whoever called him that I was imposing Radosh upon the GW department. This impression was leaked to *The Chronicle of Higher Education*, and the chairman of the Columbia History Department was quoted as saying it would be highly unconventional to fill a faculty post without a search. I agree! It would be unconventional! But there was no slot to fill! It would be Radosh with his own sandwiches or nothing! The question was, would my colleagues rather have nothing than have Radosh available to the department? I had no vested interest in the outcome except to benefit the university. The department ultimately voted that it didn't want Radosh, even if he was going to bring his own salary.

Subsequently, Professor Amitai Etzioni, a very successful sociologist at the university who runs the Institute for Communitarian Policy Studies, offered to give him an office at the institute and the opportunity to do his own work in that space. Radosh worked there for a year, then received money for another year, and ultimately left the university.

This had become an almost predictable cause célèbre. People with their own agendas used it as an opportunity to characterize the university or its leadership as behaving in some inappropriate manner—perhaps to scapegoat them. It became a public disputation over an issue in which the university proceeded with discretion and caution but was later characterized as trying to do things in an underhanded manner. It's a variation on the Duke theme, wherein faculty jumped in precipitously to condemn the university's lacrosse team.

AMERICA AS a whole has been remarkably hospitable to progressive thought, and American education has, in the past, shown great imagination. For instance, the community college is an American innovation that provides access to postsecondary school and has served our nation well. Not everyone needs a BA, but many need a two-year degree—perhaps a technical degree—to live better lives and do their jobs well. The community college has also been very important because it has provided a bridge to four-year universities for students from modest socioeconomic backgrounds.

The GI Bill of Rights was as important to America as the Morrill Act was to the land grant universities. We cannot now afford to be self-congratulatory and say the American university is the wonder of the civilized world and just leave it at that. That just won't do. It is time to make an important shift and acknowledge the role of communication. If we have the ability to teach on a statewide basis using technology, we must do so. We might find that a local professor who teaches a subject on a local campus fears being made redundant as a result. Or she may be concerned that people will think a new course, offered from a more prestigious location, is better than the local course. The unions have a phrase, "rate breaker," which refers to people who raise the standard of performance on the assembly line and cause discomfort to others who are not as productive. One doesn't have to have a great imagination to understand why people don't like change; it alters their lives, and it is discomforting. But we cannot permit this to frustrate public policy for the greater good.

If my administration was internally provocative, it was due to its taking an interest in innovation, bringing about positive change, creating new programs and schools, urging curriculum enhancement, calling for a greater emphasis on writing skills, creating an Honors Program, asking for an emphasis on quantitative skills, and offering courses in Arabic, Japanese, and Chinese so that our students could make their way in the twenty-first century. These proposals were greeted with greater or lesser hospitality by professors depending on whether they saw them as supportive of themselves or thought they might deprive their programs of attention. In a world with unlimited resources, I might have been perceived as a far more congenial president than I was in a world in which choices must be made and not everyone concurs on which are best.

There are many issues that should concern faculty; unionization and affirmative action in hiring are two. But, for example, when the faculty had a chance to elect members of the search committee to find my successor, they elected three senior white males! These were tenured, long-serving colleagues; they were all from the professional schools. There was *no one* from the school of arts and sciences—the academic heart of the university—the school with the largest faculty! It was the faculty of arts and sciences that brought down Lawrence Summers at Harvard; at my university, they didn't even get a seat on the presidential search committee.

Early in my GW presidency, I had a discussion with a faculty committee searching for a dean. I didn't think its favorite candidate was the best person for the job, and I told them so. The members got upset. I yielded. When he became dean, he concurrently received a tenured professorship—a long-standing tradition. Within two years, he had received a vote of no confidence from the faculty because he had tried to make some changes. Now they expected me to replace a dean they no longer favored. Although the search committee had insisted that he was the right choice, the members of that committee were not to be found when the tide of opinion went in another direction! It was I who had to urge him into the faculty so I could seek another dean. In the end, acceding to their desires at the outset hadn't done me or the university any good. Faculty can be very high on their prerogatives and their confidence. I learned a lot from that experience and did not make that mistake again.

During my time as president, a faculty search committee frequently wanted someone nonthreatening as dean. But I felt it was useful to constantly introduce stimulation into the system. I certainly didn't want to go out and find the most provocative person for the job, but I did not want an individual who would merely preside over the faculty and not add value. Building consensus is not a justification for license.

One of the faculty members I personally like most at GW is a man who believes that administrators are simply ministerial officials who are obliged to take instruction from the faculty and should do only what they are told. I believe that administrators are discretionary leaders who must bring vision and leadership to the job. This creates a certain tension. Possibly it is even a good tension. Still, it is useful to count votes as you do your work.

Leadership in universities is different from that in other organizations. In other organizations, the president or CEO tells people what he or she wants done, and, to a greater or lesser degree, that is what gets done. Jack Welch, who was obviously a management genius at General Electric, would probably not make a good university president. A university president has to be more of a politician than a corporate leader. A *Father Knows Best* image of management will definitely not succeed in a university, where the president is engaged in an unrelenting negotiation and constantly trying to keep an eye on where the institution should go and how he can get the stakeholders and constituents to go there willingly.

The force that cannot be overestimated in universities is passive aggressiveness. It is almost irresistible. The faculty in one of the schools of the university once passed a resolution in May demanding that the dean not do anything until they returned from their summer vacations in the fall! They wanted us to halt the decision making for that school for four months. We must realize that just as the world does not have a "stop button," neither does the university.

University administrators read *The Chronicle of Higher Education* to stay in touch with what is happening in higher education. But I don't believe many faculty read it. They don't stay current with what's going on in the academy, nor do they look too hard at what's taking place at other universities. I wonder, if they don't know what's happening, how can they make decisions? I was amused when, a couple of years ago, a faculty committee at Harvard decided that taking a semester or a year abroad might be a good idea for undergraduates. Harvard announced this idea proudly—and *The New York Times* breathlessly reported it—as if it had discovered gravity! Didn't it know how many colleges and universities all over the country have for decades been sending students to study abroad?

As a matter of law at private universities, members of the faculty are considered managers. As managers, it is natural for them to participate in steering the university and for them to be part of the overall mission. This is an important concept; their robust participation and informed cooperation are clearly vital for the future of higher education. The Yeshiva University Faculty Association filed a representation petition with the National Labor Relations Board, seeking certification as a bargaining agent for the full-time faculty members of certain schools of Yeshiva University, a private university. Yeshiva University opposed the petition on the grounds that all of its faculty members are managerial or supervisory personnel and are not employees within the meaning of the National Labor Relations Act. In 1980, the Supreme Court found that a university's full-time faculty members are managerial employees and are therefore excluded from the act's coverage. The Court held that many managerial activities of faculty affect finances because of their role in admissions and hiring standards. The same is true of tenure and promotion practice—and much more that goes to the very heart of the enterprise.

Another worry I have about faculty is the fact that there aren't term limits for officers in the Faculty Senate. Some make the office the focus of their careers. I used to look around and wonder: Where are the young people? Who will participate in faculty governance in the future? Coupled with that concern is the case for mandatory retirement of faculty. It might be good if, at age seventy-five, tenure would end. At that point, the school and the faculty member could decide whether to continue the relationship. If either party said no, there would be no fight about it. What we have now is lifetime tenure. I know that at seventy I am not as energetic as I was ten years ago, and certainly I will not be at eighty what I am now. Why do we ignore the fact of aging? It is the elephant in the room. We keep faculty on with lifetime contracts for as long as they choose to stay. Is faculty aging across the country? How could it not be? Look at it this way: If someone has a great health plan and can draw a salary, and also have four months off in the summer, what is the incentive to *ever* retire and create a space for a younger person to fill? We are favoring the elderly at the expense of the young. The question underlying all such issues is: Who is looking out for the institution and the students? Both can be equitably served by more thoughtful arrangements.

It sounds simple enough: invite faculty, persuade them, and they should gladly immerse themselves in learning how the university works and then join in. But "simple" is not the appropriate word. "Daunting" is more like it—maybe even "Sisyphean." After thirty-eight years in the academy, I conclude that many faculty seem to be uninformed about university administration. They surely know less than they should and much less than we would expect from a board member or trustee in this post-Sarbanes-Oxley era. Even worse, far too many faculty members don't appear to be very interested in learning more about university administration.

When I spoke with small groups of faculty and mentioned some of the problems confronting the university, I was more often than not met by incomprehension. And when I tried to clarify the issues in order to get some of their thinking to inform my own, I got silence. The result, alas, is a default adversarial relationship, which is neither wholesome nor profitable. The relationship can poison the atmosphere—at least on occasion—and waste time and resources. In the worst iterations of this scenario, the faculty comes to believe the administration is perfidious and greedy, while the administration comes to believe the faculty to be uncommitted and greedy. This is not much of a choice since neither statement is true.

I think I know where this problem arises. In our PhD programs across the country, we are educating people who, by and large, expect to become professors. Among the many things we do not teach our PhD candidates is anything about how the university actually works. Their goal is to become expert in a discipline. They see themselves as Mathematicians, or Physicists, or Anthropologists. It is not the fault of our graduate students that they do not receive instruction in governance or administration; at that period of their lives, do they even know there is such a thing? Why should they? They have been students bent on acquiring—as Michel de Montaigne said more than four hundred years ago—a well-filled head or at least a well-stuffed one. Their goal has been to acquire information and, I like to think, knowledge.

University governance and administration are not a topic of study except in specialized programs in higher education, where universities may be grouped with other nonprofits even though they can be very different in nature, structure, sociology, and values. It is no wonder that young faculty members arrive on campus for their first jobs with no knowledge of university governance or administration or any thought that it should concern them. It is no wonder that they don't inquire about it. In their first years they are striving to make friends, stay employed, learn to teach, do scholarship, publish, and get tenure. By the time they have joined the ranks of the tenurati, they are fully engaged with an academic ethos that I believe tends to turn them away from a focus on the specific university where they work. This perspective has been provided by David Kirp in his remarkable book *Shakespeare, Einstein, and the Bottom Line.* Kirp observes—absolutely correctly, in my view—that many tenured faculty members are primarily responsive not to their institutions or even to their departments, but rather to peers in their discipline whose approval and praise are what will gain them status and better appointments. Stanley Katz, former president of the American Council of Learned Societies, reaffirmed this view in an issue of *The Chronicle of Higher Education.*

This cast of mind, Kirp and Katz argue, leads faculty members to think of themselves as "capital" rather than as "labor." Without question, the faculty does represent the intellectual capital of a university's balance sheet. But they are not the endowment; they are senior managers in the vineyard. If they saw their situation the way I do, it might be easier to interest them in administration. The president, the vice presidents, and the deans are all workers. We could all profit from understanding—equally well—the process of the university and knowing how to make the enterprise run smoothly and without allowing friction to ruin the gears.

If we agree that young faculty have little knowledge of university affairs, there seems to be something obvious that we could do—and that we do for others: *we could teach it.* We could teach it as if we want it to matter in their professional lives.

When new trustees join the GW Board of Trustees, they are given an orientation that includes an analysis of the university's system of governance, budget, mission, and explanations of how the various board committees operate and what their goals are. When freshmen first arrive on campus, we offer them an orientation that includes just about everything we calculate they will need to know as they start at the university.

But we have only a modest orientation for new faculty, junior or senior. Departments or schools may offer something, but probably not much to do with the big picture. This diminishes the junior faculty; they don't know that they can participate or how, and so they don't. There is, of course, a small body within the faculty that holds almost the entire franchise: the faculty senators. As I have already mentioned, since there are no term limits on their service, a small number of individuals have been in charge of the faculty's contribution to the university conversation for two decades or more. After a term in the Senate, a tenured professor can simply run again—and tends to do just that.

The consequence is that the Faculty Senate—and I believe this to be true in many universities—is conservative; it likes to preserve things as they are. "New" is a word I learned never to use when I took a proposal to that group. If something wasn't done in the past, it can't be done now. As individuals, the faculty senators may not be risk-averse, but as an institution, the Senate is. This condition often makes shared governance a frustrating exercise.

President Derek Bok of Harvard once wrote, "Faculty autonomy often leads to unrealized opportunities and unsatisfactory results for want of voluntary cooperation." I think my examples of calendar reform and a four-by-four course structure underscore Bok's argument. By reforming the two-semester academic calendar and adding a third term, I believed we could get better returns on our sunk costs and save some students tuition by graduating them in three years instead of four if they chose to accelerate. It would also enable us to increase enrollment while restricting the size of GW's student body. Reform of the calendar would make GW more flexible and better able to meet its financial challenges and opportunities in the decade ahead. I also wanted to move from a three-by-five course load to a four-by-four. Doing so would add more depth to courses, free up classroom space, and actually accommodate teaching obligations by requiring fewer preparations. This would be a boon to scholars seeking time for research.

The proposal to reform the calendar was killed by a resounding resolution of the Faculty Senate that declined even to discuss the idea — ever. The four-by-four proposal was buried alive in committee after committee. I suspect that a less conventional Senate would not have been so eager to remove these ideas from among the quick and place them among the dead.

That brings me back to the younger, untenured faculty. I would like to see them participate in the Senate's deliberations. It is hard to imagine that they would be as cautious as the current Senate. This would also engage them with the university agenda early in their careers and maybe give them a longer view of the university's needs and opportunities. And maybe it would encourage their loyalty to the university, as well as to an external superego of disciplinary peers.

I am in favor of a kind of orientation for new faculty that focuses on university administration. There could even be a course of study. Anyone wishing to serve on the Senate would have to take it.

I will not argue that improving the university environment by involving more faculty, educating more faculty, and reforming some faculty from their hold on management is the only way to improve higher education. It is a means, not an end. But if something like this is not done, there may not be a university, as we know it, in the future—institutions with boundless resources excepted.

SOMETIMES DECISIONS made as a result of faculty pressure can be complicated and may have the effect of making other university stakeholders angry. One interesting example of this involves a change in our Law School, which has been a very good law school for a long time. Before I came into office, the school was still an aspiring law school, and its faculty was seeking a way to become even more distinguished. The faculty concluded that the better-regarded law schools did not have evening programs, whereas GW did. The faculty proposed to do away with GW's evening law degree so the school could be more like the upscale schools. The group thought that the quality of the students would improve without evening students. The assumption was that the evening students—who had jobs during the day—were somehow less capable than the students in the day program. The thinking was that closing down the evening program would shut the "back door" into the Law School. So the faculty voted to close it, the dean concurred, and the university president at that time acceded. The decision then went to the Board of Trustees.

In the meantime, the Law School alumni became aware of the decision. The outrage that rained down on the university forced a special meeting of the board, which ultimately voted against the change. What the faculty had not taken into account was that the evening program was a means that had allowed generations of working people to aspire to professional positions and to rise on the socioeconomic ladder. The school had accumulated a great deal of good feeling from these satisfied alumni.

A compromise was made to satisfy the faculty and still keep the program. It was decided that there would not be separate applications for the day and the evening programs. Instead, students would come from a common pool. Only after a decision was made to admit would the spaces for day and evening be allocated. In other words, the academic quality of the incoming students would now be consistent. That addressed the argument of the faculty.

The night program remains an important part of the GW Law School. In this and in similar decisions, the faculty generally disdain considering finances when making proposals and do not necessarily think about the effect of decisions on other parts of the university community. They simply had a different set of data points driving their decision making.

While I am on this subject, there is an illustrative story from my own experience as president. When I knew that I would be concluding my tenure as president, I wanted to realize a personal goal—with which the faculty fully agreed—of getting faculty salaries into the eightieth percentile of the American Association of University Professors (AAUP) rankings. I wanted to make sure that matter was concluded before I left office. My idea involved deferring raises for six months, using the float to raise some of the additional money we needed, plus getting another appropriation from the board, thereby taking the faculty salaries upward in a dramatic leap forward. After doing the calculations, I had figured that with modest sacrifice we could get the faculty to where they resolved they wanted to go, a goal we all shared. While deferring the raises by six months seemed modest given the return, the faculty insisted on reaching the goal without any pain at all.

The Faculty Senate voted unanimously that they didn't want the raise deferral. They wanted their 3 percent raises in July rather than the promised 6 percent raises in December. I sat through very heated meetings with people denouncing me. When it was all over, I thanked them and said, "Look, I am the president and I get to make this decision. I am confident that, in six months, you will see that I am right and you are wrong. If it turns out that I am wrong, you can beat me up again."

At the end of six months, the faculty got their raises, and when the AAUP comparative salary survey came out, it showed that we were in the eighty-fourth percentile for the full professors, the eighty-second percentile for the associate professors, and the eightieth percentile for assistant professors. We had more than achieved what the faculty had said they wanted—and at the cost of only modest and passing discomfort. But even after learning of the good news, the Faculty Senate was dead silent on the subject! Nobody from the faculty got up and said,

"You know, I don't want to give him the Nobel Prize, but it's important to acknowledge for our own sake as much as for his, that Trachtenberg was right." One faculty member—who had been particularly upset and wanted her 3 percent "right now"—got a 14 percent raise. I wrote on the bottom of her raise letter, "Better than three percent, right?" She never said a word. Sometimes things like that make me wonder.

The problem with being right once in a while is that it can lead you to believe that you are *always* right. So if it turns out that you have this experience early in your career, the next time something comes up, you may be tempted to believe you are right again. This time you might say to the Faculty Senate, "Look, I was right the last time, so I'm right this time and I'm going to do it." Apparently you are no longer capable of taking constructive criticism because you think that you are always right. That is a big problem because it is not as if faculty members are foolish; and they certainly aren't always wrong.

HAVING SPOKEN about some less attractive aspects of the faculty, I should also to discuss ways in which I constantly defend them. I frequently get letters in which someone has taken exception to something a faculty member has said or written. For instance, after hearing a GW professor speaking on C-SPAN, someone wrote, "I will no longer support in any way GW if this situation [arrogance and contempt for the government] is not remedied immediately."

The writer said that he thought the professor should be expelled from GW and that an apology by the university should be forthcoming. Although I do try to be diplomatic, my attempt often turns into a minilecture on what a university is all about and, specifically, what the faculty has a right to say or do. I wrote back to the writer:

> We have in excess of 1,000 faculty at GW. We pay them to talk. We like to believe that they take a moment to think before they talk, and most of them do. But, in any group of a thousand, you are going to have people who say peculiar things. . . . I have faculty on the right. I have faculty on the left. I have faculty in the political middle. I have advocates for every conceivable cause and

some for no causes whosoever. To tell the truth, it is what I always thought made university life exciting—the debate, the controversy, the disputation. Trust me—there is no single perspective at GW except that good ideas survive in the marketplace and bad ideas die from being exposed to sunlight. . . . If you were running a university, you would want [people like him] on the faculty. Look at the reaction he prompted from you! It got you thinking. It got you to write a letter. That is terrific. Would you want a whole faculty full of [people like him]? Not even his mother would want to see a thousand exactly like him. So, think of it as a pool of hundreds of people. They are all thinking and talking. Mix up all the things they think and say, and I think you will agree in order for there to be daylight, you have to have night. The contrast is what helps to define ideas. Ideas and your sentiments are all the sharper, all the more pointed because yours and [his] are in dynamic tension.

IN ANOTHER instance, an alumna wrote to complain about a GW law professor who uses public interest legal actions to combat social ills such as smoking and obesity. My reply to her gave me a chance to talk about the nature of a university:

This isn't a fraternity in which we all swear an oath of allegiance to agree with each other. It's a university. People are going in every direction. Many of them are smart, but also silly. Others are right sometimes and wrong other times, just like you and me. I suppose one could argue that we ought to hold professors to a higher standard, but higher than what—corporate executives, clergymen, public officials, lawyers? God save us. People—they're all just people. Good ones, bad ones, better ones, worse ones. So try not to let Professor Bee cause you too much grief. Or at least pity me. He's a tenured professor and I have to live with him for the rest of my career—every day. Imagine how I feel.

I wrote to the professor himself when he wrote an article in *The Hatchet,* suggesting that the university should ban smoking within fifty feet of its buildings. In the process, I also tried to steer his zeal to a more productive activity—that of combating the attempts of a group of neighbors to discriminate against students in housing.

> For whatever it's worth, I think your article in The Hatchet is wrong, but I'll fight to the death for your right to utter your remarks. You'll understand that GW's policy is in accord with those of Harvard and Yale—schools you like to call to my attention from time to time—and that they, like us, have received some of the best legal advice available on this matter. Surely you're not arguing that federal law doesn't trump the D.C. Human Rights Act. By the way, the D.C. Human Rights Act also makes it illegal to discriminate against people on the basis of matriculation. Why are you silent when the Foggy Bottom Advisory Neighborhood Commission or the Board of Zoning Adjustment rulings against GW specifically single out undergraduates as undesirable tenants in order to restrict their ability to live wherever they may wish in the neighborhood or the city?

This last comment referred to the unrelenting attempts by the university's neighbors to ban students from apartments in the Foggy Bottom neighborhood. Their hostile efforts seldom arose from fact-based complaints but seemed, instead, to be the result of a generalized dislike of young people, and GW students in particular. I wondered why such an energetic and talented advocate would choose to ignore an issue of discrimination that directly affected our own students.

When this same professor was interviewed on the TV show *Hannity & Colmes* specifically about his litigation against fast-food companies, I received an unfavorable letter from a man who violently disagreed with those views and believed that they were an insult to GW's reputation. Once again, I defended this faculty member as an important part of the university.

> . . . other folks have contacted me about students possibly being "brainwashed" by such views on controversial issues being

proffered by dynamic, charismatic professors. Most of our law students are mature men and women. We can hardly get them to agree on the most basic topics that come up in class or listen to the advice of their dean or me, let alone follow slavishly the points made by a single professor. Let's look at it another way. Think about how interesting it must be for a student to listen to Professor Bee and then to other professors and thus by comparison and reflection, come to his or her own conclusion. You and I—in a more generous mood than you apparently were when you were good enough to take the time to write to me—might actually call this "education."

I HAVE had many teachers and professors whom I revere and keep in touch with. In my early days as president of GW, one of my former Yale Law School professors whom I had a great deal of respect for, wrote the following to me:

I hope you're enjoying your new presidency. I have been in touch with [a colleague] recently concerning the ethical issues raised by mandatory retirement on reaching a certain age. I'd like your thoughts on this. Do you have a position? Does the university have a policy? Anything you have on this I'd appreciate receiving.

As I sometimes do, I let my hair down a bit too much and made remarks in reply without anticipating my former professor's negative reaction:

I think uncapping mandatory retirement will probably turn out to have been a blunder. It may have made sense to move it from 65 to 68 given the longer life span of most people and the health situation. Maybe even 70. But taking all limits away seems to me not sound. What it's induced us to do is pay out sums of money to get people to retire. We get some people who extort us. I have a particular case on my hands right now, and it may have prejudiced my vision.

I'm sorry if I sound a little cranky. Do forgive me. As far as I know, the current GW policy is: We follow the law. . . . At Boston University and the University of Hartford we continued older faculty after 65 on a year-to-year basis as long as we and they thought they were on the ball and as long as we had need for their services without blocking the upward progress of a junior colleague and as long as they were willing to carry on. The present system in some ways is less humane. We used to be able to say in the bad old days, when somebody was 60 and not working out, "Well, if we're patient for five years, it will fix itself. And it will do so without a negative judgment being passed." Today you can't wait, and you're obliged to do disagreeable things to shake someone loose.

He did not appreciate what I wrote and gave me a lesson about universities:

You sound more than "cranky." Your vision is, as you suggest, "prejudiced" and insensitive to the best interests of a university and to the dignity of those it employs. The university ought not to have to pay the price of waiting years until death or a mandatory retirement to avoid the "disagreeable decision . . . to shake someone loose." Rather than make judgments about a person's competence to do his work, you want to discriminate against those who are competent because you and your colleagues are squeamish about doing your job to make honest judgments about the capacity of those you employ or who apply for employment. Universities should be models for acting upon individual merit rather than on some non merit factor like age, color, religion. . . . I don't believe that you recognize that your vision perpetuates a discriminatory practice that is neither practically sound nor morally justified.

While I could agree that some of what I said was not a good idea, given this professor's age and concerns, I didn't appreciate the feeling that I had failed a test and wrote back to him about my feelings. But in the end, I had learned another lesson from a valued teacher.

I am most fortunate to have a friend like you who's prepared at his own initiative and without compensation to provide constructive criticism of my own clearly limited observations. . . . At first reading I thought that my late father . . . had risen to advise his errant son. At second reading I realized that the voice was one that had instructed me—sort of like a secular John Knox—for three years in New Haven and which continues to whisper in my ear, influencing my thinking one way or another to this very day. My initial reaction was to wonder why you chose to send me such a seemingly contentious communication. I concluded that you cared enough about me and your point of view to feel that it was worth your effort to try to steer me toward the path of virtue. . . . When you originally wrote to me on June 6, you presented a serious and complex question. When I responded, I gave you a hasty and too-simple answer. I should have known better. Possibly I invited, perhaps even deserved, a stern reply. Still, to tell the truth, I would have welcomed a more generous one. . . . My career has been devoted to enhancing universities and to supporting their best interests. My professional energies have been committed to supporting the life of every human being and the dignity of all in the University community and beyond. It was precisely those commitments that prompted my brief, albeit incomplete, comments. . . . Passing judgment on the continuing ability of senior faculty colleagues with whom one has worked for lengthy periods is not likely to take place without divisiveness and the very real possibility of hurting the principals involved. . . . Mature relationships will be strained and may be impacted to the detriment of all. Old hurts and conflicts will be revived. People will take sides. Who needs it? Our mutual responsibility argues for a nondiscriminatory test with no room for administrative discretion. Such a benchmark is both practically sound and morally justified. In other words, your heart is in the right place, but you're wrong. . . . I believe that society is better served by a neutral age-based rule rather than a competency test developed and administered by fallible persons and open to dispute, error, and even corruption. . . .

I am sorry if I disappoint you. . . . [But] you never said that I was taking a test. If I had been aware that you were measuring my character rather than seeking my views, I would have been more deliberate but, I hope, no less sincere. Unlike you, I hold that there is more than one way to manifest one's sensitivity and concern for one's associates. Surely we could have a neutral age-based retirement rule and some sort of post-retirement status which would permit competent, interested people to continue to work under another suitable arrangement. . . . I know how bright and able you are. Thus, I am confident that if anyone has the imagination to think of a novel approach to resolving this matter, it is you.

He did not reply, and we did not communicate for several years. And then one day I was visiting Yale Law School and we faced each other in a corridor. Each of us looked the other in the eye, and we exchanged greetings and handshakes.

The discussion we were having is a difficult one complicated by the need to comply with the rules of tenure. But I continue to believe that universities should be allowed to change their relationship with older people. They have been working longer and are, therefore, the most highly compensated. But we should be able to reassign some of this compensation to younger faculty. What we now have is a scheme wherein tenure goes on as long as life is sustained! It is a violation of everything we know about the aging process: that skills diminish with the passage of time at different rates in different people. Universities just refuse to realize the truth about the life cycles of the people who work with us and for us.

9.

SCHMOOZING FOR DOLLARS

When my mother died, her lawyer called me and said he was working on her estate. He told me he had some things that might surprise me; he was right, they did. He said my mother had named someone other than me as the executor of her will. This seemed strange since I was in my forties, I was married, I was president of a university, and I was a lawyer. Moreover, I was an only child and the sole beneficiary of her will. So the logical question was: Why did she pick someone else to be the executor of her estate, and who was it?

My law school roommate was a wonderful man, William A. Daggett. He was from Brunswick, Maine. His father had once been the acting president of Bowdoin College. Bill is a very important person in my life, and my mother was crazy about him—and rightly so. I asked her lawyer why she had selected Bill to be the executor of her will. He told me that since she had been coming to Hartford for several years because I was president there, she had noticed that I had been spending a lot of time in the company of very rich people, many of whom I was trying to induce to give money to the university. She was worried that if I suddenly came into some money of my own, I might use it to try to "keep up" with these wealthy people. Her estate was not large, but it wasn't irrelevant. She thought Bill would have a moderating effect on me if I wanted to do something unsound. It's a good thing that she told this to her lawyer and that he could later explain it to me. Otherwise, I would have considered what she did to be totally bizarre! Knowing her thinking showed me that there was tenderness in her plan. She was a mother trying to save her son from temptation.

Fund-raising does involve spending a lot of time in the company of people of means. My mother's instincts were basically right; the situation *can* introduce temptations. We have seen university presidents who have yielded to the dark side and behaved in ways that suggest that they felt either undervalued or newly entitled because of their exposure to money. I think of the recent tragedy of the president of American University. According to *The Washington Post*, he aspired to live in a manner that would parallel the lifestyle of the people he was spending time with on behalf of the university. This can also be seen in public service. Congressmen, for instance, make what most Americans might consider a good salary. Along with the salary come various benefits and privileges. But many elected officials find that maintaining a home in their district as well as one in Washington stretches them financially. And so we have seen people destroy their careers for what seem to be modest sums of money. It is not as if someone said to them, "Here's a hundred million dollars; if you get away with this, you will be able to go to Brazil and live like Croesus." Instead, some of these people put their entire reputations and family happiness at risk for small change.

I collect antique wristwatches as a hobby. I do this while fully conscious of the fact that I can live perfectly well with a $100 Casio. I would not put my professional life and reputation at risk for a Rolex. Yet I read about people who will! They sell themselves for a boat or jewelry or a fancy car; even football tickets! It seems absurd and pathetic to me. Now, if someone said to me, "Smith got caught stealing $100,000 to pay for his wife's heart transplant," that statement would say something oddly positive about Smith. It might also say something negative about the distribution of health care in America and how it turned a good man into a thief. But taking an automobile as a bribe? I don't know what kind of serum you would need to take to insulate yourself from that type of moral slippage.

As I have said many times, a major preoccupation of a university president is money. I can't help it; my university is many things, and one of them is a business. With an annual budget of about three quarters of a billion dollars but without a state legislature or an endowment the size of the endowment of an Ivy League University, funds were a continuing preoccupation for me as president. I spent a lot of time thinking about whom to ask for money, schmoozing those people, listening to their interests, thinking about and suggesting various ideas to induce their benefaction, listening again, schmoozing again, hoping for a positive answer, and repeating various steps of the process until I got some sort of closure. Food makes people more responsive to a president's petition. One result was that I ended up eating for a living; almost every time I met with a potential donor, there was a meal to be consumed. University presidents frequently gain weight on the job; this is one reason why.

I am an eternal optimist and never turn down an opportunity to meet with a potential benefactor or someone who can do something good for the university. Even after the presidency, I still believe that around the next corner lurks the person who will give the university $50 million or $100 million. But it didn't happen to me! In three decades, I never turned down a single opportunity to meet with a potential benefactor, no matter how inconvenient or unlikely. Living as I did in a world without Saturdays and Sundays, if a benefactor showed up in town on a weekend, I always got up and shaved and went to have breakfast. Even now, as president emeritus, I keep hoping to land the great gift that will transform the institution! I can only assume that many other university presidents have similar fantasies. I live in the hope that what I have done to plow a rocky field will be rewarded—perhaps a generation in the future. I worked hard to make life good for the students who were here during my tenure; my dream is that they will give as generously as they can when the time is right for them.

My view on fund-raising is existential. I see it as a variation on se-duction, the sort of behavior that people engage in when they are court-ing. For instance, despite my concern about gaining weight, I think a fund-raising activity always does better if food is involved, and plenty of it. Something in the subconscious makes people feel safer, warmer, and more comfortable when they are eating. When their stomachs are full, people are good-natured and more accommodating—maybe even grateful for their well-being, to a certain extent. This is probably why we have phrases like "wining and dining" in our culture, a term associ-ated with courtship or wanting to get another person into an agreeable state. Food has kind of an aphrodisiac, soothing quality about it. Of course, then there is my mother's view that food is love. When I talk about fund-raising for the university, it means sitting down, having a meal, and talking about the university we love, the Colonial athletic teams, dear Professor Smith, the Law School, etc.

STANFORD HAS announced the start of a $4.3 billion capital campaign. I always wonder about numbers like that. Why isn't it $4.1 billion or $4.5 billion? I suspect it's because Stanford's fund-raisers want to make the number look like the result of precise planning. They want to give the impression that all the departments of the school thoughtfully re-viewed all their needs and figured out exactly every dollar it will take to meet their goals. There is a charm to such inexact precision.

If a president is to lead a complicated organism like a university, it is impossible to please everyone. If everyone loves you, you are failing. The reason is simple: a president of a college or university has many constituencies, all competing essentially for one thing—*money*. They may articulate their desires or demands differently. They may say, "We want more faculty members" (or more books or more computers or more scholarships or more croquet wickets). It doesn't matter. All these things are bought with the same coin.

Balancing the legitimate needs of competing stakeholders is no easy matter. You always have to come down on one side or another. You have to do something today that will help students—perhaps more financial aid. You have to do something tomorrow that will help faculty—perhaps more money for travel to professional meetings. And so on. No matter where you place your chips, inevitably you will make someone unhappy; perhaps even several someones. Every decision creates a number of unhappy critics and one ingrate. Whatever else you are doing in the university, you are always, always thinking of money and how to get it and invest it. Fund-raising is always in your mind, and you are always engaged in elaborate dances with potential benefactors. It is the ever-present fact of a university president's existence. In my case, even after I left Boston and Hartford, I continued to try to get money for those institutions because my sense of having a responsibility to help them never ended. Even now, for instance, if I meet a graduate of the University of Hartford and find out that she has a capacity to help, I will call the current president of the university, give him the name of the alumna, and suggest that he contact her and seek support.

I think to have even moderate success in fund-raising, a president has to have a flame within; part of that flame is a taste for selling, which is a big part of fund-raising. You have to sell yourself and your faculty and your university to get donors interested. Of course, there are people who are simply looking for a way to minimize taxes, but the vast majority of benefactors want to be involved in something affirmative and uplifting. As president, it's up to you to point them at their best aspirations. If you are at Harvard, it looks as though you don't have to do much selling to get people to want to give money. But if your institution is hungrier, as mine is, you have to do more, talk more, and sell yourself more while asking potential donors to add value; to do something important and meaningful with the university.

One of the challenges of my fund-raising activities at GW was answering this question: If you don't have a proximate constituency to go see, how do you create new opportunity? GW does not have a large local population of wealthy alumni. Much of the money in the city was made elsewhere. Therefore, elsewhere has a claim on people's hearts and charitable budgets. For instance, there might be a transplanted family with a lot of money now living in Washington but with roots in the West. The family may have ties to a church back home and regularly contribute to it and also give money to other good works there. That family might not necessarily feel about the Washington community the way people in Hartford, who made their money in Hartford, feel about that community.

Washington, D.C., is a uniquely hard community in which to raise money. This could be because, as is often said, no one is actually *from* Washington. Many people who have a lot of money went elsewhere for their education and give money to that alma mater. Since GW was a commuter institution for a very long time, even the people who went to GW back in the day might not have the same feeling about the institution as they would if they had been at a residential institution. The GW of old did not spend a lot of its time hugging its students in order to get them to care more for the campus. Of course, this isn't the kind of thing the board and the faculty want to hear from its president. True or not, it sounds like an excuse.

I remember being in Manhattan one December and running into Virginia Smith, who was then president of Vassar College. She was sitting in the lobby of a hotel with a big sack of mail and a letter opener. I asked her what she was doing, and she said, "I am opening Christmas cards." She added, "I have to be very careful when opening these cards because with the holiday greetings, there are often donations to the college." In all my years as president, I don't recall a single Christmas card that contained an unsolicited donation for the university!

THERE ARE institutions where the idea of talking about money is considered vulgar. To them, it diminishes the purity of their commitment to the arts or to learning. Look at the case of Antioch College in Yellow Springs, Ohio. It has long been famous for its innovative and progressive values, but in June 2007, it suddenly announced that it would have to close its doors by July 2008 and start laying off its staff and faculty. The following is from an article by Scott Carlson in *The Chronicle of Higher Education* (June 21, 2007):

> So the question is: While so many other poorly financed, little-known liberal arts colleges stumble on, why has Antioch fallen flat?
> Over the decades, Antioch had many opportunities to secure

its financial future. But raising money and building an endow-
ment were never given the attention such activities get at other
elite colleges. A full-time development office was established at
the campus only in the past year.

At Antioch, and also at other small elite, tuition-driven institutions like Sarah Lawrence and Bennington, there has historically been little effort given to building up an endowment. This could be seen as a philosophical preference. In other words, the pursuit of money was seen as anticultural, an attitude that helped to define the values of the institution. I remember when one president of a university stepped down. During his time there, he had raised more than a billion dollars. Yet it was said about him at the time of his departure that he was "Only a fund-raiser." In other words, he was not "A man for all seasons." And that fact made him less.

I find it astounding that the trustees of Antioch were apparently not in communication with the alumni and weren't talking about the university's problems long before they announced the demise of the college. Now, at the eleventh hour, they are trying to raise money. But this is a last-ditch effort. Raising money when you are on the threshold of closing can be futile. A single infusion of money will likely not be adequate to get the institution back on its feet for even a year. What is needed is a steady infusion of money that helps to undergird the budget on an ongoing basis. It is one thing to say, "Oh, my alma mater is about to close; here's a thousand dollars to help." It's quite another thing to say, "I'm committing a thousand dollars a year for the next twenty years." When this happens, maybe the president can get enough people to do that and then get a lot of people to give $10,000 or $20,000 or more *each year*. I have seen schools that have been saved at the last minute and manage to struggle on. Schools can be very resilient and feisty and survive for a long time on short rations. Antioch is a sad story. The condition it finds itself in can get to be a little overwhelming. It certainly needs the help of professional fund-raisers. It is strange that the notion of a development office is new at Antioch.

•   •   •

I HAVE a favorite story about a man who was driving in the countryside and stopped to ask a farmer for directions. While he was at it, he chatted up the farmer about a cow he saw. He asked, "How much milk does that cow give?" The farmer said, "She don't give any. You've got to take it away from her." That has been my experience as a fund-raiser. There is little spontaneous giving to my institution. You have to go and ask people in order to get what you seek. And if your roster of alumni and past givers is modest, it is harder and you do a lot more retail to get it.

All presidents who are involved in extended negotiations with many potential donors often make a cost-benefit analysis of the time and effort it took to arrange for a gift. Some wonder about their time if they personally engage a donor for an amount as modest as $100,000. But I couldn't afford to have too high a threshold. I would gladly go to lunch and work retail with a person for a smaller sum. In other words, unlike many university presidents, I was totally promiscuous and would go with anyone if there was a glimmer of hope.

Fund-raising has to do with history and context. Ivy League presidents raise huge sums of money. This is not necessarily because they are inherently good fund-raisers, although they may be. It is because, given the nature and sociology of the institution, the alumni want to give money because they hope to continue to be part of the place. Knowing this, I used to say to Ivy League alumni who lived in Hartford, "It is all very well to give to your alma mater, but you should give something back to the community in which you earned your money."

Whenever I thought of someone new to ask for money for GW, I had to be able to see some promise of success. I didn't follow someone who made no indication of interest in GW. I did go to my famous fat Rolodex and used it for making connections for the university and for finding new benefactors. Speaking of my Rolodex, if I were a twenty-first century man, I would go through it, throw away the cards of dead people and the people I haven't heard from in twenty years, and put it all into an electronic file. But for me, going into my Rolodex is kind of like going into the stacks at the library, something I have always enjoyed. When I was a student, I would search for a book and then get happily distracted looking at the books on either side of it as well. I spent entire days at the library in this manner. I *like* the smell of book dust and the spin of an old Rolodex.

When a GW donor saw my name on her call list, it wasn't hard for her to figure out why I was there. I could have been acting simply as a matter of friendship, but a GW donor recently told me, "When you are no longer in office, I would like you to come visit my wife and me at our farm." In other words, *when we can be friends without another agenda*. The truth is, that will never happen because as president emeritus, I still want to be helpful to GW, just as I feel an obligation even now to the University of Hartford and Boston University.

One of the university's greatest benefactors is a woman who never went to college. I met her through her lawyer. He had been trying to persuade her to make a gift to his own alma mater, not GW. She is a wonderful woman who knows her mind and is not easily dissuaded from what she wants. In the long run, that was an advantage for GW. I knew her husband had made his money in Washington and wanted it to stay here. So I called her. At the time, she was being besieged by numerous institutions, and I knew I had to get myself to the head of the queue. In the end, I am not certain whether I was the one who got the gift or if it was my institution that appealed to her. In any case, I regularly went to lunch or dinner with her. This was a substantial time commitment for me; if I went to her club, it would take a whole afternoon with a long drive out and back added to the actual lunch. In the long process of getting help from her—or anyone else—I had to give some options, assist her in evaluating them, and listen for possible variations I could offer that would make the opportunity appealing. Of course, she had ideas of her own about things that GW simply couldn't do.

Fund-raising takes time. This donor gave a lot of money to GW over our extended association. Sometimes getting a commitment involved a very long negotiation process, but when she made up her mind, she decided on the gift and the next day the check would come. But sometimes, before she made up her mind, the deal was complicated by the arrival of a lawyer and an accountant and I would have to work with them because, more than likely, each would have other charities they thought worthy. Because our benefactor had a foundation, I also had to work with the board members of that foundation, who had their own agendas as well.

There is one potential benefactor who has successfully eluded me for my entire tenure here. He wouldn't even meet with me because long before my time at GW, when he was a student, he made a vow that he would never give a cent to GW! He was angry at the university. He is a graduate of GW and has been very successful in his career. As it happened, in getting his BA, he had done so well that the GW Law School offered him a full-tuition scholarship. A condition of this accommodation was that he would devote himself completely to the study of law and could not hold a job while a student. The school's reasoning was that, by waiving the tuition, they were taking a burden off his back so that he could have a better chance of becoming a source of great pride to them. He was so thrilled to get the scholarship that apparently he didn't pay attention to the conditions that came with it. He married and, feeling a responsibility to support his wife, became a part-time student manager at the campus auditorium.

The dean of the law school at the time heard about this and called him in. He reiterated the terms of the agreement and told the man that he would have to choose between the law school scholarship and the position. The man protested, pointing out that he was married and wanted to help support his wife. As a result of all this, the man's new father-in-law suggested that he leave GW, move to Chicago, and go to Northwestern Law School instead. And that is what he did. For twenty years he has refused to meet with me. We are both from Brooklyn, and I feel that had we met we might have liked each other's company and that he would have enjoyed coming back to GW as a successful alumnus. It's too bad. That dream is dead. This is a sad and frustrating story for me and a real loss for him.

SOMETIMES I saw an unusual opportunity that appealed to me, but my vice presidents might not have shared my enthusiasm. One generous donor owned a pet cemetery where some celebrity pets are buried along with many ordinary pets. The donor asked if I would accept the cemetery as a gift to the institution. I would have taken it gladly because I could imagine a situation in which we could say to pet owners who wanted a resting place for their dog or cat that in addition to paying a maintenance fee, they would have to make a donation to GW; for example, to our medical center. I thought it could have served a need and raised some money for the medical center. I told my vice presidents about this idea, and they thought it was a bad idea and laughed at me. I agree that it might have been a little odd, but some time later, I read of a university that actually has a pet cemetery! We could have done it, too, and it would have worked out just fine.

NOT WANTING to paint too dreary a picture of the difficulties of fundraising, I should mention that it often produces pleasant surprises. It is unusual for me to receive an actual handwritten letter. I might receive a brief handwritten postcard from a student on spring vacation, but generally nothing serious comes to me on personal stationery. But in this case, I was in the office alone on a Saturday going through accumulated mail when I saw an intriguing little World War II–era thin blue airmail envelope with a postmark and stamp from Ireland. Inside was a short note, scribbled in an uneven hand, apparently offering the university a parcel of real estate. I wondered if this was like the proverbial offer to buy the Brooklyn Bridge. After briefly scanning the letter, I decided it was a crank—perhaps the Irish version of the chain letter from Nigeria that begins, "I know you are a wonderful person and perhaps you can help me get my money out of a U.S. bank." I crumbled the crinkly blue paper into a ball and threw it in the trash.

Several hours later, something made me take that letter out of the wastebasket and look it over again. The writer claimed to be a GW alumna living in Castle Gregory, a village on the western coast of Ireland. She had been born and raised in Washington, D.C. Decades ago she had inherited two town houses from her father, which she now wanted to give to the university. I looked her up in the alumni roster and learned that she had earned her undergraduate degree from GW in 1932 and graduated with the class of 1937 of the GW Medical School. No one at GW had heard from her in twenty-five years. I wrote back and asked how we should proceed. She replied, saying something like "It is nice to hear from you; the matter can keep a while; I'll be visiting Washington in the near future and will call on you."

I put her on my watch list for follow-up. Two months later, an elfin woman appeared at my office door. She was a sweet-looking elderly lady, about four feet, ten inches high, with sparkling eyes and thin wispy hair. She was clutching a cardigan sweater around her shoulders and carrying a small tote bag. She said, "I'm the lady from Ireland. Can we chat?"

Dr. Catharine Birch McCormick was one of only a few women in her medical school class and had been engaged in her own practice in Washington when she married a ship's captain. The couple lived together in Washington for several years. Then, in 1964, when Barry Goldwater lost the presidential election to Lyndon Johnson, Catharine and her newly retired husband, apparently disillusioned by the politics of the time, moved to Ireland to the most picturesque town they could find and where the U.S. dollar could be stretched.

Within a few years, the captain died and Catharine was alone—a widow and an expatriate. She led a secluded life but still came back and forth to Washington to go to the dentist! Her investments were handled by a local D.C. attorney, and on her visits she usually stopped in to say hello to him.

Now in her eighties, she began making plans for her estate and transferred the two parcels of land in Northwest D.C. to the university. She came more regularly over the next few years and often visited me. I introduced her to some university colleagues and to my wife. I sent her books. We wrote to each other regularly. On one occasion, I invited her to come home with me for dinner, and I called ahead to ask Francine to prepare something for us. That night, Francine served us dinner in the kitchen: scrambled eggs and toast with sliced oranges, a cup of tea, and a plate of cookies. When she saw the dinner, Catharine's eyes lit up, and she cleaned her plate eagerly. After dinner she said, "I dislike the wasteful overabundance of food provided in restaurants, and I appreciate a university president who doesn't waste resources." Then she added, "I have another gift to give GW."

Catharine had only one stock—Coca-Cola—which she had kept

from the time she was a young physician. She had held on to it and the
shares had split; then she held on to it and the shares went up, and still
she held on to it. When she transferred it later that year to GW, it was a
donation of $5 million, enough to endow a chair at the medical school,
scholarships for women medical students, and more.

The next year, Catharine asked Francine to come to Ireland to in-
ventory her household possessions. It was a simple home, furnished
with the wrought-iron accessories made by Catharine's father when he
was a shop teacher in the D.C. schools. There were lamps, tables, a set
of dainty Limoges china, some silver serving pieces, and a roomful of
books. There was nothing extraordinary beyond what one would find
in most homes. Catharine took out a small box and said she had a few
pieces of jewelry she thought the university could sell for a donation
to the scholarship fund. They were a broken watch and pins and rings.
While nothing seemed particularly valuable, each piece came with a
story. "This," Catharine would say while picking up a piece of jewelry,
"was given to me by a handsome Russian count when I met him in
Spain. . . . This ring came from a Frenchman whom I met once in
Switzerland. . . ." With each piece of jewelry came a new story about a
beau accompanied by a packet of letters. Catharine had been quite a
popular young woman!

Within a few years of our first meeting, Catharine grew frail. She
wrote to me and said she was making a small change in her will. She
was bedridden, and several local folks in Castle Gregory were giving
her special care. She wanted to leave her home to the woman who
was nursing her. She hoped I didn't mind this change. I wrote back
and said I understood her desires. I also asked for a portrait of her in
her thirties that hung in the dining room of her house. She had been a
beautiful young woman. After Catharine's death, her solicitor sent me
the painting. It now hangs in the GW Medical School.

We sold the real estate for $6.5 million and created two more chairs
at the medical school. Catharine would be thrilled. If all the university's donors came with the wit, charm, and personality of Dr. Catharine McCormick, the burden of fund-raising would be elevated to pure
pleasure.

• • •

UNIVERSITY FUND-RAISING is a waiting game. As president, you have to constantly hope that eventually a potential donor whom you have been courting will give the university something. Someone once tried to figure out how many years you have to wait to get a million dollars from a person. The conclusion was that you just don't live long enough! Of course, the chances might be improved if the university were in a city with great wealth and a large population like New York and a strong tradition of giving. A disproportionate amount of the Washington population consists of poor people. Manhattan, on the other hand, has a large number of people with great wealth—something you begin to see when you read *The New York Times* real estate section and society pages on Sundays! It is not surprising that Columbia and NYU are emboldened to run billion-dollar capital campaigns. Fund-raising in Washington focuses mainly on politics.

According to an article by Mary Beth Marklein in *USA Today* (February 22, 2007), "Charitable contributions to U.S. colleges and universities reached $28 billion last year, up 9.4 percent from the year before, a survey says. It adds that alumni giving, which represents about 30 percent of such support, grew by 'an impressive 18.3 percent' last year, to $8.4 billion." This good news was tempered by Ann Kaplan, director of the survey for the Council for Aid to Education, who is quoted in the article as saying, "Voluntary support could never grow sufficiently to become the primary solution to budgeting challenges." And of course, it was the wealthiest universities that pulled in the largest amounts. Stanford, for instance, received $911 million, the greatest sum ever collected by a single university. Harvard ($595 million), Yale ($433 million), and the University of Pennsylvania ($409 million)—all large research institutions with medical schools that attract private support—were the recipients of the next largest amounts.

10.

SEIZE THE DAY

While fund-raising takes patience and time for building relationships with potential givers, there is another set of traits useful to presidents that are almost the reverse. These involve the ability to see an opportunity and act on it quickly and decisively. Universities are generally not good at taking spontaneous action, because they are so process-oriented. I have had my share of seeing a chance to do something, doing it, and then going back and being made into an "honest man" retroactively by my board or faculty. Sometimes, being gun-shy from a previous experience, I have hesitated and missed an opportunity. Specifically, to my regret, I have sometimes hesitated to buy real estate for the university.

Once, a wonderful piece of real estate opened up on Nineteenth Street, N.W., near the heart of the campus. It was a building that was in the estate of a friend of the university. That building was located near the World Bank and the International Monetary Fund. I saw where it was and thought, That is where our business school should be located. I developed a rationale for purchasing that building. It seemed to me that the main reason for proceeding was that in a single real estate initiative, we would define by its location the case for greatness of our business school, making it preeminent for international business. Not only would we have nearby the two world-famous financial institutions I just mentioned, but we would have the White House and the Congress up the street—and the business school address would be Pennsylvania Avenue. So I called the vice president in charge of such things and left a message that we should buy the building. He was out of town for a few days, and when he got back and returned my call, it was too late; the building had been sold to a law firm. I should have acted without him, because timing was a very important element in this opportunity. Win some, lose some.

I believe that building not only would have uniquely positioned our business school, but it also would have solved another problem. The university is located in Foggy Bottom, a neighborhood that is technically largely residential, and there are zoning regulations that limit our enrollment in ways that would not be applicable in a commercial neighborhood. Had we moved the business school to that site, it would have been in a different but adjacent neighborhood and we would have been able to transfer some of the student census to that location.

You can beat yourself up about the opportunities that got away. There is nothing wrong with having our business school on the main part of the campus, where there is a critical academic mass. In fact, it now has a splendid new facility. Nevertheless, had we been able to locate the business school on Nineteenth Street and Pennsylvania Avenue, we would have added value. It just didn't happen.

That was an opportunity we didn't seize. We also didn't immediately grasp the chance to acquire the nearby Mount Vernon College when it closed, and it escaped us once. Located relatively near our downtown campus, it is a highly desirable piece of real estate with a number of facilities that, at the time, were suffering from severely deferred maintenance. The second time it became available, when the little college had reached the end of the road financially, we moved with alacrity and acquired the site. Of course, we were able to do this because the timing was excellent. Between the two opportunities—one missed, one taken—the International Monetary Fund had approached us to buy a piece of university property, for $100 million. Because of this sale, we were able to acquire Mount Vernon College without having the board become nervous about the cost and without the faculty raising issues. In the years to come, as people look back on my tenure, some may say that the Mount Vernon decision was among the best I ever made. It substantially added to our size and physical resources.

Unless your strategic plan is to be always on your toes and prepared to take advantage of a contingency that presents itself, you cannot plan for these opportunities. It is in the moment! Every time I have acquired a piece of property in Washington, it has been a good thing to do. Every time I have decided not to acquire property, it has been the wrong decision. We were offered the opportunity to buy a building on F Street and turned it down, saying it was too expensive. The owner then sold the building to a real estate investment trust (REIT). We have always regretted that decision. It would have been a wonderful location for nonacademic support services. For instance, we could have put day care services there. Because of the difficulty of finding new space in Foggy Bottom, we are increasingly moving nonacademic services away; some have already been moved to Virginia.

The point I am making is about planning and entrepreneurship. Universities are overly committed to how things get done and insufficiently aware of chance, and so they tend to be "get-along" institutions rather than "get-up-and-dance" institutions. It is in their genes. But sometimes there is a president who takes a university ahead a couple of chapters rather than a step at a time. I like to think I have been that kind of president.

I OFTEN think that presidents of universities are a lot like the untouchables in India. The role of the untouchables is to do the work that must be done but nobody wants to do. Burying the dead and collecting trash are two examples. But because they take on dirty jobs, the untouchables are themselves considered dirty. There are things that have to be done for the benefit of universities, people that have to be seen, and issues that have to be addressed that have nothing to do with you yourself but rather with the office. You have to deal with things that make you unpopular—and there are times when you have to get up in front of people and be accountable on behalf of the university. Sometimes people are personally abusive and say disagreeable things. You have to be steady and calm and not let those things into your heart; then you have to come home and get your wife to give you a hug because you are feeling unloved. You have to keep doing that because, as the president, you are the visible representative of the institution.

People often get very angry when something they like is taken away. They assume the worst intentions on the part of the administration that did the subtracting. I received a letter from a parent that was written in overheated prose. He was dismayed that we had stopped giving "free" copies of The Washington Post and The New York Times to any student who wanted them, and he actually accused me of stopping an "historic" practice in order to save money.

I pointed out that we had been engaged in this process for only seven years. It was not a historic tradition; in fact, the program had been my baby! I had thought of it. So if anyone should be sorry about our decision, it should be me. I explained that, despite our best efforts, the cost (about $50,000 per year) exceeded the benefit and we had other pressing needs for the money. Many, many of our students can afford to buy a paper if they want one, and, of course, the library subscribes to and makes available many newspapers. I told him that we had found that the number of papers actually being read by the students was declining and we had been gradually whittling down the number in proportion to this lack of interest. Despite that process, we still ended up with large piles of newspapers to haul away at the end of the day. Clearly, more and more students were getting their news online or elsewhere.

Nevertheless, when we stopped the practice, there was a student protest. We told the students that we were willing to give the project another year to see if readership would pick up, and we did so. Unfortunately, readership did not pick up over the course of the additional year, and we concluded that the students who wanted papers could get them on their own—either by buying them or by going to the library to read them—and allow us to use the money for other things. When I wrote to this father, I offered to raise $25,000 if he could help raise the other $25,000 to continue the project for yet another year. He didn't write back.

I never expected that father to give us $25,000. I was trying to make a point that money—which invariably comes from tuition dollars—must be respected and that, if you have a program that students are ignoring and that results in a waste of resources—both in cost and in paper being wasted—it is reasonable for us to conclude that those dollars should be reinvested in something that will benefit more students. There are an infinite supply of good ideas and a finite supply of money. It is not sufficient for students to merely say they want something; they have to vote for it by actually using it! The fact is, contemporary university students are not newspaper readers. Apparently, even getting a newspaper free is not a sufficient inducement.

When you are running an institution, you make larger decisions by making smaller decisions. You have to decide: At what point do I have to take this expenditure—and the potential waste of tuition resources—seriously? I am still respectful enough of what it takes to earn $50,000, and the amount still seems like a lot to me.

As president, I was usually more responsive to suggestions for improvement if those who made the case showed some dedication to the cause and a willingness to contribute. For example, some students came to my office saying they wanted the university to divest from any company doing business in Darfur. I told them I had heard this proposal before in different guises. I call it the "Pontius Pilate solution." Pontius Pilate, while distancing himself from Christ's fate, washed his hands and put the responsibility elsewhere. In other words, I didn't do it. Other people made me do it. What these students wanted was for GW to do something so their hands would stay clean. But they themselves weren't making a commitment to solving the problem.

I said to them, "That is not a useful device. We have no Darfur stocks, but even if we did, the people in Darfur wouldn't be any better off if we were to sell all the stock. Other people would simply buy the stock and life would go on. This is not a positive idea; it's a negative idea. I have an alternative." I asked them how many of them had summer jobs. About five of them didn't. I told those students I would pay them $150 a week for up to ten weeks in the summer if they would do a positive project for Darfur. I told them they could research how many universities would be willing to provide tuition for a student from Darfur to enroll. With thousands of universities in the country, I thought that if they could get a hundred scholarships, it would be really impressive. I also said that, to make the job easier, I would pledge the first scholarship. Then I said, "So now you only have to get ninety-nine scholarships."

Even if they didn't get any scholarships, their engagement would show them that while doing this kind of thing is very challenging, it is nonetheless worth the investment. Out of it could come some good, both for people from Darfur and for them. I thought they would learn a valuable lesson about taking a positive approach to life and not just handing over the responsibility to another person or entity. Many students want to feel they are making a difference and making the world a better place. But often they don't understand that making the world a better place is more complicated than getting your father (in this case, the university) to say yes to your request.

This group is still working on the project, which they call "Banaa." It is a scholarship network designed to give young Sudanese the tools for lasting peace. The group is now organized and committed and is determined to keep working until they have raised operating funds and scholarships. In the process, they have learned how hard it is to make a program like this successful.

On that subject, contemporary university students are more persistent about finding ways to add experiential training to their academic experience than earlier students were. I see this when I review the dossiers of Rhodes Scholarship applicants. More and more students are looking for ways to get engaged in public service or charitable work. Like anything else, sometimes the commitment can have more to do with résumé building than with self-sacrifice, but, by and large, it is a good thing, because the needy recipients of these activities do benefit. I once mentioned that contemporary students are astonishing because they find lepers and then they read to them! Thomas Friedman found some value in the remark and quoted me in his *New York Times* column.

• • •

BECAUSE THE president is a flesh-and-blood human being and also a symbol, the job can be a rather complex juggling act. People expect you to be doing many different things, often at the same time. If for example, you are always on campus, someone is likely to think: Who is visiting the Ford Foundation on behalf of the university? Who is seeing the alumni in Chicago and Los Angeles? On the other hand, if you are away a great deal, people wonder why you are "never on campus." They ask each other, "Where is he?"

If you are never on campus, you can't keep up with your constituency or talk knowledgeably about what the university needs. Your advocacy must be informed by observation and by participation in the daily life of the institution. But if the president is always on campus, he is not out in the world. Think about a small manufacturing business. Two partners are necessary. The partner on the inside has to make sure the goods get made. The outside partner needs to sell the product. The company can't market what it doesn't make and can't make what doesn't sell. A university president has to be the inside person *and* the outside person, and that is often hard. You really have to be both a high-energy person and a social person to achieve a dynamic balance.

A conspicuous example of the importance of a president "being there" was Benno Schmidt, the president of Yale University from 1986 to 1992. His life was complicated by the fact that his family remained in New York City while he worked in Connecticut. Since Benno happened to like his wife and children quite a bit, he regularly went to see them in Manhattan. Thus, not only was he often absent for this purpose, he was also absent because he was traveling extensively to raise money for the university in places far from New Haven. At some point, the students missed his presence and became resentful. Yale students were soon wearing T-shirts on which was printed, "Where's Benno?" This became a hot issue on campus and led to other conflicts and disagreements. Ultimately, Schmidt decided he didn't really like the job as much as he had thought he would, and he stepped down after six years to do something else.

It was said about Father Hesburgh of Notre Dame University that he was a very active participant in the affairs of America, nationally and internationally, during his long tenure as president. The question was posed, "What is the difference between God and Father Hesburgh?" The answer was "God is everywhere; Father Hesburgh is everywhere except at Notre Dame." Of course, this wasn't true. Hesburgh was an extraordinary president, and his presence everywhere else uplifted Notre Dame accordingly. Regular people simply couldn't believe he was actually doing all the things he was.

A faculty member once wrote about me in the student paper saying that I was "invisible on campus." Curious, I went back, looked at my own diary for the period he mentioned, and found that I had been to ten public events in the two weeks preceding his letter. At each of these gatherings, hundreds of people had been present. I had spoken to the Freshman Convocation (I assume he was not there), I had walked the streets welcoming incoming students to the dormitories as they arrived (perhaps he wasn't there because it was raining!), I had spoken at a 9/11 memorial event (I guess he was not there), and I had hosted President Pervez Musharraf of Pakistan at a public forum and luncheon at which hundreds of students, staff, and others had showed up (apparently he was not there either). I can only conclude that there are people who believe the reason they do not personally see you is that you are never anywhere and therefore are an invisible president. No matter how hard you run and how many events you attend, there is only one of you, and you cannot possibly touch all those people wherever they are. And so it is possible for them to think, He's never here!

I remember going to a student concert once and, about halfway through, realizing that if I left at the intermission I could make the last act of a student play being performed at a nearby venue. So I slipped out at the break and saw the end of the play. Because I had left the concert, I was able to attend both of these student events. The next day I got a letter from the student who had given the concert. He said I had "stalked out" of his concert. He said how upset he was that I hadn't stayed until the last note. I felt bad about his perception of indifference on my part. Clearly he did not realize that I had come to the concert, had a nice time, listened attentively to the first half, and left for another student performance. I told him that my leaving during intermission had to do with the nature of my life and had nothing to do with his performance, which I had enjoyed very much.

There are some fundamentalist groups on campus; some students from one of these asked me to a prayer session. I was touched by their invitation and joined them as they prayed. They asked me to come back on a regular basis. I said I couldn't do that but was gratified by the request. They understood and said they were pleased I had come. So was I. As president, I always wished I had more time for such events.

I love to meet people, especially students and parents. During the high season for looking at colleges, I frequently stopped groups of high school kids touring the campus and talked with them. They were always astonished when they learned I was the president. At Hartford, I used to stop my car, pick people up, and drive them around campus, showing them all the new buildings and talking about our academic programs.

The presidency is a political race in which the election never comes. The president is always in campaign mode. Just as if you were running for Congress, you are constantly reaching out and embracing people to bring them into the university community. Meanwhile you still have to make sure the community itself is being nurtured and taken care of. Nobody can do that alone. Having a great team of vice presidents, deans, and professional staff is imperative. And at the top of the A list are the professors. Whatever you want to do, you can't do it unless they want to do it, too.

I THINK that by and large, search committees for presidencies of universities haven't the foggiest idea what the job involves and what they ought to be looking for in their president. They publicly and privately consult stakeholders in the universities as if the multiple stakeholders knew what the president ought to be like. And then there is the effort to reconcile mutually exclusive views from different sources in order to come up with a presidential ideal. So what you get is a statement something like "We want somebody who is academically outstanding but willing to abandon an outstanding academic career in order to do totally nonscholarly things like going to fund-raising dinners." Or

"We want someone who likes to read but has no time to read because the person goes to basketball games and makes appearances at student concerts and plays." And "We want someone who is thoughtful and reflective but also who is outgoing and warm." Essentially the list reflects blended magical thinking from individuals projecting onto some invisible screen their own deep anxieties and ambitions. Of course, there is a reactive quality in which search committees look for strengths that were absent in the previous president and a new collection of weaknesses that serve their agendas.

When the search for my successor began, open meetings were held at which students were asked what they wanted in the next president—good optics, although I personally doubt that a college sophomore knows much about what a college president should be like. Professors were being asked what they thought was needed; but does a professor of chemistry know what a college president does from day to day? What you find with this sort of process is that nobody really knows what is needed—but everyone has an opinion.

The point to be made is that while everyone is entitled to an opinion, the opinion that holds more weight is the educated one. If you have two friends—one a lawyer and one a doctor—and you don't feel well, you may be courteous to the lawyer when he tells you what is wrong with you, but you are going to be more attentive to the thinking of the doctor because she, presumably, has an educated opinion. In fact, all the people who attend meetings leading up to a presidential search tell you what they want in a university president, but they tend not to know what one does. It's a harvesting of the opinions of the uniformed. But it has great optics and appears participatory and transparent—an end in itself.

I can't remember the last time anyone came to my office and asked, "What do you do for a living?" My own Board of Trustees, searching for my successor, never asked, "What have you been doing for the last eighteen years, and what do you think you are leaving undone, and what would you have us do next?" If I were trying to find a new president, I would surely ask the sitting president what he or she thought. Then I would do what seemed sound.

I was chosen for this job because I was just about as different from my predecessor as one can get. He was a tall, slender West Virginian who was soft-spoken. He was a transactional president who had held the job for twenty-four productive years. The longer I served, the more I grew to respect him and his accomplishments. The search committee looking to replace him wanted someone social who would engage stakeholders and students in his home. The faculty, I suspect, made the mistake of wanting someone more like them. They always confuse the president with the notion of a superprofessor.

Not long before I left the presidency, I went to my biweekly lunch with a group of faculty and we discussed the search for a new dean of arts and sciences. One of the members of the search committee said, "First of all, we want somebody scholarly." I asked, "Why?" There was a pause. I said, "Surely your goal is not to have a dean who is writing a book. Your goal is to have someone to help faculty write *their* books." She said, "Well, we want someone who understands our problems." I asked, "Do you believe that only someone who has had a heart attack can be a cardiologist? Or is it more probable that someone trained and experienced as a physician is going to give you better care?" It is a mistake to take someone whose life has been devoted to scholarship and say, "Congratulations, you have been so good at this that we're not going to have you do it anymore! We are going to assign you something that will call on a whole new set of skills that you may not have!" But we do this again and again. Faculty search committees know how to search for professors and are comfortable doing that. Faculty may search for a dean only once or twice in a lifetime, and so they don't bring any experience to that assignment; they only have experience searching for people to be their colleagues. They take the background they have and bring it to the search for a dean. And what they get is a history professor! Turns out that person may not have a vision for the entire college or a grasp of how to administer an entire enterprise, doesn't raise money, isn't a good leader—in effect he brings a whole different basket of skills to the job than is needed—or not. Universities are the most peculiar places in this way.

In the last couple of years there has been a question at GW about having students on the Board of Trustees. I wonder, does anyone know of organizations other than universities that would seriously think of putting an eighteen-year-old who has never earned more than $3,000 in his entire life on the board of an enterprise that has an operating budget approaching a billion dollars? They would probably wonder at the lack of experience and wisdom. Certainly, you can't hold an eighteen-year-old accountable for the actions he or she has taken on a board of such an institution. But when putting that person on the board, the institution assumes that liability! The faculty rejected the notion of the eighteen-year-old board member out of hand. But some members of the board found it a tantalizing idea. The chairman agreed because as a young man he had been a student politician and enjoyed serving his undergraduate university. I lobbied against it. I pointed out that we had already put students on all the committees where they brought added value—Student Affairs, Academic Affairs—but students can be of little use on the Audit Committee or the Development Committee.

The faculty wanted to have a representative on the Development Committee, and there was a struggle between the vice president of Development and the head of the Faculty Senate. The Development person said, "We would be delighted to have a faculty member on the committee, but it needs to be someone who has been a financial contributor to the university." The head of the Faculty Senate wanted the person to be a professor who chaired one of the Faculty Senate committees. The vice president said, "We don't just randomly put trustees on the committee; it is a position that calls for certain interests and skills. For us to fill the job mindlessly with whomever happens to be filling that position on your Faculty Senate committee is not a smart thing to do if we care about how it all comes out. Can we instead choose someone from the faculty with a demonstrated interest and capacity to do this kind of work and a record of having, themselves, been generous to the university?" The answer was "no"; the Faculty Senate leader wanted it to be an automatic process, not one in which choices were made based on qualifications. And she prevailed.

I have already listed the ideal traits of a university president: the kindness of Mother Teresa and so on. But I was asked by the American

Council on Education to write seriously about this subject for its magazine, *The Presidency*. The following was extracted from my article "No Magic, Little Sleep, and a Lot of Luck" (Fall 2006):

> *While it is difficult to rank personal traits, I give pride of place to a* composed temperament. . . . *Faculty, students, staff, donors, alumni, trustees, parents, the media, city officials, and neighbors all need a different touch. . . .*
>
> *The second trait essential to a successful presidency is not inherent, but learned—often the hard way. For want of a better term, I will call it style, but I also could call it the ability to* think first, speak second. . . . *I maintain that no utterance of a university president, however banal or routine, goes unnoticed or unquestioned. . . . Presidents learn this lesson quickly or they serve briefly. . . .*
>
> *The third component . . . is patience in faculty relations. . . . Robert Brown, the president of Boston University, once said, "Many university presidents have died on the mountain of change.". . .*
>
> *Patience is also required for the fourth quality . . . that is, the ability to raise funds. . . . Money is [not an] end in itself. Money is fungible and is redeemed by its use. . . .*
>
> *The fifth quality . . . that I consider a sine qua non is the ability to be a generalist. He or she must know how to talk to donors, students, faculty (when they are in the mood to listen), parents, reporters, and so on . . . [and] also needs to know something about the hundred or so programs on campus and should remember that Professor Ines Azar's work on Cervantes is still progressing and no one has touched her accomplishments in 40 years. . . .*
>
> *The sixth characteristic . . . is* luck; preferably good luck. . . . *It is only by luck that a sex, money or athletic scandal does not blow up in a president's face.*

11.

DESCARTES GOES INTO A BAR AND ORDERS A MARTINI

I did some speechwriting for John Brademas when he was a U.S. congressman, and for Harold Howe when he was the U.S. commissioner of education. During my presidencies I made countless speeches, remarks, or public talks, sometimes two to three times a week, and was on my feet in front of people all the time. Through experience and inclination, I became pretty comfortable with public speaking.

In my last year at GW, I gave a talk at an event celebrating the tenth anniversary of the School of Public Health. The school had prepared some remarks for me. I was to follow the dean's remarks. As she spoke, I realized she must have been the person who had drafted my text because the two were functionally identical! I thought, This is a disaster; I can't use this outline. So on the spot, I crafted a twenty-minute speech. After giving a lot of speeches, one learns what people want to hear under various circumstances. First I told the people from the School of Public Health that they were terrific. You never get into trouble saying this to people. The two predecessors of the dean were sitting in front of me in the audience. The school had been through its share of struggle and strife in its early history, and these two had been bruised during that period. So I talked about that a little and got people to laugh about past controversies. Everyone in the room who was aware of that rough history was probably a little surprised to hear me bring it up, but it seemed that doing so took the tension out of the air and allowed me to publicly praise two good people for the dedicated work they had done.

The speech went over well, but it went on too long and they had to cut me off. That was thoughtless on my part. A speaker has to have respect for time. If you are up in front of five hundred people, you should do the math. Five hundred people times fifteen minutes of listening to you speaking is a lot of person-hours! At almost any hourly rate, it represents a real resource investment.

If you speak a couple of times a week, you have to have the humility not to think you can always wing it. But you should also not think you can actually write all of your own remarks while also holding down a full-time administrative job. Generally, I would outline the speech and list the stories I wanted to relate and the message I wanted to impart. Then I would have someone work on a preliminary version for me, and I would edit the final presentation to fit my style and preferences.

Always anticipating that I might have to speak as president, I collected vignettes, clippings, and stories with points and morals. One joke that I used for many years tells the story of the philosopher Descartes going into a bar and having a martini. The waiter came and asked, "Mr. Descartes, would you like a second martini?" Descartes replied that he would. Then, when Descartes finished the drink, the waiter returned and asked, "Mr. Descartes, would you like a third martini?" Descartes said, "I think not," and he disappeared! It's fun to see how many people know that it was Descartes who wrote, "I think, therefore, I am." Some people just don't get it. But the people who do are always very pleased with themselves—especially academics.

My rule is, if you make the speech, you own it. You can't hide behind the speechwriter. I heard a wonderful story when I was in law school about a distinguished professor who had written a definitive book. The book was done with an associate, and both names were on the cover. We'll call them Brothers and Fellowes. A case came up, and Professor Brothers was testifying. During cross-examination the opposing attorney asked, "Did you write this book?" Brothers said, "Yes." Then the attorney said, "Did chapter four say this?" And he quoted the text. Brothers said, "Yes." Then the attorney said, "Well, doesn't that contradict what you have just said in testimony?" Brothers said, "Ah, yes, but Fellowes wrote chapter four!" Speakers can't get away with that.

SOMETIMES UNEXPECTED things happen when you are making speeches. One of the most memorable incidents in my entire speaking career occurred when Dorothy Height was on a platform for an event honoring the memory of Reverend Martin Luther King, Jr. Mrs. Height is an African-American leader who has been an administrator, teacher, and social activist. She enjoys monumental esteem in the black community because of her long and distinguished record. She stands out physically in a crowd because she is a robust woman who wears large and significant hats. On this occasion, I was on a platform with her along with several others. She was a senior citizen by that time.

Mrs. Height was sitting quietly in a chair while I was speaking. Suddenly there was a noticeable rustle of fabric, and I turned around in the direction of the sound. Dorothy Height had completely disappeared from the platform. Gone! There was a space between the stage and the wall and in that space was a row of flagpoles with draped flags. Mrs. Height must have moved her chair in such a way that the rear two legs went off the stage and the chair tipped back. Apparently, she and the chair just tilted over. The sound we heard was Dorothy Height sliding down those flags while still seated in her chair! The flags had lowered her gently to the ground. We all ran off to the back of the stage to see what horror awaited us. Mrs. Height was still cheerfully in the chair, lying backward and quietly looking at us faceup. She was perfectly calm! We picked up the chair with Dorothy Height in it and put it back on the stage, pushing it forward so it wouldn't go over the edge again. Dorothy remained completely unfazed, composed, looking as beautiful as ever, and still wearing her amazing hat! She is a blessing.

• • •

WHILE IT is common sense that a speaker must always be prepared for unforeseen events, I confess that I never anticipated the intervention of Mother Nature until once when I was making a graduation address just days after my father's death. My mother and I were sitting Shiva after his funeral. This is the Jewish ritual mourning period, which generally runs for a week after a passing. It can be interrupted if the Sabbath or certain holidays come before the end of the week. In this case, we had sat for about three days and then the holiday of Shavu'ot came, ending the mourning. I had been long scheduled to give a commencement address that Sunday at Ethel Walker School, a girls' private preparatory school outside of Hartford, and mentioned that to my mother. She thought it would be good for me to honor my commitment, and so I drove back to Connecticut from New York for the event.

The ceremony was outdoors. All the girls were dressed in white, it was a beautiful day, and these attractive young people and their parents were walking around campus; it was a Ralph Lauren scene from a Polo catalogue. I had a very nice talk prepared and was looking forward to giving it. After an introduction, I got up and started to walk to the microphone. Suddenly an enormous bumblebee came along. It was flying in my face and buzzing. It was the biggest bee I have ever seen; to me it seemed the size of a loaf of bread! I was having trouble getting past it to the microphone. Finally, I swatted it away and tried to begin speaking. But it came back. This happened several times. People could see the bee and were starting to giggle at the sight of me battling a big bug.

I decided to sit down. When the microphone stood vacant, the bee went away! I got up again and returned to the microphone. The bee returned. I thought of smacking the bee and killing it. But I concluded that it wouldn't be seemly for me to be stomping on a bumblebee in front of such an audience. Eventually, I got to use the microphone long enough to say, "I do have a commencement address and I would like to give it. But the bee keeps coming back. Clearly it doesn't want me to give this talk."

Then I explained that my father had died during the week and it seemed to me that he had been reincarnated as a bee that was trying to

frustrate me from making the speech. Perhaps he thought it disrespectful to his memory. So I thanked the audience and promised to send
them a printed version of my text by mail. I sat down to a standing ova-
tion. When the next person got up to speak, the bee was nowhere to be
seen. I know this is a little crazy; but maybe it *was* my father . . .

WHEN YOU are a president, you are constrained to treat the relentless
stream of complaints that come before you as a welcome and worthwhile part of the continuous process of improvement you are expected
to lead. But I am flawed and human, and every once in a while, I am
moved to complain about complaints and complainers. I was invited
once to join an exercise in which speakers were asked to decide what
they would say if they were giving their last lecture. Although my "last
lecture" is a few years old, I think it still works.

Learning to Live in Heaven

*Since this is going to be the last lecture I ever deliver, I'm having
to deal with feelings of sheer intoxication. Finally, I can shoot my
mouth off with no fear of consequences! Five months from now, no
columnist for* The Washington Post *or the* GW Hatchet *will take
me to task for disgracing my profession. No member of the United
States Congress will cite me from the floor as typical of the problems facing American higher education today. Nor will I have to
write a long and abject letter to the ambassador from Mongolia
to explain why my reference to Genghis Khan just couldn't take
account of the latter's humanitarian aspects and was confined to
his military exploits.*

*In short, I am free. The opportunity to present my very last
lecture has liberated me from the constraints of a lifetime. I'm free
of fear, free of guilt, free of shame, and free, above all, of having
to pay any price for even the most outrageous of my pronounce-
ments.*

*And so, having found myself in Speaker's Paradise, I ask my-
self: "What have you really been dying to say to your fellow hu-*

man beings? What have you had to clamp down on again and again because it could get you and/or your university in trouble? What act of cognitive and oratorical suppression has sent your stresses repeatedly soaring? And now that this fruitful collaboration between GW's Campus Ministry and the Western Presbyterian Church has opened the doorways leading to your heart and soul, what thought or series of thoughts is really begging to be let out into the light of day?"

Having asked myself questions like these, I'm now going to deliver my last lecture, which I hope you won't find too horrifying.

Tell me, please, why do we spend so much of our time complaining? I mean, I spend hours at my desk every day, reading not just the mail addressed to me personally but communications of many other kinds, and there are times when I feel as if I'm drowning in the grouchings and grousings of my fellow human beings. This is wrong. That could be improved. And the other, in the corner over there, falls disgracefully short of perfection.

There was a time in my life, now known as "my younger years," when the chorus of complaining so typical of the human race usually got me into a sympathetic frame of mind. Back then, I couldn't imagine that a chorus of such volume and intensity could be other than justified. And so, like most members of my generation, I paid instant and respectful attention. Even when the complaint struck me as on-the-face-of-it ridiculous, I assumed that if you "dug deeper" and took the nominal subject as just the symptom of some deeper form of despair, you'd sooner or later hit pay dirt.

No, the fact that the university that employed me was repaving its interior roads wasn't the real reason for all those picket signs and processions. But the university was part of the military-industrial complex, wasn't it? The university had taken almost five years to divest itself of all stocks involving South Africa. And there was no question about it; the university had yet to hire a professor or even a dean or vice president born on the island of Guam. So if the university could only move into the forefront of *the struggle to change its nation and its world, and could become a major force in realizing the universal ideals of justice and goodwill, then its current repaving of all the roads, which required equipment to move through so many neighboring streets, would no longer be represented to the media as a racist plot worthy of Simon Legree. And the students sitting in at the Sports Center to show their support for the community might actually return to their classrooms.*

So much for the world of my younger years. Alas, those years didn't stick around. I got older and older. And now, here I am — staring in disbelief at the Big Sixty that's headed in my direction and will strike at the end of this calendar year. And from the perspective of age fifty-nine, quite frankly, the complaining that goes on all around us these days is starting to rub me the wrong way.

So in this my last lecture, I'm going to try out a hypothesis that I've never before revealed in public. It's the notion that what's really bothering so many of us is the fact that we are living in heaven. Yes, I mean it — Heaven.

Summon to the bar of our court most of the human beings who have ever lived on this planet, and ask them for a definition of heaven. Their answers are likely to be: a place where there's enough to eat, a place where you can sleep without fear, a place that's devoted to pleasure rather than pain, and a place where it's considered unusual when one of your children dies. I won't bore you with one more recapitulation of all the human suffering that generated such wishes for the afterlife. Heaven, most human beings have tended to agree, must be a place where the rules of life on Earth — on an earth of limited resources, where the powerful seize whatever they can whenever they want — no longer apply. Above all, Heaven must be a place where those with power and wealth no longer oppress, rob, humiliate, and brush aside their fellow men and women. It must be a place where even the humblest person is regarded as full of sacred meaning, and beloved of God.

I don't have to give you a lecture on the extent to which this

vision of heaven inspired Jewish, Christian, and Muslim thinkers, who used it to draw the most biting contrasts with what human beings have achieved, and are used to doing, right here on
Earth.

No government, no church, and no representative of law and
order has escaped bitter criticism for falling so far short of heavenly ideals. Those for whom the words of the Bible have not suf-
ficed for their chronicling of injustice and human folly have been
able to turn to King Lear or Samuel Johnson's poem "The Vanity
of Human Wishes" or Voltaire's Candide in order to make their
point. And that point can be summed up as the utter miserable
failure represented by human life—the way we all have of betray-
ing our youthful hopes in order to attain our middle-aged wealth
and our later influence.

But now take a step back and look again at the definitions
of heaven that have bound our species together, and see whether
heaven is not where we're living right now. I'll confine my observations to the United States of America, and since this is my last
lecture, no one will feel tempted to denounce me as a craven na-
tionalist excusing his homeland for its imperialist thieving of the
world's choicest goods.

We are living at a point in time when the existence within our
borders of a single hungry child is regarded as a national disgrace.
We are living at a point in time when the incredible life spans
we have already achieved are regarded as mere preludes to even
longer ones. Perhaps, if we unlock this or that secret with regard to
our genetic inheritance, we can succeed in living forever, like God,
or taxes, or tuition rises.

We are living at a point in time when the aesthetics of our
entire country, and the ecological viability of its every nook and
cranny, are ceaseless concerns to our media and ceaseless policy
issues for our government. To all of the rights in our Bill of Rights
we have added the right to live in a decent shelter within a pollu-
tion-free environment, while being ruled by a government that is
devoted to our individual and collective well-being.

Heaven must be, by definition, a place where every human soul finds happiness in the happiness of its fellow human souls. This suggests, in turn, that heaven is a place where the unhappiness of even a single human soul is a cause for concern. Well, pick up an average issue of The Washington Post *or* The New York Times. *These days, as you'll soon become aware, a reporter in a foreign land who has a bit of free time on his or her hands is likely to be traveling around the countryside reporting on misery or hunger or injustice — and, once in a while, on a successful program that's actually increasing the sum total of happiness enjoyed by local residents.*

If we now ask ourselves what standard *that reporter is using, more often implicitly than explicitly, in his or her articles, the answer would appear to be: the standard taken for granted in the better-off parts of the United States, which now represent our ideal for this planet as a whole. Look back only a few decades, and compare the standards that used to be applied where most of our fellow human beings were concerned. The "suffering millions of China" would go on suffering into the foreseeable future, most Americans and Europeans believed. The murder rate in American cities could only go up; there was no way of reversing our remorseless slide from perfection. The nuclear race between West and East would probably end in the kind of mutual destruction envisioned by a movie like* Dr. Strangelove. *This or that disease, this or that chronic condition, would prove to be the one for which no cure was possible.*

And above all, the standards of democracy and justice developed by a country like the United States would almost certainly turn out to be the unique result of our rather unique history. Take out the long sequence from the Magna Carta to the Bill of Rights, take out the heritage of our Founding Fathers, and what hope could reasonably be entertained for a higher vision of human possibility, especially where a particular society's politics are concerned?

But the world has refused to cooperate with these visions of only a short time ago. Internally, here in the United States, we have succeeded in producing a concern for justice, equity, and democratically distributed well-being that is virtually limitless. It has been symbolized in our legal system by the "class action suit," which is based, by definition, on a very broad vision of damage. Even the corporate sector of the American economy, once regarded as a temple of greed and moral indifference, has learned to ask itself, in advance, the kinds of questions formerly leveled only by its political critics and other adversaries.

Meanwhile, we seem to have developed a vision of foreign policy that differs in the most remarkable way from the visions of half a century ago. Back then, you'll remember, it was fashionable to assume that a world of pure threat would never cease to keep our anxieties high. Always there would be a Stalin or a Hitler, whose smiles would keep the curtain drawn over mountains of bodies and pits filled with the remains of their victims. Always, the capacity to obliterate such violent and rapacious figures would determine our own continuing survival. Always, our scientists would be financed mainly through the quest for better ways of destroying the other members of our species, or averting the weapons they were aiming at us. And, always, the decision to go to war would represent a mere subtext of the eternal need to stop aggression in its tracks, which would also represent the long-term purpose of every one of our foreign policies.

And now look at the directions in which American foreign policy moves at the present time. Without a vote having been taken in Congress, without a proclamation by any U.S. president or a constitutional amendment, we have actually made the pursuit of freedom and happiness of our fellow human beings into central policy aims. The fact that people are suffering, the fact that they are hungry and/or terrified and/or sick, suddenly has been and is being redefined as intolerable—an affront to our new and heavenly definition of a proper global norm.

Remember the time when it was common to hear conservative denunciations of "bleeding-heart liberals?" That particular phrase hasn't been heard of late. And one of the reasons it has faded away is because the adjective "bleeding-heart" has come to be perceived as a synonym for empathetic. And to feel empathy for another human being, to be able to see the world from their point of view, has become as central for conservatives as it is for liberals. Where they're likely to differ is on questions of policy rather questions of merit. The fact that another human being is suffering, another human being in any part of the world, is now universally regarded as regrettable. What we've collectively lost is the capacity to respond to misery by simply turning our backs. And if necessary, if the suffering displayed by our media reaches a point we collectively can't stand, our military forces will be "sent in" to somehow bring it to an end, and to restore to the inhabitants of that distant land the possibility of freedom and happiness.

Like most of us, you've heard references to what's now known as "compassion fatigue." Why must the media assault our sensibilities with the sufferings of our fellow human beings? the enemies of "compassion fatigue" plaintively inquire. Well, the answer to that question is fairly obvious. First of all, the prerequisite for suffering from "compassion fatigue" is necessarily to feel compassion. Meanwhile, the media rush to depict suffering in every corner of our planet because they know from experience that a suffering *human being, unlike a human being celebrating a happy birthday or anniversary, immediately attracts what's known as audience attention. We see the suffering. We identify with it. The thought goes through all of our minds,* That could happen to me, and thank God that it hasn't. *And this is followed by another thought:* Why doesn't the American government do something to stop it?

Well, that's not exactly the Golden Rule, but it's close. Feel about others the way you'd like them to feel about you, *and get your government to help them the way you'd like to be helped if you found yourself in a similar situation. What we now regard as our preferred values where our fellow human beings are concerned, are values that come close to being biblical. Meanwhile, where our own personal lives are concerned, we regard anything short of happiness as a failure of some kind. The right pill, the right psychotherapist, the right boyfriend, girlfriend, or spouse, and our "happiness shortfall" will finally be abolished.*

And so, inevitably, we go on complaining. In a more expressive, and in some ways more classical, state of society, our first act upon reaching the office in the morning might be to unroll a prayer rug, get down on our knees, and thank the heavenly powers for giving us both work to do and the health that enables us to do it. But like all of those who live in Heaven, we'd of course like to be members of the inner circle of angels, who are really getting a charge out of divine presence. We have a nearly limitless capacity for envy. Somebody's always got something that's even better than the big heap of things we have. And so we shrug off the most important feeling of all, the feeling of gratitude, and substitute for it the grouchings and squabblings that make up so much of our daily life.

Well, I divulge to you, the attendees at my last lecture, that I'm trying hard to make myself an exception to this general rule. I'm very grateful to be serving as the president of The George Washington University. I'm very happy to be a part of my splendid family. I'm as glad as I can be that my two sons are so terrific in their respective ways. I greet with joy the students who continue to flock to my school, and the faculty members who so devotedly teach them. And in general, in every way, I'm amazed to discover that, having been born in 1937, I'm still around, well, and fully functional, 60 years later.

Having allowed myself to utter these outrageous thoughts, I'm now going to say "conclude" and head back to my office. There, I have no doubt, the top item in my in-box will be a heart-stricken complaint. Mr. or Mrs. Average Washington has just gotten sick and tired of walking across the GW campus and spotting young men and women, students, presumably, whose hormones appear to be raging out of control. Not only are their hands all over each other, but they're obviously longing to rip off their clothes and do something awful all over the neatly clipped grass. How can I, as the president of The George Washington University, abstain from getting this situation under control?

And my reply will run along the following lines: Though my superhuman strength is a matter of common record, I still fall just a trifle short of the capacity to alter the hormonal endowment of our species. Its long history testifies to the remarkable power of its reproductive inclinations. In my next meeting with God, however, which is scheduled in the Board Room three days from now, I will ask Him or Her for a staff or wand that will cause GW students to keep a proper distance from each other during business hours, and perhaps after business hours as well. *Mr. and Ms. Average Washington should keep his or her eyes glued to* The Washington Post, *which will surely feature me on the front page as God grants my humbly expressed wish.*

And taking care of one more complaint will add yet another nice touch to a day that has begun so enjoyably, with this my very last and absolutely final lecture.

EVERY ONCE in a while I am flattered by the inclusion of one of my speeches in a book about speech writing. The following speech appeared in *Executive's Portfolio of Model Speeches for All Occasions* by Dianna Booher, published by Prentice Hall. I gave it in 1987 when I was president of the University of Hartford. A. Bartlett Giamatti—formerly the president of Yale University—had recently been made the seventh commissioner of Major League Baseball in the United States. Bart was a wonderful friend of mine, and I enjoyed roasting him gently at the Diamond Club Dinner in Hartford.

In Honor of Bart Giamatti

It's a pleasure and an honor for me to welcome you to this evening's program, and to welcome our distinguished guest A. Bartlett Giamatti, president of the National League.

Bart Giamatti needs little introduction from me, given his standing in the world of major league baseball and of American athletics. He has added a new and illustrious name to the pantheon that includes Abner Doubleday, Lou Gehrig, Babe Ruth, Joe DiMaggio, and Mickey Mantle.

Indeed, Bart's identification with baseball and athletics is so complete—his passion for sports so total—that it has given birth to some envy. And envy, as always, has given birth to some rumor.

The rumor being spread by those who cannot stomach his successes is that Bart, like some kind of superspy out of a James Bond novel, is a man with a secret past. Bart, it is whispered, far from having always been the sportsman and athletic raconteur we see before us today, was once—of all things—a university president.

And not the president, let me add, of a muscular school like Ohio State or Notre Dame! The president, rather, of an effete eastern snob school that produces the kinds of graduates who don't like Ronald Reagan, or Cheerios, or Blondie, or engagement parties or bridal showers.

When I heard this rumor the first time, I was shocked. I regarded it as one more example of the kinds of slurs that are always being flung, alas, at those of Italian-American descent. It seems that no matter how many years go by there are still those who cannot see a last name ending in "I" without suspecting that the person it denotes is a representative of the Mafia with a colorful past and a switchblade in his pocket.

I heard the rumor a second time. I heard the rumor a third time. That left me no choice but to go straight to Bart's office and to beg him for an explanation.

I don't have to tell you what palatial quarters he occupies today. Making my way past a battery of secretaries and personal assistants, each of whom asked me for my driver's license and Social Security number, I admired the trophies in their glass display cases, the medals, the inscribed photographs of major athletes and the many other signs of a long and satisfying career in sports.

When I was finally admitted to his mahogany office with its elegant recessed bar and he had given me a snifter of fine cognac, I posed the question to him.

"Bart," I said, "what about these rumors that you were once the president of—uh—forgive me for saying this—Yale University?"

It took Bart a few minutes to recover his composure, and then he offered me the following explanation—which I am happy to present to you today.

Bart admitted that his Italian-American origins had played an important role in his life. But far from seeking to model himself on such figures as Al Capone and Marlon Brando, he had chosen as his personal godfathers the two great Italians known as Dante Alighieri and Niccolò Machiavelli.

Initially he studied them in college and graduate school—to such an extent that he even received a PhD in the field of Romance Languages and Literature.

Then, discontented with the abstract nature of his confrontation with these two cultural greats, he decided to test their outlooks and their philosophies in actual practice—in the world of grim reality.

Machiavelli, as we all know, was the author of what the Germans call Realpolitik. *What that means is that you have to be prepared to do things that are necessary rather than things that are merely pleasant or moral. "And that," Bart said to me, "is what Yale University is all about."*

True, he did serve as the school's president for a number of years—but only to experience what Machiavelli was getting at in his most famous work, The Prince. *Let me quote the words Bart actually used in his mahogany office:*

"Steve," he said, "I played that role up to the point at which I could feel Old Nick smiling upon me from his studio apartment in the Inferno. *At that point, I knew that I had absorbed*

the very essence of his outlook, in a manner that might be called Applied Humanities. When I received a note of commendation from Education Secretary Bennett, telling me how well I had embodied the values of the Western tradition, I knew it was time to quit."

Specifically, it was time for Bart to live out the values of Dante as laid out in The Divine Comedy—especially the books called Purgatorio and Paradiso.

"Purgatorio," Bart explained, "was when I announced my resignation from the presidency of Yale and had to sit through the resulting farewell dinners. You have no idea what a high-cholesterol dinner will do to you when it is followed by one-hundred-year-old port and fortune cookies."

Paradiso, on the other hand, is his present job as the president of the National League and all-around sportsman. Again, let me put it in Bart's own words:

"Steve," he observed with a blissful smile, "I can't see a baseball sailing up into a blue sky without thinking about Dante. After getting a little bit of a boost from Virgil and from his own beloved Beatrice, Dante took off into the wild blue yonder, where goodness reigns supreme. And that, it seems to me, is what baseball is all about. It's why baseball has done so much to shape our wonderful American psyche. It's why baseball is so closely identified with joy, love, loyalty and peace."

By this time, I must confess, I was in tears. Bart led me, blubbering, to the door. And my closing image of him, framed in the mahogany doorway, was of a figure of tradition, not only of Dante, but of Fiat, Ferrari, Frank Sinatra, and Olivetti—all of those products and traditions that have made our lives melodious and stylish.

Bart sits here today as a man who has passed through hell and reached the world of eternal bliss. He has earned his smile, as well as his PhD, through almost unlimited tolerance for pain. He has even emerged with a grin on his face, from the presidency of Yale, a school that is still trying to compete with the Uni-

versity of Hartford in areas like fund-raising and intercollegiate athletics.

We welcome you tonight, Bart. We welcome your smile and your neatly trimmed beard. We welcome the athletic values that have made you a folk hero in your time and an example to us all.

12.

THE VIRTUES OF
COLLEGE ATHLETICS

B ecause of the Duke lacrosse excitements of 2006, there are
indications that some colleges and universities will view athletes
as potentially dangerous characters and will be putting more
and more restrictions on them. I wonder when it will cease being fun
to be a college athlete. Should we be viewing athletes with suspicion?
Caution? We are already doing drug and urine testing and trying to follow all the rules the National Collegiate Athletic Association (NCAA)
lays down for collegiate athletics. If I am a college athlete, do I want
to feel that I have fewer civil rights because I am on a team? Am I to
be treated differently from a chess player? I don't think for a minute
that college athletes shouldn't be held accountable for their actions.
But how should universities deal with these issues? Maybe we should
limit big-money Division 1 athletics. Where on campus does this get
talked through? What duty do professors have to their students on this
issue? These are agendas that remain unresolved in the university community.

Very able academic students often like to attend a school where
there is a strong athletic program, which partially explains why Duke
and Stanford and others invest as much money as they do in their ath-

letic programs. I distinguish these schools from Indiana or Nebraska, where the university is many things to the people of the state. Land grant schools are often the pride of their respective states, and so Nebraska football means a lot to people throughout the state, many of whom may never have matriculated. This is distinguishable from most universities in New England, for instance.

I wouldn't want to see intercollegiate sports disappear from college campuses. But having an athletic program is a question of tone, perspective, and the place of athletics in the value system. People argue about the role of sports on campus from both ends of the spectrum. Some professors think athletics should be banished. They may be annoyed with the compensation paid to some coaches. And they might make a good case that sports are a distraction for their students. They might also object that special accommodations may have been made to attract and maintain athletes, just as we make special accommodations to get students who are otherwise blessed — for instance, terrific mathematicians, musicians, and others. Getting a mix of talents and aptitudes in your student body seems to me to be a good thing. It's just that college athletics, like other things in our society, has become overblown and overinvested and may have involved some scandals, such as cheating, or situations that arise from excessive drinking by spectators and others.

Part of this lamentable situation has to do with pressure that universities put on their coaches. As a university president, I was of two minds on this. Certainly you want your coach to produce a team that wins. On the other hand, coaches are ultimately teachers; you want them to have the values of the academy, and winning a game is not the overriding academic value. I am just happy that football was blessedly gone from my university by the time I became the president of GW because it is very expensive and, at an urban university like mine, difficult to accommodate. But I also admit that I sometimes wondered if fund-raising at GW is harder because we don't have a football team. It can help with school spirit.

Don't get me wrong. I like football, but it calls for great investment. It requires a large staff of coaches and trainers and costly facilities and equipment. You need facilities for practice and a stadium in which to play. The worst part is that the football budget distorts the allocation of athletic resources between men and women's sports. If you are trying to honor the Title IX laws giving opportunities equally to both genders, football puts a disproportionate number of men's dollars into football, leaving too little for the other men's teams. On the other side, a lot of money is allocated to the women's sports to balance the football budget; and that amount of money might not always be necessary, given the number of women who play competitive sports in college. So, as it turns out, if you take football out of the equation, you can bring equity to men's and women's sports far more easily and efficaciously.

Lou Little was a famous Columbia University football coach for many years. He was a handsome, well-spoken man who was always ready to meet a photographer. Unfortunately, his teams lost far more often than they won. In the postgame interviews, Lou would say things like "Yes, it is too bad that Princeton beat us again, but it is important to point out that Columbia graduates who played football on our past teams include two rabbis, two brain surgeons, two Supreme Court justices, etc."

Lou was always proud of the extraordinary accomplishments of the team members *after* they graduated. But on the field these team members were often not the athletic stars in the league! I always thought, How does he get away with not having to explain the team's defeats? Think of it this way: What if a group of chemistry majors were doing work that was less than hoped for, but their professors nevertheless touted all their other outside accomplishments? Would the university say happily, "Yes, the chemists are wonderful dancers and they have beautiful manners"?

Coach Little always reminded us that the game was character-building, good for sportsmanship, created strong bones and strong teeth, and so on. And that was certainly a message we could probably hear more of today. Columbia graduates still talk about a few standout victories in the 1930s; this is likely because they don't have enough great contemporary victories to point to.

I never understood why a high school coach would send a talented student athlete to a Division 2 school. A student is either good enough as an athlete for a Division 1 school or is an academically oriented kid who is also a good athlete and would like to play for a Division 3 school with a good athletic program, intramural or collegiate. The major distinction between Divisions 1 and 3 is that Division 1 gives athletic scholarships. However, this rule is often honored in the breach. Division 3 schools might give a scholarship based on need, or they may discover that the applicant-athlete also plays a musical instrument.

I believe in cutting some slack for intercollegiate athletes. What I mean by this is that we should maintain academic standards for them but give them all the help and encouragement needed to meet those standards. These students are often on the road for games and obligated to miss classes. In this situation, universities must provide almost unlimited support services for student athletes. I have been very impressed by the dedication of our athletes and have been especially impressed by the women; they are not only marvelous when they play, but they are generally outstanding in class as well.

Athletic teams teach many virtues, such as bonding, the satisfaction of accomplishment, physical fitness, teamwork, and time management. While I think sports are an asset overall, I think maybe there is altogether too much emphasis on winning for the universities and not enough emphasis on the individual. Are universities sufficiently concerned about what pressures are being placed on these young people, and are they giving them what they need to compensate for what they miss because of sports? We need always to keep the students themselves first in our minds. We need to think of them as our children. Presumably, we know something they don't and can share some of this wisdom. It is more important that we educate an engineer than that the university win a game.

Having pointed to some of the shortcomings of collegiate athletics, I should say that I feel certain that if sports were dropped at the university, the environment would not be the same. It would be sadly diminished. You can be deviant, which is to say, not have football, and still be a contender. But at some point, if you are nonnormative and go too far in this direction—like also not having basketball—you are then changing your profile and have to appeal to a totally different constituency. There are schools that may be able to thrive without having football or basketball or other intercollegiate competition. Most cannot.

I like sports and think that universities have some obligation to help all students develop sound bodies along with sound minds. As president, I was pleased to encourage all manner of intercollegiate and intramural sports. I think lifelong sports—like golf and the racquet sports—are great. But I would like to make sure that students stay active throughout their lives. Unfortunately, some who are injured playing sports in college develop arthritis and other problems as they age—and often this is related to undergraduate sports.

I THINK basketball is a wonderful game for both men and women, and I have been an enthusiastic supporter of our teams over the years. In the case of GW, the basketball team is an important element of campus life and, because of our recent successes, has become an exciting enhancement of our reputation. Having said that, I have often worried that basketball, which I consider one of the parallel aspects of the university, is an area in which we seem to recruit African Americans in a way that—if we do not act with care—may exploit them. Given this concern, it seems a bit ironic that one of my biggest crises as president occurred as a result of our efforts to attract a talented African-American basketball player who got into serious trouble in high school and as a result saw some of his opportunities for higher education and a basketball career slip away. This tragic tale came to be known as the "Richie Parker incident" and was highlighted in the media all over the country, particularly in Washington and New York. It was just the sort of nightmare that university presidents dread; it certainly was mine.

The Richie Parker story was best told in the June 24, 1996, issue of *Sports Illustrated*. SI's reporter, Gary Smith, took six months to research all aspects of the case, and I can attest to its accuracy and balance. We had a high school basketball player with some real talent whom we were interested in attracting to GW. But we were very concerned that while he was in high school, he and another young man had made a terrible mistake and sexually abused a classmate. Parker confessed to the act. This later became the focus of an attempt to define his basket-ball—and college—career. Since we wanted to bring him to GW, we were very careful about researching the incident thoroughly. In doing so, we found that he had no prior record. Also, he seemed to be in deep contrition and we saw no virtue in his being banished from society or denied an opportunity for an education.

Our scholarship was a chance to get Parker out of New York, where he lived, and into a new environment. We planned to require that he meet with professionals to assess whether he understood the gravity of his past acts and was ready for college, and we were going bring him to GW and then redshirt him for a year (in other words, he would not be allowed to play basketball in his freshman year). Assuming he did well enough academically, we were going to have him join the team as a sophomore. Moreover, we were going to see that he got appropri-ate counseling and supervision, and he was to live with the family of a local clergyman. In our planning, we took pains to cross all the Ts and dot all the Is. Of course, underlying all of this was the expectation that he would add value to our basketball team. It was a plan for GW to do good and do well.

We had consulted with his family, his pastor, and the court that had sentenced him. There was a good deal of encouragement for what we had in mind. I am a believer in the potential for personal reinvention, and this was surely a case where a young man might, with our help, earn his way to a better life. Looking into the case, it seemed that his act, while most grave, was not beyond redemption.

But the case became a huge media event. Feminist groups saw our offer as an unjust reward for a sexual criminal. There was uninformed speculation in the press, combined with interviews with GW students and GW faculty, who are never shy about their views, opinions, and comments! The stories were full of opinions. None of the stories said anything about our plans to address the situation with all the serious-ness that it deserved. Under NCAA rules, we were not allowed to talk publicly about a person we were thinking of recruiting. We followed those rules and didn't give statements.

We had a review committee ready, chaired by a retired family court judge, and representatives of all the concerned constituencies. We hadn't even announced these plans when the attacks started. The situation became so dramatic and so political that our Board of Trustees chairman called me and asked me to back off. I was reluctant to do so, but he told me that this was an instance that called for the wisdom of the board. He told me that I was too close to the situation; I was too committed. Reluctantly, I acceded.

I learned a couple of bitter lessons from this episode:

1. Doing good does not come free.
2. If the press doesn't have a story, they make one up.

About two years later, Richie Parker was admitted to a college. The president of that college was an African-American woman, herself a mother of daughters. Because of her race and her gender, she had the standing to bless Parker's matriculation into college that I did not. I was pleased for Richie Parker that it worked out.

At the time, the optics of our involvement had become a big problem. I guess that in the end, it was appropriate for me to back off. But I still believe that the young man deserved the chance we wanted to give him. William Raspberry of *The Washington Post* wrote a very thoughtful column about the situation, and, ultimately, it put an end to all the talk. I was not being a good Samaritan—after all, we were trying to get him for the basketball team—but I thought Richie Parker should be given an opportunity. He had been stupid and committed a crime. But the court had said that going to college would be a good thing for him.

Had this young man not been a basketball player, and if he had been from a family of means and not in need of a scholarship, I believe that after the court put him on probation, he would have been admitted to a university and could have attended if his parents could pay his tuition. In fact, he could have come to GW and no one would have even known about the incident. Universities don't do background checks and security clearances on students. We rely on letters from teachers and others to recommend applicants.

In spite of my feelings about the righteousness of offering this young man a place on campus, I admit that I experienced more self-doubt about this case than others involving contending constituencies. It was almost overwhelming.

MY UNIVERSITY funds twenty-two men's and women's sports. To do so, the university seeks help from alumni, parents, and friends of the programs. Our coaches know that fund-raising is a part of their responsibilities. The head coaches have some flexibility in deciding how to budget their programs. So, for instance, in the case of men's rowing, the coach might decide that the top priority is a competitive schedule that will provide high-level experience for his rowers. As a result, the university funds he has might be invested in travel and equipment. But that is not all we have to think about. For instance, for the past two decades we have worked hard to get a new first-class boathouse for the crews. Because the university is in Washington, D.C., this task is a bit daunting. We have to gain permission from the city and the National Park Service to build our boathouse, and this is not an easy process. After twenty years of unrelenting effort, we still were not able to do so by the time I left office.

Our men's basketball is the team that brings the most attention to the university, and it has been a very successful program. I wrote the following letter to the GW men's basketball coach, Karl Hobbs, a few seasons ago. I think it pretty clearly outlines my view of athletics in the university environment.

Congratulations on a wonderful season. 18–11 ain't chopped liver. I'm proud of you, and I'm proud of how we got to where we got this year. And it goes without saying that I'm keeping my prayers in place for next year when I'm hoping we're going to be doing even better. But I want you to know that as important as it is for us to win, it is even more important that we do it straight-up, which is to say I like to go to sleep at night knowing that I've got you as my coach and that we've got our heads together about what we believe in and what we value.

I've got nothing but compassion for the President of the Uni-

versity of Colorado, a fine university administrator, a learned academic with two PhD's. But there she is up to her knees in alligators perhaps because her football coach got confused about what it's all about. Thinking about St. Bonaventure just gives me a migraine headache. If we can win 18, 19, 20 games once in a while and have players who go to class, finish their coursework, get their degrees, that would be terrific. And if once in a while we made it into the NCAA and once there—what the heck?—went up the ladder to the Sweet Sixteen or the Elite 8, all the better. But first and foremost is the nurturing of student-athletes. It's easy to figure out how to do it right—just treat the players as if they were your own children, which in a manner of speaking they are.

When our team had an even more rewarding season, I wrote to Coach Hobbs about my reaction to a specific game:

I knocked over a cup of coffee during the last couple of seconds of the Dayton game on Saturday. You're going to kill me. An old man like me can't take that much excitement. Is there any chance we could win the rest of the games with a 10–12 point lead rather than closing on the last shot? The stress is going to wipe me out. You're doing a great job.

Coach Hobbs later wrote to me and said, "Thankfully, we have had great successes, both on and off the court. I could not be more proud of the four athletes who graduated on time last year and I look for similar outcomes for my players of today. Thank you for trusting me." When I receive a letter like this from a coach, I find myself becoming even more enthusiastic about college sports. Hobbs has both talent and class. He is a teacher and a gentleman.

SEVERAL YEARS ago, a GW graduate sent me a letter exhorting me to develop a stronger basketball team than that of Georgetown University, our friendly nearby neighbor. I tried to reassure him that these things take time:

I haven't been following GW basketball as long as you have, but I've been doing so for fifteen years with, I think, an enthusiasm built on a vested interest. And I have done everything I can and should do from the President's Office to enhance the quality of our men's teams and our women's teams in basketball, and in all other sports. I have invested a great deal of money and energy in coaches and balls and equipment and playing fields, and into bringing us into compliance with Federal Title IX laws and regulations. So, you can imagine that if you're disappointed, I'm disappointed.

That said, I have some appreciation that when it comes to improving universities at almost any level, whether it's the Psychology Department or the School of Education or the Law School or the basketball team, there are multiple ingredients that have to be mixed. One of them is patience. Georgetown has been a basketball power for some considerable time. . . .

But all these things are going to take a period of gestation. If you cook soup too quickly, it burns. Babies take nine months. University basketball programs take a few years and then, even then, it doesn't always work out, which is why I come back to the word I used at the beginning of this letter—patience. But you could add prayer.

13.

THE BRIDE IS TOO BEAUTIFUL

Some of the people from the Foggy Bottom neighborhood near the university didn't want to be seen coming to my office. So they came in the dark of evening to offer to sell us their houses. After years of complaining—with or without reason—about the university, they nevertheless assumed they would get the best price from us as they prepared to move to Florida. But they didn't want to be seen by other neighbors while visiting GW. After all those years of negativity regarding the university and its activities, they were embarrassed to be seen consorting with the enemy, especially when something as vulgar as money was involved.

Since as president of the university you carry the flag, it doesn't matter if you are a devil or a saint; your office and role are what it's about. The neighbors turned on me within weeks of my arrival in Washington—nothing personal, of course. I attended my first Foggy Bottom Association meeting and sat quietly in the back. When they started discussing an issue, I knew enough about it to get up and introduce myself as the new president and say, "I think the issue is being misstated here, let me try to explain it." *Bam!* They started shouting at me, "Shut up! Sit down!" And so on. I waited a minute and then tried again. They started shouting again. I went to a few more neighborhood meetings but soon realized that my mere presence was disruptive. Apparently, I had become a catalyst for uncivilized behavior. Unfortunately, the discourse ended soon thereafter and the GW vice presidents had to continue the conversation with the neighbors in a formal fashion.

My mother used to say that there are some people who are so critical that they will go to a wedding and complain that the bride is too beautiful. Here's a perfect example of how the neighbors complain about the bride. There are some ornamental gates on the approach to the medical school. When we installed them, the members of the Foggy Bottom Association complained to the city that we had put up a gate (actually, since the gates aren't meant to close, it could more accurately be described as an arch) and requested that the city force its removal. They argued that the gate/arch appeared to demarcate university property and such symbolism was contrary to their understanding of community access to the university. The fact that the constantly open archway made entry even more inviting and more attractive escaped them. They were complaining that the bride was too beautiful!

The situation with the neighbors has to do with matters that go back ninety-five years to 1912, when GW moved to Foggy Bottom. The name of the area is said to have come from the industrial fog that cast a shadow on the neighborhood and hung there in the swampy atmosphere near the Potomac River. In those days, the neighborhood was the home of many of the laborers at the local glass factory, gasworks and breweries and auto repair shops. Many of the houses were simple, narrow town houses, one to two rooms deep. Some were slums. I think the greatest oversight on GW's part when it relocated was not having enough money to buy more real estate in the neighborhood. Instead, the university merely got a toehold and had to grow incrementally from there.

If we could have acquired large pieces of property when the neighborhood was depressed, we might have become known as the savior of Foggy Bottom. Since that time, the university has had the effect of uplifting the neighborhood and making it an attractive place to live. The real estate values have all gone up enormously. But some of the neighbors say the university's growth is a negative rather than a positive. They are concerned Foggy Bottom will become a "university neighborhood." My response to that was: Where is the bad in being a university neighborhood? Why not, as long as people get value for their property, let the university buy up the property others want to sell? They reply, "Old Foggy Bottom (a unique residential portion of Foggy Bottom) is a historic neighborhood." I say, "Yes, and we don't own or seek a single house in Old Foggy Bottom!"

The university owns the old Howard Johnson Hotel that was made famous by the Watergate scandal. It is now called the Hall on Virginia Avenue (HOVA). We used it for undergraduate housing for six years—without incident. When we first acquired it, neighborhood critics came up with a whole list of horrible things that would happen as a result of GW having some of its undergraduates there. Half a dozen years passed, and none of those sad predictions happened. Nevertheless, the neighbors' allegations hung in the air almost as if they were real, and municipal decisions were made based on invented concerns expressed half a dozen years earlier, none of which had turned out to be valid. The neighborhood is safer now because we keep a police car and officer parked in front of the building; a good thing for the residence hall and for the neighbors. The facility backs up on a busy street, a gasoline station, a park, and a highway. There are no neighbors living close by, and, to my knowledge, there have been no valid calls made by neighbors to complain about noise or other problems with the students. Nevertheless, the city, at the urging of the Foggy Bottom Association, insisted that we not use our property for undergraduates.

As a result, in 2006 we put medical students in HOVA instead of undergraduates. It will be hard for the neighbors to come up with a complaint about our baby doctors! Aside from inconveniencing the university, there will be no difference whatsoever to the community whether there are medical students or undergraduates there. However, we have now been obliged to build additional undergraduate housing to make up for the loss of HOVA. If we had an infinite amount of land, building more housing would not be a problem. But we have a limited amount of land in Foggy Bottom, and when we use vacant land to build student housing, we consume space that could otherwise be used for academic purposes. At some point in the foreseeable future, we will have exhausted the ability to build in the neighborhood and the university will have to put more and more of its enterprise—probably its research facilities—elsewhere; perhaps out of the city. That's too bad. If now-vacant parking lots could be used for academic facilities rather than for housing, more of the heart of the university could be here. All this would be a more rational usage. But the situation with the neighbors has always been emotional and political rather than logical. Ironically, many of the people who complain are renters, not owners. Maybe if they owned property in the neighborhood, they would be happy to see the value of their property increase because of the presence of the university.

Since this is Washington, the neighbors have a world-class understanding of how to organize and file complaints. They hone that skill and raise it to an Olympic level. For some of our neighbors, fighting the university seems to have become the reason for living; we have given them a purpose! While president, I tried to be forthcoming to the neighbors by providing access to the university for courses, athletic events, lectures, art openings, theater, concerts, etc. But very few of our neighbors took advantage of our offer.

Every university is perceived as slightly intrusive. I remember that in Hartford, we put a satellite dish on campus. I got a letter of complaint from a man who claimed the dish was making him sterile. What do I know? Maybe it *was* making him sterile! Since I did not have the answer, I sent the letter over to the health department and asked them to consider the problem and give me advice. The public health people said there was no harm being caused. I wrote back and told my correspondent what I had been told. He wasn't satisfied and continued to argue that the dish was making him sterile. I think it is absolutely necessary to treat people with respect. But I also think you should treat them with the respect they deserve. If it turns out the complaints are unwarranted and there is nothing else to be done, you have to move on with your life.

I sometimes dream that the neighbors have prepared signs that say, FOGGY BOTTOM ASSOCIATION IS AGAINST _____. When "something" comes up at the university that they want to complain about, they fill in the blank space with that something! Generally, whatever it is that we are in favor of, they are opposed to. I suppose that a feeling of helplessness drives their irrationality. They can't listen to what we are saying because the blood is pounding in their ears. Sometimes I became irritated when we fixed something in the neighborhood and the neighbors suddenly coveted it. On one occasion, I wrote the following about neighbors' activities to our executive vice president, who handles the university's money:

> *Remember when we spent $300,000 renovating a field that the city said we could use to play soccer on? It was covered with glass and wire and acres of trash. Then, when we fixed it all up, the neighbors decided it looked good, so they got the city to throw us off so they could use it. It's happening again on [name of another field] . . .*

TRASH WAS a favorite subject of contention during my administration. One man wrote to complain about the noise of trash collection in the Foggy Bottom neighborhood and blamed it on the university. His letter began with the subject line "RE: Your continuing aggressive assault upon your next door neighbors," and it went downhill from there. It was one of the rudest letters I have ever received, and, since I knew I would be leaving office soon, I did not feel compelled to sugarcoat my reply, some of which follows:

> *. . . The truth is that there are a variety of things that go on at GW that I myself don't personally know anything about. The collection of garbage is very high on that list. I am personally ignorant of when trash is collected and what sort of noise may or may not result. Having lived in cities most of my life, I do know that the urban condition can be noisy. Traffic, pedestrians on the street, and yes, trash collection do give a less-than-pastoral background to metropolitan environs. I guess that in the country they have other problems. Mooing, perhaps. Still, while I cannot promise*

*you that it's possible, even with a magic wand, to do away with
the sounds of life, I can assure you that I will look into the issue
you raised and find out whether some mitigation is possible.*

*I do know that whatever is happening is not personal. I am
confident that nobody is trying to pick on you. I suspect that the
rubbish people have a route that they follow and in order to get
the job done they move from place to place during the night so
that they are not doing their work during the day and inconveniencing traffic and raising issues that inevitably would follow. It
is also possible that the collection is done by contractors and not
by my grounds people as your accusation suggests.*

The subject of trash came up in another way when a neighbor who
wrote to me fairly often demanded that we remove two public trash
cans we had put adjacent to a walkway. It seemed to be just a case
of a well-intentioned act on the part of the university (presumably, to
provide a receptacle and keep people from dropping rubbish on the
street), but the writer seemed to see something more sinister in our
placement of the trash cans. She wrote:

*. . . Unfortunately for us—it seems you guys just don't get it—or
maybe you really do and then come up with solemn pleas of innocence. It is not trash cans, nor call boxes, nor emergency phones.
It really is GW's incursions onto public spaces, without notifying
the neighborhood or public space officials, and without obtaining
permits. Permits?? What a novel idea!*

*[The GW employee who put the trash can there] assured me
his intentions were "well-intentioned," came from a resident's suggestion, and I believe him. That resident, however, did not ask
him to put GW trash cans on public space, only expressed his
regret at an overflowing public trash can near HOVA [Hall on
Virginia Avenue]. He never asked him to disobey the law . . .*

This is the kind of letter I was accustomed to, but for some reason, I
continued to try to make some sense of the situation and wrote back:

If I were a sensible man, I'd probably just not respond when you write to me. I'm confident that would serve my purposes best. . . . I know that you're [complaining about something trivial] largely either to provoke me or because you're looking forward to getting a souvenir for your Trachtenberg file, or to reassure yourself that you're still a player in the Foggy Bottom conversation. . . .

I don't mind, if I may say so, writing back to you. It's fun. We get some sort of perverse pleasure out of playing "Punch and Judy." When other university presidents tell me about their problems, I'm in a position to assure them that nothing they've got tops [your letters] and I can document my representation with stories that you have provided. And on your side, as it's clear from your most recent note, you have exercised power. You wrote a letter, you got trash cans removed. The world is a better place and you made it happen. . . .

I think of what you might have accomplished in Foggy Bottom and what you still might accomplish in Foggy Bottom if you put your energies to work in a positive rather than a negative way—if you looked for ways to work with [GW employees] to add value to the community, to see GW as a resource, even if it's only at the level of putting a trash barrel in a place where it would be good to have one. You spend too much time, if I may say so, being cranky.

Keep on working on behalf of Foggy Bottom. Anything you actually do to enhance the neighborhood is ultimately to the advantage of George Washington University; an irony that I am sure hasn't escaped you.

I learned some time later that this neighbor had been hospitalized briefly in our new GW Hospital. She had opposed the building of this hospital, and I was surprised to hear that she was among the first to use it. I asked her in a letter how she had been treated there and invited her to lunch. She replied in a predictable manner:

Yes, I did enter GW Hospital, for the last time if I have anything to say about it. I am unable to say anything nice; because of the

treatment I received I filed a letter of complaint which resulted in
the censure of an employee. . . .

As for lunch, no thank you. The invitation was kind of back-
handed.

I never like to give up on these things and once again wrote to her
in an attempt to get her to participate in a more positive relationship
with the university:

I do hope you'll reconsider my lunch invitation, which was most
earnestly proffered. . . . We are on the threshold of a new, more
positive relationship between GW and the Foggy Bottom/West
End community. The development of Square 54 [a square block
of land where the old hospital was torn down] is going to help to
define how we interact in the coming generation. You need to look
to the future, face forward, be a pioneer, have a new vision, or
run the risk of becoming irrelevant. The historic mode of dialogue
between persons such as yourself and the University is an obsolete
artifact. Witness the changing sociology of the ANC [Advisory
Neighborhood Commission]. Constructive engagement is increas-
ingly imperative. Get on board and make a wholesome contribu-
tion. You can do it, if you really want to.

14.

YOU CAN'T ANTICIPATE
EVERY CRISIS

Universities have not been exempt from violence in the twentieth and twenty-first centuries. However, far from becoming used to such experiences, Americans still find them abhorrent. From the shootings at University of Texas by Charles Whitman in 1966, to the bombing of the Army Math Research Center on the University of Wisconsin campus and the National Guard shootings at Kent State University in 1970, to the shootings on the Virginia Tech campus in April 2007, it seems that bloody, murderous attacks upon the academic communities of American universities have become a horrible, inexplicable part of campus life. A boundary has been breached by such violent acts, and the "hallowed halls of ivy" are no longer a step removed from contemporary life—if they ever were.

We have seen campus violence in other countries as well as our own. There was a bombing in the cafeteria on the campus of Hebrew University in Jerusalem in 2002 that killed nine people, five of whom were Americans. In September 2006, a shooter on the campus of Dawson College in Montreal, Canada, was apparently copying the Columbine High School shootings when he shot and killed one woman and wounded nineteen other people. And then, in January 2007, we learned of the lethal combination of suicide bomber and car bomb at the Mustansiriya University, a once-prestigious Sunni institution in Baghdad. Institutions once considered special sanctuaries even in war—hospitals, mosques, and universities—are no longer held sacred or inviolable when terrorism is the goal.

I believe that an attack on an institution that represents the values and aspirations of a society—a university—is in some ways different, and more unspeakable, than other instances of violence. When there were attacks at the two universities in Gaza, they ripped the already torn fabric of Palestinian society and in this way did more harm than if the rival gunmen had simply been firing at each other in and from two ordinary houses or office buildings. A Hamas leader seems to have confirmed this idea when he said, "When we saw the university burning, it was like our hearts were burning because this institution is very dear to us."

CONTEMPORARY UNIVERSITY administrators have to take campus security very seriously. This is true not only in urban centers but also in pastoral environments. Wherever the threats occur, sadly, they can come from the inside as well as from outside the campus walls. Whenever you have a community of people, there is some statistical chance that someone is going to do something untoward. In fact, many of the more consequential cases in this country touching on university safety have taken place in small, rural environments where someone—either from off campus or living on campus—has committed a rape or a murder or other crime against a member of the university community.

Students are young, healthy, and energetic. When one of them dies, the event diminishes the student body's sense of invulnerability and forces individuals to face their own mortality. It changes their worldview. I have watched the effect of suicides, fatal accidents, and crimes on students. They come together in an almost primitive ritual—often candlelit—to celebrate the life of the departed. Many of them get up and, in a Quaker-like fashion, testify about the life of the dead student. Someone has been plucked from their midst, and those left behind must try to make that knowledge real by coming close and talking about it until the reality is accepted or at least understood.

University presidents constantly try to make their campuses as safe as possible. We have a sense of personal and institutional responsibility. And of course there are legal obligations that are expected from the institution. Institutions like mine have their own professional police departments. The GW police patrol on foot and by car, checking the buildings, the open areas, and the streets that enclose the campus. Ours is a porous campus, accessible by public streets and sidewalks. Anyone can go through without being stopped. Nevertheless, we have tried to enhance security and make it visible, without making too much of it and making people apprehensive. For instance, we put up call boxes around the campus that make it possible for students to quickly pick up the phone and instantaneously be connected to campus security. Likewise, we placed alarm boxes throughout the campus to allow students who sense trouble to punch an alarm that will bring help. Up until 9/11 this all worked reasonably well and we had no more incidents affecting student safety than is statistically predictable for an urban environment.

But after 9/11 we enhanced our security even more to give a greater comfort factor to the campus community and to the families of students, faculty, and staff. We hired an outstanding supplemental security person to head the effort. He had just retired as a captain from the U.S. Navy and was perfect for the academic community because he held a PhD from an excellent university and understood the nature and culture of academe. Also, he understood important security issues at a level beyond what we were accustomed to considering. He did a review of our campus security and preparedness. His work led us to purchase additional hardware and vehicles, do more staff training, and get upgraded computer software. In all ways, we upgraded and rethought our security plans. This made us realize even more clearly that campus security has to be reviewed constantly, reconsidered, and rehearsed routinely; and that we were always at risk.

Campus security is the sort of thing that universities can never, ever get exactly right. A person wouldn't congratulate himself for bringing an umbrella to work to keep off the rain when the umbrella works perfectly. But if the wind is too strong for the umbrella and turns it inside out, making it useless, self-recriminations ensue. The umbrella didn't function properly, and in spite of the planning and preparation, the umbrella owner got soaked. As long as things were going well, whatever he did or did not do to protect himself was sufficient. But when things did not go well, his preparation, however extensive, was inadequate.

AFTER THE Virginia Tech shootings, I thought the people rushing to judgment about the university president were an embarrassment to themselves. Clearly they didn't remember that only a matter of months earlier, others had been rushing to judgment about the president of Duke University and declaring what he should have known and should have done with regard to the dreadful accusations surrounding a men's lacrosse team party. When tragedy strikes, critics come up with proposed solutions that no one ever thought of before and that would generally be impossible, even if they seemed plausible. For instance, when someone suggests — in a cascade of Monday-morning quarterbacking — that the Virginia Tech campus should have been shut down after the first murders were discovered, I do not know what they are talking about. A campus with 2,600 acres, hundreds of buildings, and thousands of people living and working inside it is a small city. It cannot be slammed shut like a bank vault door. Even if it could somehow be closed, who knows if that would be the best solution for whatever emergency is taking place? Depending on the situation, it could be that ordering everyone to leave the campus immediately might be a better solution than a lockdown. Of course, no one disputes the need for excellent preparation. The university has to have a plan that can be explained logically and must have resources dedicated to carrying out that plan. But the notion that if someone gets hurt, the university is automatically to blame seems an impossible stretch of the imagination.

The tragedy at Virginia Tech leaves university administrators with a dizzying array of questions. Could it have been avoided if the shooter had been dismissed from campus or forced into counseling months earlier? I am reminded of the case I mentioned earlier about the suicidal student to whom we gave an involuntary leave from campus because we believed he was a possible danger to himself or others. We were criticized and then sued for taking this action. We believe a life may have been saved. But can anyone know this for a certainty?

For the Virginia Tech administrators, similar questions abound. Why did the shooter commit these horrible acts against students and faculty at his own school? How might the loss of life have been prevented? When he received treatment, why didn't it help him and why didn't he return for more? Was there a way the shooter's family could have helped the university discover his troubling mental state? Were there things that the university could have done within the legal guidelines to take more definitive action based on the shooter's dark writings? This is a very sticky question; after all, Stephen King, a writer of some of the more violent and bizarre fiction in contemporary America, was presumably an undergraduate somewhere, too. When is creative writing just creative writing?

Media reports can be quite facile in offering retrospective, clear-cut solutions to such complicated and difficult issues. Professional judgments by trained psychiatric personnel are never so facile because they see the legal and psychological complexities. When a person is suspected of being abusive or homicidal, we are told we must still give proof of a threat or a violent act before enforcement officials can arrest and hold the person. Such ambiguous situations certainly create conflict, anxiety, criticism, and, unfortunately, sometimes tragedy.

The Virginia Tech situation informs us of an uncomfortable but immutable truth; few people can be prepared for the news of murder and massacre. A campus is no different. Even when we have sophisticated plans in place for calamities, it is inevitable that there can be confusion, emotional dizziness, and a legitimate questioning of the reliability of the news before the machinery comes into place and police pick up the trail of the perpetrator of the crime. Upon hearing the news, we might even try to avoid taking severe action in the event that we are operating on hearsay or inaccurate reports. We are hesitant to cause panic and instead might take a deliberative pause before acting.

These days, news arrives by text messaging, cell phone, e-mail, blog, Facebook, YouTube, and television or radio, and it spreads quickly—

and often incompletely. University administrators must sort through the selective nature of these communications quickly and decisively. My university has a recorded information line and a Campus Advisories Web site where anyone can go for information during an incident. We also participate in Alert DC, a free service through the District of Columbia that allows subscribers to select how they would like to receive emergency alerts and notifications. But technology is merely the channel, not the message. We must still deal with a bewildering conundrum: how to get and share accurate information during a crisis while also addressing the desire for immediacy.

WE LIVE in a time in which everyone seems to think that for every question there must be an answer. We want those answers now. Moreover, we don't want to live with the contingency that bad things happen, people get hurt, people die. When the older people in our society were children, they existed in a world in which the reality of mortality was omnipresent. They were taught prayers like "Now I lay me down to sleep, I pray the Lord my soul to keep. If I die before I wake . . ." With the recitation of such words, children became somewhat conditioned to the inevitability of death. In those times, proportionately far more children were swept away by disease and accidents than are today, and numbers of parents had to bury their children. Whereas children once had to listen to stories in which Jack and Jill went up the hill, fell down and broke their crowns, and little children got baked into pies by witches, now we have stories about little trains that think they can, think they can, and don't fail. And they never roll backward and hurt somebody!

I wonder if modern children are at all attuned to the recognition that life is not always as accommodating as we would like it to be and that there are going to be tragedies. If they do not develop the ability to deal with that fact, they will be immeasurably shocked and aggrieved when confronted with melancholy reality. Of course, it can also be said that today's children have had to deal with a mind-numbing and constant barrage of TV reports about such innocence-shattering situations as 9/11, the Virginia Tech shootings, the ongoing Darfur genocide, and the constant and continuing violence in the Middle East.

We have greatly reduced many of the threats and causes of death brought on by accident and disease, and that is a good thing. But, in our efforts to get it right, we have managed to set the standard at the level of perfection, and I am not sure that is sound. If something bad happens, we tend to look for someone to blame.

I think we aren't all that different from the people who were wandering in the days of Abraham, Jesus, and Mohammed. For instance, there is a commandment that says, "Thou shalt not kill." What that tells me is that back in the past, there were murderers. Otherwise God wouldn't have taken the trouble to say, "Don't do that." There were adulterers, and there were thieves. And children were being disrespectful to their parents; even in the long ago! All of those things called for a set of commandments to prohibit them. A central value of reading the classics and scripture is that they inform us about such things. We can see that, while there are amazing technological developments in human society, the nature of human behavior seems not all that new or different.

MANY INSTITUTIONS of higher education in Manhattan were affected by 9/11. These included Columbia, NYU, the New School, and Pace. Here in Washington, there was also fear in the local universities close to the Pentagon, the White House, and Capitol Hill, all of which were said to be targets of the terrorists. In the reporting on 9/11, there were even incorrect stories in the media describing a hit on the State Department, which is right down the street from our campus. There were reports on TV about billowing smoke coming from there. Because of all this, concerned families were desperate to contact their loved ones on campus and, as was true in New York City, some of our communications systems were quickly overloaded.

The upside of contemporary communications is that everyone who cares to knows everything all the time. The downside is that the insatiability for constant communication, upgrading, messaging, updating, and so on, create fear and anxiety when the communications fail. Parents, accustomed to being able to pick up a cell phone and talk to a son or daughter in Washington immediately, were unable to get through and were traumatized by the communications void. We learned a lot at GW during that crisis about messaging parents and about communication in general. As a result, we are now better prepared to keep people informed. We know that transparency and constant communication are watchwords in this kind of situation. A university does not want to ever be silent. Our lesson learned was: Keep talking, keep answering questions, keep putting messages on line, keep putting out press releases.

The 9/11 experience showed us the need for improved on-campus communications, and we realized that there were some competing needs we had to get straight. For instance, we thought it was important to keep common places open so that students could come to them and feel safe. But in specifying the library as one of those gathering places, we found we were in conflict with the librarians, who felt it was best to close up shop and go home to their own families. There wasn't the kind of communication in place then to deal with that. As a result, there is now a rule that no one is permitted to close a campus unit without getting in direct communication with our central command. No one would want to have a situation in which students end up running through the streets looking for safety, having been closed out of university shelter and gathering places. Maybe we could have foreseen this situation, but we didn't. You do the best you can, and after learning about the problem, you put an answer in place for the future. You simply cannot anticipate every crisis that can assault a campus and prepare for it. You can devote your entire university budget to preparing for the worst.

There is a great temptation in modern life for scapegoating. When something goes wrong, we look for someone to blame. Doing so makes us feel in control. If we can identify a miscreant and say, "If only he had acted correctly or more quickly," it makes us feel less threatened by the unknown. We live in a world in which there are many things that cannot be controlled, and I am afraid we just have to live with them. But wouldn't it be nice if, whenever something bad happened, we could identify a malfeasant and sacrifice him? We could say, "Okay God, we're going to burn this offering." Every culture has had ways of keeping horror at bay; for instance, giving maidens to the dragon, offering up the lamb, Abraham preparing to sacrifice his own son, Aztecs extracting human hearts. The list goes on and on. Scapegoating serves the same purpose. But I think society needs to control its expectations. If our expectation is perfection, we will always fall short and will need to point fingers. If we can control our expectations, we might be able to more fairly decide whether people have behaved irresponsibly and blundered or if they have done as well as they possibly could under the circumstances.

Earlier societies had castles, moats, and superthick walls. Enemies came along and figured out new instruments to shoot arrows farther and higher to get over the walls. And then they figured out they didn't have to just shoot plain old arrows; they could set them on fire and shoot them over the walls and cause even more damage. Then they figured out how to make catapults to shoot large flaming bundles of matter over the walls to destroy the castle. The point is that technology advances—both the technology of progress and the technology of evil—and it is a never-ending story. We will hardly ever be ahead of the curve unless some magic occurs. University presidents certainly are not capable of magic. What do we want of them? Is there a whole package of expectations that we need to call on in different times and for different things? We cannot afford to say that unless we get it right every time, *Woe is us!* As it is, we have such a "gotcha" culture that people may be avoiding positions of responsibility because they don't want the level of opprobrium that comes with them. We need to have people who are accountable, but where is the balance? How can we do this in ways that do not raise the stakes for participation too high? It is a dynamic world. We need to stay alert and awake, but we cannot pull rabbits out of the hat. We can only do our best.

15.

THE BENEFITS OF BEING
A TWENTIETH-CENTURY MAN

I readily confess that I am an unreconstructed twentieth-century man. I use old-fashioned fountain pens and an ancient Rolodex, I don't care much for e-mails, and I enjoy writing letters that will be sent by the U.S. Postal Service. I can't help it, that's the way I am. I once had a publicly available e-mail address of my own and received communications from hundreds of students and thousands of alumni, and God only knows how many parents and neighbors and faculty—all with something to say—so I went incommunicado from e-mails.

A university president gets a lot of correspondence from all sorts of people. If someone took the time to write to me about their concerns, I tried to personally answer each and every one. I felt obliged to do so. People usually don't like to be disagreed with, especially when they write seeking redress from some perceived injustice or mistake on the university's part. But many letter writers relaxed a bit when I replied to their letters and did so in a mellow tone. In this way, I picked up several regular correspondents over the years and came to enjoy our conversations.

I often shared these documents with the appropriate people in the university so they had some sense of what I or the letter writer thought on a particular issue. Some university colleagues flattered me over the years by telling me they kept copies of some of my letters and used them as models for their own.

If a letter got to my desk about a problem, I was often tempted to try to solve it personally, and I did a lot of retail that I probably shouldn't have as president. For instance, I once received a letter from an alumnus who enclosed a check for $1,000. He explained that he was trying to settle with that check all his debts to the university; these amounted to $10,000. He wanted to have a transcript and get along with his life, but he said he didn't have the $10,000 and worried that we would send his account to a collection agency.

I was away on a fund-raising trip when that letter arrived, and my assistant drafted my reply. It said, "I have your letter, I sympathize with you, but the rules are the rules and you owe us $10,000 so I am sending back your check." My philosophy has always been, *Never send money back*. So I changed the draft to read, "I have your check for $1,000, but it is not in full settlement of your $10,000 debt; you must realize you cannot make this decision unilaterally." I knew that if we were to send the problem to a collection agency, it would charge us a fee to get the money. So I added: "If you send us another check—for $4,000—within five days, I will mark the file paid in full." Three days later, we got a check from him for $4,000. I now had 50 percent of the debt. Maybe he had all the money and could have paid in full. As it worked out, he went away with a bargain and we ended up richer than we would have been if the case had gone to a collection agency. It was a fair enough deal on all sides.

Obviously, I didn't want it made public that all one has to do is write to the president to get a debt reduced! But I thought this graduate had made a good-faith effort to honor his obligation. Chances are, if I had sent him the letter drafted by my assistant, he would have written, "I don't have the remaining $9,000!" Maybe he borrowed the other $4,000 to pay us; who knows? The main point is, we closed out the case—and it's done. He never sent me a thank-you note, but somehow I think he was grateful.

•　•　•

I DIDN'T get many congratulatory letters from strangers. But several years ago I got a letter from a Columbia University graduate from my era; he had fallen flat on his face on a city sidewalk near our campus and, bleeding and dazed, was helped by two GW undergraduates. The man wondered if I had somehow imparted to GW students the concern for others that he and I had "picked up at Columbia." I wrote back to him:

> *I hesitate to claim the sunlight when I know that tomorrow some GW youngster is going to do something that can be characterized as the rain, and having taken credit for the sun, I'm going to be obliged to own the rain. I have a feeling that these students were properly taught by their parents or their schoolteachers long before they got to GW and that we got lucky. But I don't want to go overboard with this humility thing, so maybe—just maybe—we deserve a little of the credit.*

PARENTS OFTEN wrote about problems that were quite legitimate, and I was glad to receive these letters. If the parent hadn't taken time to write about the problems they had experienced, I might not have known about them and couldn't have done anything to fix them for all the other students who might be similarly frustrated. Some parents have strange ideas about how we operate in a university and ask for inappropriate consideration; others are just earnestly trying to get the best for their children.

A father wrote to tell me that he was humiliated because his poor investment decisions had resulted in an unfortunate depletion of his daughter's college fund. He was writing to ask us for financial help. His list of troubles was long, and many of them were well beyond my ability to address. I did try to help where I could:

> *I'm writing to say that I have received your communication and that I'm going to turn it over for appropriate research and initial response. . . .*
>
> *We will, of course, try to explore every nook and cranny and*

try to be as forthcoming as we can. Obviously, we haven't brought Carrie along this far to lose her now. . . .

But let me not get ahead of myself except to say that the last thing in the world you want to do is be humiliated by reaching out on behalf of your daughter. What are parents for if not to try to assist their children in making their way in the world? You're okay in my book. I hope we can help.

I look forward to making your acquaintance, God willing, at Carrie's graduation from GW if not before.

A FATHER wrote complaining that although his daughter was guilty of not paying a fee to the university, he was annoyed because she had to go through a difficult bureaucratic process to resolve the matter. In this case, I decided to break my rule—*Never send money back*—and try to soften his harsh opinion of us:

Most of the people who write to me complaining about a prob-lem never acknowledge the slightest possibility of culpability, but you're different; you agree that Alexis owed the fee. Still, because some of our folks were either rude or inefficient, and because you'd never encountered any problem getting transcripts before, it seems to me our culpability may be greater than hers.

So, I'm going to ask that her $52 be refunded—cheerfully! . . .

By the way, when people do write to complain they almost never mention the fact that they did indeed benefit from their days at GW. I'm glad you did; I'm glad you participate in affinity pro-grams. I hope you'll forgive us this lapse.

Another father wrote to me complaining that his daughter's name had been left off a list of commended scholars in our graduation pro-gram. He speculated that the reason his complaints had not been heard was because he was not a university benefactor. I was concerned about this and wrote back:

I do want you to understand that we don't differentiate among

*parents or students who have legitimate beefs with us on the
basis of whether or not they are "benefactors." We try hard not
to make mistakes, but when we do slip up we try to correct them
in the individual case and to resolve any systemic problems.*

*I hope you didn't allow our failures to diminish too much your
enjoyment of the commencement ceremony itself or your delight
in Jen's accomplishments and bright future. Indeed, I hope your
experience was like our weather—overcast at first, brilliant at the
conclusion.*

I LIKE to add historic markers to the university campus that are unique
and tell something interesting about our location in Washington. I
think they are important in giving a university a sense of place. Sometimes I don't get much feedback, but one father wrote:

*We enjoyed discovering the American Meridian Plaque which is
just below our daughter's dorm window.*

I was delighted that he had noticed and replied:

*I love you. I love your observation. I'm the instigator of the Ameri-
can Meridian marker which is located near New Hall, and in
all the time it's been there, you're absolutely, positively the first
person to comment on it to me. Thank you. I can't ever go past it
without smiling.*

SOMETIMES THE letters are over-the-top shrill. A parent of a GW
alumnus objected when she found that a controversial art show in a
small venue on our Mount Vernon campus had been canceled. She
accused us of removing the show because "someone from the Saudi
Embassy found it objectionable!" Among other things, she said: "How
much Saudi money does it take for you at GW to trash sacred values"
(invoking the memory of George Washington); "Shame, Shame,
Shame!"; "At GW, Arab money trumps freedom of speech!"; "Perhaps you need some Danish friends to help you make braver, more

moral decisions." She further accused the university of threatening to fire the person who had made the arrangements to mount the exhibit, and she even mentioned Hitler to describe my management style. I didn't much like her letter but tried not to respond in kind:

Your story tells of a Manichean struggle between the forces of virtue on the one hand and the spawn of Satan on the other. Dear me! Suffice it to say that the agenda that prompted you to write is far more interesting than the anecdote you have reduced it to. You make representations that are news to me, and that I have no reason to believe are accurate.

As a matter of fact, I did see the show. I thought it was very interesting. I also thought the paintings were beyond controversial. I am [not] satisfied that nothing in the show could be characterized as an insult to Islam. Not being a Muslim myself, I am not sophisticated in the subtleties of the faith, but I do have eyes and I can tell you that if a comparable show about Jews were hung [elsewhere], I would be writing letters to somebody complaining about the characterization of . . . my religion. It is possible, as you can imagine, for great art to also be offensive. Different people will view different works as offensive. You are probably familiar with the controversy over the artist Goya and his painting of The Naked Maja. Within the context of its time and place, there were those who thought it was outrageous. Public art is always a source of debate. And, yes, I thought the crucifixes in jars of urine displayed as art in New York City a few years ago were equally offensive—surely as offensive as if the artist had displayed Stars of David or mezuzahs in urine.

One can ask where in the world did you get the stories about Saudi Arabian money having something to do with [the art] show? And how did Hitler get into the act? I don't mind a little criticism once in a while but yours is uninformed and overheated. . . . The notion that people were threatened with the losses of their jobs is fiction. . . .

It is clear you believe in free speech. But the defense of free speech doesn't require you to say ugly things about people—particularly when they are not true. So, if you are going to contact the press despite [the artist's] request that you not do so, try to get the facts right. Otherwise, you will end up embarrassing yourself and ultimately, through your implausibility, reflect badly upon the First Amendment and all the important and strongly held sentiments that apparently inspired you to write to me [at the outset]. . . .

As you can tell from what I have written above, I am annoyed with you—not for writing and caring, since I think the matter you wrote about is important. I am annoyed with you for going off half-cocked without getting all the facts straight, without making sure that all the information was accurate. It is supposed to be look-aim-fire. Not fire first. But we can discuss all these things further when we get together which I hope we will. Come see me, please.

AN ALUMNUS wrote to tell me he had been shocked to hear me mention during a radio interview that I enjoy a cigar from time to time. He added that he was dropping any plan he might have to leave a bequest to the university. I had to speak up:

Yours may be one of the most puzzling communications I have received in years. I refer to your letter of February 19th, which you began with a long recitation of your GW ties that go back to 1956. . . . You represent that you did well at GW and loved your four years at the university, went abroad as a Rotary Fellow, went to law school, and then returned to GW to get a Master's degree in International Economics. All of this, you say, has given you a good professional life which has made it possible for you to have not one, but two homes. . . .

In the next paragraph you say that notwithstanding all of the above, you're prepared to turn on a dime and repudiate The George Washington University. You advise that you are no longer considering making a bequest in your will to the university because you heard me say that I like to smoke a cigar from time to time.

I am frankly astonished at this report, and equally at a loss for words. I don't know whether I am more shocked or disappointed. Surely if I choose to smoke a cigar in the privacy of my own home from time to time, this is my private affair.

Why don't we start again? Why don't you reconsider? In return I'll promise to try to cut back on my cigar smoking, even in private. Maybe it will do me good. I'm down to only two or three a week as it is. Reducing a little more will make my wife very happy.

I do apologize for shocking you. You can imagine that was never my intention.

Unlike many of my detractors, the letter writer then wrote back to me. This time, he had a slightly remorseful tone and seemed to want to elevate our conversation. Here is part of his reply:

I'll bet we're going to be friends after all. Each of us was "shocked" by what the other had to say. So now that we can get over our shock and go on with life, I'd wager that we probably share more in common than seemed apparent from our initial exchange.

I compliment you on the beautiful and very accurate recitation— even though with a bit more braggadocio than I intended—of what I had written you. You took a few words of mine and made an essay. I've got things to learn still.

But I do want to hasten to correct on the feeling that comes across in your letter. I did not say that I was shocked that you personally smoked. I do care, in a health-sort-of-way, but it is none of my business what you do in private. I still believe strongly that you have an obligation to young people, in particular, not to praise the virtues (the word I used) of smoking, in 2003. That's what came across in your interview. It just didn't seem right to me that the influential president of a great university (. . . with a now-famous hospital) should be out promoting those virtues on the airwaves. I apologize for being a puritan on this issue but I do have my well-intentioned reasons.

• • •

AN ALUMNA wrote to complain that she had received an invitation to the GW Inaugural Ball, to take place during the inauguration of President Bush and Vice President Cheney. The Inaugural Ball is an event we hold on a regular basis at the university, regardless of which party wins the election. It is a campus celebration that the students love. The writer said she would no longer contribute to the university because she objected to the expenditure of university funds for such an activity. I wrote back:

> We have been holding inaugural balls at GW for some years—in fact, every four years—through a variety of presidents, Republican and Democratic. Ours is not a partisan initiative. It's a celebration of the President of the United States, who, regardless of his (or in the future, her) party affiliation, is the chief executive of our nation, our republic.
>
> So why did it surprise you that George Washington University, located as it is a few blocks from the White House, would see the inauguration of a new president as an [opportunity] to hold a party? . . . The ladies put on gowns and the guys put on tuxedos. They all look beautiful. They get together; they drink non-alcoholic beverages, dance until all hours, and have a wonderful time. If you think a subvention for an event like this is a frivolous use of university funds, then what do you think about cheerleaders or parties to celebrate the winning of an athletic contest? We host an annual party to celebrate George Washington's birthday. He was a President of the United States too . . . and we even named the university after him. . . .
>
> You don't want to help us any more, but perhaps you'll allow me to help you. I'll be glad to provide you with an absolutely free ticket to the inaugural ball. Come, be my guest, meet the students, see the event that seems to trouble you and make your judgment in an informed way. I'd be pleased to hear you're going to join us.

The writer took exception to some of the comments in my letter and protested that she was not against parties. She seemed to believe that any contribution she might make to GW would be used for some purpose she opposes. I replied:

If you don't like the way the university is spending some of its money, make your gift in a restricted manner that you approve of. How about books for the library? It's hard to oppose that. And since you're not against parties, it's silly for you to be against this party. To put it another way, 4,000 students have purchased tickets to come to the Inaugural Ball. If there are 4,000 Republicans in the student body at GW, I'll eat my hat. These people aren't voting for or endorsing a candidate. They are putting on a tuxedo or a ball gown and going out dancing. They are being 18- to 22-year-olds. They are having a good time. This is in no way contradictory to wonderful lectures in English literature or concerts in Lisner Auditorium or going to art exhibits. Life is not all black or white. . . . Surely you understand this and are just giving me a hard time because you're annoyed that your candidate didn't win the race for president . . .

You are absolutely right; the other universities weren't holding inaugural balls. It's a GW innovation and as I pointed out above, the students love it. And yes, people are dying, and we're at war, and yes, there is a huge deficit. And yes, you may be right that the Bush administration is going overboard in their celebration. . . . That's not an argument against [GW] having a party. I'm sorry you didn't accept my invitation to attend the inaugural ball at GW.

I LIKE to send treats to friends of the university and members of the university community. In one case, I sent a congratulatory gift to a professor and he wrote back that somewhere en route, my gift of knishes had turned into a nasty, spoiled surprise. My reply:

You can't ever take your eyes off the knish people. No sooner do I go on vacation that they send out bad knishes.

This sort of thing happens from time to time with packages of food; particularly in the summer. . . . I myself received a box of steaks for Christmas last year as a gift . . . they had been wandering around in post offices between here and Johannesburg for a month or two. When I opened the box I had the feeling that our colleague . . . who digs up famous dead people and does forensic autopsies and DNA testing to find out how they actually died and if they're who the headstone says they are . . . had sent me a clinical sample of his work. It was like visiting a morgue in August during an electrical shutdown.

I WROTE to a colleague who had written an op-ed piece in *The New York Times* in which he decried the decision to dig a trench at the new memorial in Belzec, a German death camp in Poland, where the remains of at least 500,000 Jews had been dumped into mass graves. The trench was being dug to allow people to go deep into the earth and walk among the dead. The project was meant to "intensify" the tourist experience.

My concern is that we not smack people no matter what they do. In other words, if they ignore the Holocaust, we smack them for neglect and being uncaring. If they recall the Holocaust, we smack them for doing it wrong or messing up somehow or being disrespectful. That leads to frustration. And frustration—as you know better than I—unresolved brings unhappy consequences. My reading of world history tells me that after you and I and the generations of those who remember the Holocaust—who can actually close their eyes and smell it and taste it and touch it—are gone, it will, for better or worse, become history of another outrageous example of man's inhumanity to man, of our species' capacity for brutality, a unique one; perhaps larger, more articulated, but in the end one in a chain of such incidents that makes us skeptical about Planet Earth and its inhabitants. But I am getting moody and melancholy as I go down this path, so I'll cut it off here to say that I appreciate the work that you do and your dedication to the victims.

I remember some years ago being engaged in a disputation in Hartford, Connecticut . . . [a man] was raising funds for a Holocaust Memorial Statue to be built in West Hartford. I thought that rather than another stabile, the money would be better invested in scholarships to help educate the young about what had transpired in order to give meaning to the words, "Never Again." [The man] was a millionaire. I was just another academic. He prevailed. There's a [very] nice memorial in West Hartford in front of the Jewish Community Center. But every time I drive past, I think of Shelley's poem "Ozymandias."

THE FOLLOWING is a conversation I had by letter with John Silber, President Emeritus of Boston University. I meant to send him a copy of one of my speeches. Somehow, he received several copies and wrote this to me:

I've written you favorably with regard to your speech. Were my comments unresponsive or unacceptable? The reason I ask is that I have now received by separate mail three copies of this speech. Supposing it is your wish, I have read the speech now three times, and if you send me another copy, I suppose I will read it a fourth time. I would be pleased, nevertheless, to know why you have sent me this bountiful supply of copies, or if perhaps I have failed to be adequately appreciative. I thought I made it clear that it is a very fine speech, so good in fact that I wonder who wrote it for you, although I know from the style and content it is vintage Trachtenberg. But, please advise.

This tone was characteristic, and I responded in kind:

I thought you'd perhaps keep one for yourself and give the others to your two friends. Actually, I did appreciate your kind words about the text. I was sort of pleased with it myself and will probably use it again or look for a place to publish it one of these days.

All's good on this end. I'm taking your advice about a variety of important life decisions, so I hope you know what you're talking about.

He continued the repartee in his usual fashion:

Looking at that picture of you with [a college president], I offer this advice: don't wear shades for important photographs. You appear to be either blind or a Mafia capo.

Norman Lear lent his copy of the Declaration of Independence to GW University for students to view. A man then wrote to me to remind me that he himself was the owner of George Washington's personal copy of the document. I immediately replied:

I did know that you had the Declaration of Independence . . . Surely, I've raised the question with you about having it prominently on display in an appropriately designated place on The George Washington University campus. I know you've made some representations about giving that along with other parts of your collection to the University of Virginia, and I would never say anything mean-spirited about the University of Virginia. . . . But you can't give them everything. And what's one little Declaration of Independence between friends? You could carve it out from the rest of the collection, and I'll bet they would never even notice.

Mr. Lear was kind enough to give us some other artifacts.

As the time came closer to my departure from office, the fund-raising and speaking engagements increased. I was gratified and touched by the outpouring of wishes for my future and the thanks for what I had been able to accomplish at GW. I wrote to two of our generous donors about the physical effects of our efforts:

I have your good letter of October 26th, which was waiting for me upon my return from a goodwill visit to Boston, New York and

Philadelphia, during which I shook 2,000 hands. Even as I am
dictating this note I have my hand in a bucket of ice water, other-
wise I would reach out and shake yours. I am gratified by your
kind comments.

WHENEVER I conferred an honorary degree on a person, I was certain
to receive numerous letters about our choice of recipient. More often
than not, the letters were critical. When this happened, I always responded to the complainant. In one case, I wrote this to someone who
complained about our choice of Kofi Annan:

Yes, of course, Kofi Annan is imperfect—maybe even imperfect-
plus. And, yes, there's a contradiction in my saying that and hav-
ing acceded in awarding him an honorary doctorate from The
George Washington University. So, you are right and I plead
guilty but I plead guilty with an explanation.

They are all imperfect. I have been giving honorary degrees
to people as president of a university for three decades and they
all had something wrong with them. And no matter who I gave
honorary degrees to, I can count on one thing: getting critical
letters from people who think we should have given the degree to
somebody else or not given the degree at all. I don't know where
all the mail is that came in after we gave an honorary doctorate
to Hillary Clinton—I think it took up an entire landfill in West
Virginia. And, more recently, George Bush (#41).

There are a variety of risky initiatives in life—getting married
is one of them, having children another. They make us humble
with their gravity and inadequate data with which we decide. Lo-
cating public art is tough too, and honorary degrees. What can
I tell you? Even people with clean hands and pure hearts can do
something embarrassing. We once gave a degree to the President
of Korea who was later convicted of taking bribes and sent to the
slammer. What to do? Only Mother Teresa is special and perfect
and safe. But also dead, and thus, not a lively speaker. And even
when she was alive, there was only one Mother Teresa.

As President of the university, I am obviously a player in deciding who to give honorary degrees to. I am also responsive to other stakeholders. In the case of Kofi Annan, faculty at the Elliott School of International Affairs and the Dean were the initiating advocates. I agreed, so I am in the loop. For what it's worth, the student body came out in vast numbers and was glad to hear him.

Once, about a year after we gave an honorary degree to President Hosni Mubarak of Egypt, I came out of a meeting in Cairo (with President Mubarak) and was reminded of the honorary degree by a reporter who asked me why we gave it. I said we didn't give it to Mubarak although he was the recipient; we gave it to the Egyptian people. We honored Egypt in history for all it had meant to culture and the arts. We honored the men and women of this consequential nation. Presidents of countries are, of course, themselves but they are also more than themselves. People constantly remind me when I say something foolish, or occasionally wise, of my responsibility as the spokesperson for George Washington University.

So in honoring Kofi Annan, are we honoring the United Nations? Well, yes and no. The United Nations is currently deeply flawed. If I could [improve] the UN, would I do so? You bet. But—and here's the but—I am not prepared yet to walk away from the idea of the United Nations. I remember when it was founded. I remember the vision we had at the time for what it would be, for the good it could do, for how it would engage our better angels. It hasn't all worked out. Do we abandon it exasperated? Where would that get us? And so, we continue to strive to make the UN and Egypt and our own beloved country better, more committed to our vision, to our original mission, to our mandate, to the aspirations of our people. And we continue to give it a hug from time to time with an honorary degree that allows the Secretary General to share his thinking with university students in the marketplace of ideas, and permits his thinking to inform the students and their thinking to inform him.

Yes, there's compromise and relativism and self-justification in all that I have said above, but if we didn't give Kofi Annan an honorary degree, how would you have known? Would it have made anybody think? Would they have noticed? Would they have asked why GW hasn't given Kofi Annan an honorary degree? Would it have made the world better, the UN better, you happier, me less skeptical? Think about it.

I OFTEN get letters from students. In my replies to them, I try hard to teach them something. I once received a long letter signed by a list of students who had, as part of a class, interviewed a cross section of university employees. Their interpretation of the resulting data resulted in a degree of moral indignation about the plight of workers who toil at the lower end of the pay scale. They wrote to me to complain as a group about what they saw as injustice. In their letter to me they said:

Upon compiling the data from these interviews, we were struck by how different the responses of J-Street [food service] workers were from the responses of [university] administrators. For instance, while one administrator we interviewed said she liked to ride horses on her farm in her free time, a J-Street worker said, "Free time? I do laundry and take care of the kids." In response to the question about day-to-day interactions, a J-Street worker said, "Most of us aren't happy to be at work at all. It puts us in a bad mood." In sharp contrast, an administrator replied, "We have a constant collegial relationship.". . .

We implore you to use the privileges that have been granted to you as a result of your hard work and your social location to make GW a campus where J-Street workers, janitors, administrators, faculty, and students alike feel this is an excellent environment for working and learning.

Our class put up over 1000 posters around the campus of GW to bring attention to the inequalities that exist here between J-Street workers and GW administrators. We write this letter specifically to bring your attention to these inequalities. As a class we feel that something must be done. We do not charge you with intentionally and individually creating these inequalities. Rather, we challenge you, as one of the most well-respected and influential individuals on campus, to prioritize these inequalities and encourage others to participate in the struggle for equality. We ask you directly, what will you do to address the discrepancy between J-Street workers and administrators?

I wrote this reply to them, hoping to help them expand their thinking:

Thank you for your thoughtful letter about the kitchen workers.

I was glad to see that GW students are concerned with social issues and pleased as well by the evocation, if not quotation, of Karl Marx's famous statement: "From each according to his abilities, to each according to his needs," an idea, by the way, that he appears to have borrowed from the French writer Louis Blanc. All points of view should flourish on our campus, and evidently they do. . . .

[Y]ou have hit upon a problem of what we call "distributive justice," the most troubling issue in any civilized society. In other words, how do we make things fair and equitable for all? Sometimes, it's not hard. For example, when my sons were young and wanted to divide a piece of cake in the refrigerator, their parents gave them a method: the first son would cut the cake and the second son would choose the piece he wanted first. This guaranteed a fair cut and served justice.

But obtaining distributive justice in the real world is not a piece of cake. It would be fine if people who had agreeable jobs, like the horse-riding administrator you mention, earned less and people who had less agreeable jobs, like kitchen workers, earned more: psychic benefits could replace cash. But that is not the way the world works. And GW, though a not-for-profit university and not a for-profit capitalist enterprise, is not free of normal economic imperatives. That being said, the University does try to deploy its

*resources as equitably as it can and undertake policies that argu-
ably could be liberating for all its employees.*

*However, before I begin a further explanation of this state-
ment, it is important to distinguish between two groups of people
who work at the Marvin Center. Let me explain. "J-Street workers," individuals who prepare and dispense food at J-Street, are not
GW employees; they work for [an outside contractor] who oversees
all matters of compensation and working conditions. Individuals
who operate and maintain the Marvin Center are GW employees
and this later group receives a benefit package that is indistin-
guishable from any other staff at the university—administrator,
office worker or facilities personnel.*

*First, GW is competitive with almost any employer in the
District. Second, we give tuition remission to our own GW
employees and their children. This benefit makes it possible for
current workers to improve their education and, consequently,
their employment prospects, and it is certainly even more likely
that their children will have better educations and thus better
jobs available to them. This idea was nicely encapsulated by the
worker you quote as saying she would break her back to make sure
her kid goes to college. Good for her. Immigrants and people at
the lower end of the labor market have been doing that in America
for years. Third, we are, after all, in a competitive marketplace,
where factors such as education, work experience and competition
for like positions affects pay scale. We compete against other universities in the metropolitan area as well as with schools around
the country. In any enterprise, higher salaries frequently reflect
the capital investment the individuals made in themselves to get
where they are. Fourth, people with less education and fewer skills
are less competitive in the labor market and are obliged to take
lower paying jobs—and jobs, as your survey shows, that sometimes they may not like.*

*These are the social and economic facts and apply just about
everywhere in the world, though perhaps Cuba and North Korea
are exceptions. The inequity you have researched and described*

is a universal challenge, not unique at GW, and I believe you understand that. Distributive justice remains an ideal, not a practice.

Still, you ask me, with extremely good nature, to address this issue. I must confess to you that I am not sure how I can do more than I have already stated. There is not much more that GW can do about pay; as I said, we are already virtually making the market for this particular work. For the most part, neither the J-Street workers, the GW Marvin Center staff, nor the school's administrators come to work because they are feeling benevolent toward GW, though some may. They come to earn a living, which is in "their own interest." There may be some more things that one can do to make actually working on campus even more rewarding, and I'd be grateful for any suggestions and I remain open to all possibilities. I would like to see the results of your survey, which might offer me some clues.

Perhaps it might be helpful if I recommend some books dealing with distributive justice, beginning with Marx's Das Kapital. *I commend as well Alan Wolfe's* Moral Freedom *and Michael Walzer's* Spheres of Justice. *I also think everybody should read Adam Smith's* Wealth of Nations, *published in the interesting year of 1776. Toward the beginning he writes, "It is not from the benevolence of the butcher, the brewer, or the baker that we expect our dinner, but from regard to their own interest."*

IN ALL my years as a dean and as a university president, I have tried to teach and treat the next generations in a way comparable to the way I was treated by my many excellent teachers who saw something in me, spent time with me, and took the time to teach me valuable lessons. But when I try to teach a student a lesson with the same benign intent as my teachers from the past, sometimes the lesson backfires on me. One such situation occurred when I received a letter from a student who wanted to go to dental school after graduating from GW. She didn't take biology as an undergraduate and then discovered that she couldn't get into dental school without it. In her letter to me, she tried to make the case that it was because of her adviser's neglect that she could not get into dental school. I suppose I could have just written to her and said, "Dear Ms. Smith: No!" But, I saw the situation as a teaching moment. So I wrote back to her saying:

> *In the tradition of bat and bar mitzvah, the Jewish notion is that at age 13 people become adults. What that means is that from the age of 13 on, you have some duty to take some responsibility for yourself. I assume that you are 21 or 22 now—older than 13. You must have known that if you intend to go to dental school, you need to take Biology. As a pre-dental student, you had some duty to look at the catalogue of the dental school you would apply to in order to find out what undergraduate courses you have to take. You can't unload this responsibility on the advisor. The advisor doesn't tell you to brush your teeth in the morning. There are some things you are supposed to know or find out on your own.*

Not wanting to write a completely cheerless letter, I told her that if she took Biology 101A and did well, I would pay for her semester in Biology 101B. I got a letter back from her immediately. I didn't expect her to thank me for the lesson. But, I did think she might thank me for the offer of a free semester in Biology. However, she now wanted me to pay for Chemistry 101, Chemistry 102, Organic Chemistry, etc., etc.! I wrote this message back to her and said, in effect, "There are limits to my tolerance and apparently no limits to your chutzpah!" Sometimes my style works, sometimes it doesn't. The aspiring dental student apparently figured it hadn't hurt to ask the first time and wouldn't hurt to ask for more after I reinforced an unfortunate tendency of hers with my offer. I have since heard from her. She told me she was admitted to a dental school.

An MBA student wrote to me, castigated me for using humor in a speech, and lectured me about my duties as a university president. Here is an excerpt from his letter to me:

I was embarrassed for you and GW when I read your comments in The Washington Post. *I would have rather read that you had energized those people . . . with lively discussions of the benefits of higher education. And I would have been impressed if you had listened to complaints about higher education and contemplated solutions. Unfortunately you took the easy route and the one from which only your ego will benefit.*

I hope you will reconsider your approach to introducing yourself to others, and more importantly your responsibilities as a university president.

Alas, he had not read my entire talk and had a misperception of the tone and intent of my remarks. I wrote to him to try to get him to expand his perception of the uses of humor:

I have your altogether too serious letter of March 28. You need to mellow out a little bit. The quotation attributed to me in The Washington Post *. . . was part of remarks that I gave to the Washington, D.C., Board of Trade at their most recent annual meeting. University presidents are supposed to give such talks — [but] they are not obliged to make them deadly dull. On the contrary, if they can introduce some humor while making their point, they tend to get remembered better and are generally more persuasive.*

Fortunately, in context at the Board of Trade meeting, the story . . . was that universities are too often underestimated by the business community because they are perceived as not-for-profit. In fact, the not-for-profit world is a major component of the American economy and increasingly needs to administer itself in cost-effective ways that will minimize the expenses of running them and permit them to be more efficient and effective in the application of resources. That's how tuitions get held down. That's how waste is eliminated and money is found to provide scholarships and faculty and staff raises and to paint laboratories and classrooms and to buy computers and art materials and books.

Anybody who is a candidate for a master's degree in business administration has surrendered a certain amount of his standing [if he is] embarrassed by the remarks I made. Exactly what are you preparing yourself to be when you finish up with your MBA—a monk? . . .

Even if you interpret my words in the worst possible way, I am confident you remember the phrase attributed to Aristotle in Nicomachean Ethics, "One swallow does not make a spring." If you want to pass judgment on me, that is your privilege. If you want me to take your judgment seriously, you need to do more research.

A HIGH school student was incensed that we decided, after admitting him, to withdraw our offer when his senior-year grades tanked. His letter was imprudent and a bit callow. I tried to give him a little practical advice while also offering him an opportunity to reinstate himself as a candidate for admission in another year:

My colleagues and I have been thinking about you a lot. We are trying to figure out what is in your best interest in the coming year. Unhappily, what we concluded is probably not what you yourself would recommend.

We are going to protect a place in the sophomore class for you starting in the fall of 2007. In other words, we are NOT inviting you to join us as a freshman this September. I know you are going to see this as bad news and maybe it is, but it has a happy side. You are on our radar. We know who you are. We want to see you as a student at GW, but we are not sure you are ready to take on that particular challenge. You disappointed yourself and us with your recent grades after we put you on notice that this was going to be a "make or break" semester. We know you have a lot of balls in the air. . . . You are not alone in this circumstance. You have your story, but many of our students have their stories. . . .

Chris, don't use the word "shit" in letters to universities. You don't know who is reading the mail. Some people would think you

were bold and courageous. Some would think you were a dope.
A cost benefit analysis tells me that you want to make the smart
move. Hang in. We have faith in you. We have confidence in you.
We need a little more proof than you have given us that when you
get here, you are going to be ready for success.

ONE UNDERGRADUATE started writing to me as soon as she reached campus about her concerns regarding the university's shortcomings in the area of workers' rights. Over the four years she was here, she wrote numerous letters to me and lobbied for various causes she wanted me to support. Here are some excerpts from our ongoing conversation:

Student: . . . *the work that I am most involved in has to do with the struggle for worker's rights. We met last year to discuss the issue of GW affiliating with the Worker Rights Consortium (WRC). Since that time, GW has still not affiliated with the WRC, and no dialogue has continued on that issue. Yet, as I write this, workers all over the world are sewing GW apparel under conditions that are not only inadequate, but are unlawful. I am not claiming that all of the factories producing for GW are "sweatshops." This is impossible to know. However, there is no real mechanism in place at the moment for GW to know the conditions under which its logo apparel is made.*

SJT: *You're right; the real issues are those having to do with the lives of people working in dreadful conditions. But there is absolutely no evidence that "workers all over the world are sewing GW apparel under conditions that are not only inadequate but are unlawful." That's an unsupported assumption you make based on our reluctance to join the WRC. As I have explained to you, we do have mechanisms in place to ensure that we do not offer merchandise produced in sweatshops, and as you know we debarred a company for that reason just a couple of months ago.*

What we disagree about is whether the only way GW can truly live up to our word and our principles is by joining this particular organization. I met with you last year, and I thought we had an interesting conversation. But there's nothing in your letter that advances your argument that WRC affiliation is a sine qua non without which our good works and good faith are meaningless. We are on the same side; we share the same values; we don't agree that GW should follow your instructions on how it should advance workers' rights. For now, I think you're going to have to settle for two out of three.

She sent me another letter accusing GW of doing something wrong by not affiliating with her organization. I wrote this letter in reply:

The burden of proof is yours—not the University's. Our job is not to prove ourselves innocent. Yours is to prove us guilty of something. As far as I can tell, you are terrific at suspicion, skepticism, and unproven allegations. But you're not as strong on demonstration. You claim that GW is guilty of some malfeasance, but you offer no evidence, largely I think because we are not guilty. . . .

This is America. The Constitution provides us with freedom of association, which means we get to choose whom we want to associate ourselves with, and we don't have to associate ourselves with those we don't want to associate ourselves with. I don't want to associate with groups that you select for me. I don't tell you what clubs you should belong to, and I think it is elitist and even a little totalitarian for you to be so robust in trying to force me into doing something I don't want to do. . . .

I am confident your heart's in the right place. I think we share similar goals. You must think you're doing the right thing in coming back to me again and again on this subject. I myself am feeling that it's somewhat coercive, and I would urge you to devote your energies to something else. As for Isaac Bashevis Singer, he once said to me, while eating dinner (I recall a boiled potato with sour cream) at my home in Hartford, that sometimes thinking is more important than acting. Action without thought is often worse than no action at all.

The student continued on several occasions to get me to affiliate the university with WRC, and I continued to answer her letters:

As far as I can tell there is no reason for a new look [at WRC] since the last look, but as for you, I'll be glad to meet with you— you alone—if you'll come by the office and talk to me person-to-person. What I'd like to do, frankly, is to follow up with you on the last note I wrote to you in which I said we could continue, if you insist, on banging heads over the WRC, or we could try to find an agenda that we agree upon and try to do whatever good we can. Now, that would be starting the new school year, as you put it, "a bit differently." Surely the Worker Rights Consortium is not the only thing you've got on your mind. There must be something on which we can make common cause to the benefit of all.

Our ongoing correspondence ended only when this student graduated. In order to publicly salute her commitment and sincerity, I invented an award just for her and formally presented it to her at Commencement. The citation mentioned that she had "most significantly challenged the social and intellectual conscience of the university." We also gave her a small cash prize. I never found out what she did with the money.

IN A somewhat less positive written exchange with a student, I wrote to a contributing editor of *The Hatchet* because he had written in an editorial that GW's next president should be "a better-connected president" and encouraged students to let administrators know what they would want to see. Here is a portion of his editorial:

[Trachtenberg] has also made himself somewhat of a stranger to the average student here. Most of my rare glimpses of our president roving the streets of campus revealed him socializing with University administrators or well-connected members of the student body, not that kid from your Political Science class with the pack of Skittles and the trendy Urban Outfitters shirt.

The person I would like to see as our next president is someone who is highly connected to the student body. Someone who takes the time to pop into random classes during the day and sit with students he or she doesn't know while getting lunch every week in J Street. One of the most memorable moments of my freshman year was Late Night with the President, where Trachtenberg took time out of his busy schedule to spend an evening with us, the lowly peasants at this school.

He also took the opportunity to refer to my offices as "lavish." I wrote the following to him with some measure of sadness and hurt feelings, but also with a resolve to try to help him become a more rigorous and truthful reporter:

I am curious at your strange text, which seems to have been crafted from whole cloth. Let me put it another way. What the heck are you talking about? I can't tell from what you have written whether you ever visited my offices or have merely dreamed about them. Do you truly think my space is luxurious, grand and opulent? Compared to what? I can only despair at the circumstances of the other people whose offices you may have visited. What exactly is it about my office that you find extravagant? Electric lighting? Indoor plumbing?

As for [your claim about] my being a stranger to the average student at GW. . . . I wonder at the way you have appointed yourself Mr. Typical Student and base your arguments exclusively on your own "rare glances" of me on campus. When did being seen by you become the litmus test? Your proposal that a university president should "pop into random classes during the day and sit with students" would, of course, offend almost all the faculty and be disruptive to the classes. . . .

I will leave it for others to say, but I would be astounded if you found that other university presidents were spending any more time with undergraduates than I have conventionally done for the last thirty years at two universities. There is a record. You can look it up.

After he replied defensively, I tried to explain some of his responsibilities as an opinion writer:

> You don't have to be scientific, but that doesn't oblige you to be wrong—to be uninformed. You could actually get it right! People read opinion pieces because they are interested in the thinking of the writer, but they like it when the thinking is based on fact. You may be right that my office hours aren't common knowledge. That of course, I blame on you. If I had a column in The Hatchet, I would put in it that Trachtenberg has office hours, and then more people would know, but you keep it to yourself and you don't let the knowledge inform your opinions. When you say it does not seem to be common knowledge around here—do you mean at 616 23rd St. or do you mean at The Hatchet? In any case, since The Hatchet regularly publishes notices about my office hours, don't you think that as a member of The Hatchet family, I can hold you accountable for knowing things that are printed in the paper? . . .
>
> I meet with the Student Association leadership regularly. I recently took the president of the Student Association with me on a business trip to Hong Kong. We were together on the plane each way for seventeen hours and in each other's company over meals and meetings from morning until night.
>
> As for meeting with student groups on campus, you [should be] aware that I have accepted every invitation proffered by a student group that has been physically possible for me to respond to affirmatively in eighteen years—in good days and bad—in crisis and calm—town halls, open meetings, resident hall sleepovers. You really need to check the facts.
>
> On the popping into classes [suggestion]—trust me, University professors do not want the president or the dean popping into their classes. They would see it as a violation of their space and their sovereignty. They would see it as a violation of academic freedom. They would think it would have a chilling effect on their professorial endeavors. Again, check it out. Go talk to a half dozen professors. . . .

Even as I am writing this letter, I should be someplace else honoring other commitments. I [write] it because I think it is constructive and is part of my responsibility to you and to the University. . . .

I am trying to demonstrate that I respect you. I don't listen to people who I don't respect. You need to respect yourself [and] form your opinions on the basis of fact. You need to make them bulletproof so that when I say I don't have a luxurious office, you are not vulnerable. Before people take you seriously, you need to take yourself seriously.

16.

THE IDEAL UNIVERSITY?

I am not sure there is such a thing as an ideal university. St. John's College in Annapolis, Maryland, is a small, intimate, teaching-oriented, classics-focused institution that is sometimes mentioned as one ideal. I remember when in 1954 a St. John's representative came to speak to a parent/student meeting at my high school in Brooklyn. As interested as the parents were in what the man had to say about the college, it was clear that they were needlessly concerned that if their kids chose St. John's, they wouldn't be able to get into medical school. To them, it was, perhaps, too unconventional a place that was following a curriculum they perceived as too far from the norm to be recognized by professional schools as providing a legitimate education. But for many other people, St. John's was and still is the very best form of undergraduate education, a chance to immerse oneself in the most important ideas of our civilization.

There are aspects of a culture that are handed on and create nationhood and help to define an educated person. In spite of this, very few undergraduate curricula of our colleges have specified a common core curriculum. As a result, it is daunting to find consistency in the requirements for a BA degree. In fact, it is difficult to say what the universal elements are when graduates from different institutions earn the same degree. There are similarities, but not enough to call it consistency. Maybe we wouldn't want a national curriculum, but there must be more things we can agree on that ought to be part of the national discourse about higher education.

Harvard has emerged from a four-year process designed to rethink the curriculum guidelines. Included in the recommendations are the following categories: Societies of the World; Anthropology and International Relations; Ethical Reasoning, a Practical Approach to Philosophy; and the United States in the World, a course that is likely to include offerings from several departments like Sociology and Economics. Commenting on the new curriculum, interim president Derek Bok said, "Students will be more motivated to learn if they see a connection with the kinds of problems, issues and questions they will encounter in later life" (Jeremy Caplan, "As Harvard Goes . . . ," *Time*, February 22, 2007).

At the professional level, of course, there *is* agreement on a consistent—or national—curriculum. In fact, law schools have sometimes been criticized for being too much alike and not flexible enough. This is because the American Bar Association has had a major influence on what is offered at all accredited institutions. Law schools are starting to become somewhat more elastic, but there is still a single model for what a person must study in order to pass the bar examination and become a practicing lawyer. If you haven't taken courses like Torts and Contracts you are a layman, not a lawyer.

Likewise, there is a body of agreed-on information one must have to become a physician. You have to pass exacting exams to prove you have mastered those things in order to get the MD. But for the BA degree, we do not require a national exam. This raises questions about accountability and leaves open the question of whether we have sufficiently impacted people during the time they have spent in our company. Shouldn't we know the effect of our efforts? Have we added value? If some graduates majored in drinking beer, took random minimal courses, and received Cs in them, haven't we taken their tuition money year after year under false pretenses?

There is a lot of confusion about the role of a liberal arts education. People aren't always sure how much of it exists to enlighten and liberate the mind of the individual and how much of it is preprofessional training—a station on the way to law school or dental school or medical school. To my mind, too much of the notion of an "ideal" university is driven by the focus of many people on the economic investment they are making. Parents want their sons and daughters to choose the school with what they have been conditioned to think of as the best brand, with the idea that this will pay off in higher income and status in later life. This notion has been reinforced by *U.S. News & World Report* in its annual college and university rankings. But these scores tend to be based on criteria that have very little effect on the quality of the experience a student has in college. Alas, in spite of their inappropriateness, these rankings have a powerful effect on choices and on a university's view of what must be offered in order to attract good students.

If you ask someone, "What is the ideal suit?" The thoughtful answer is likely to be "You haven't given me enough information." At a minimum, determining the ideal suit requires knowing the conditions under which the suit is to be worn and the preferences of the wearer. And so you might decide on a flannel or a tweed suit for the fall and winter, and seersucker or linen for the summer, with another criterion being which suit fits the wearer best. Likewise, in choosing an ideal university, a student should take into consideration primarily his or her own inclinations and needs.

There are almost four thousand colleges and universities in this country, a number that includes a broad spectrum of community colleges. We have a large, pluralistic society made up of people with widely differing goals. And they are fortunate to have many different models from which to choose. *Not every college needs to offer everything.* Harvard is the wealthiest academic institution in the United States, and it does not offer all academic disciplines. Further, what it offers may not always be the very best that is available in that discipline. Many institutions have programs that are better than Harvard's in a variety of ways. Even if an institution has a $35 *billion* endowment to implement its program, there is always going to be somebody doing something better!

Are research universities the ideal universities? We have confused two different university functions. One is the teaching of our young people, and the other is the nurturing and advancement of scholarship. It seems that having research and teaching in a single institution with a single faculty has created tension. In the last half century the place of teaching has been downgraded while promotion and tenure are awarded largely for the books published and articles written. I have often wondered if we might be better advised to house more research in research-only institutes doing pure scholarship and teaching institutions doing instruction more robustly. On the subject of teaching versus research, Christopher Shea wrote in *The Boston Globe* (January 7, 2007):

Lindsay Waters, executive editor for the humanities at Harvard University Press, dubbed this growing pressure to publish "the tyranny of the monograph." The demands to produce books are increasing even as academic publishers say they don't want to publish them. Libraries lack the money to buy them or just don't think they're important enough. . . . [Waters] sees "colossal bad faith" on the part of older professors who vote to deny tenure to 35-year-olds who've produced far more than they themselves ever had to. And more than fairness is at stake. "If you find a university where the faculty is foolishly chasing after numbers"—of pages and books—"the faculty members are not going to be happy, and you're not going to get a good education."

The following comes from a news report by Lois E. Beckett of *The Harvard Crimson* (January 24, 2007), in which she comments on a report by the Harvard Task Force on Teaching and Career Development that offered a number of proposals to encourage teaching at Harvard:

The report paints a sobering picture of Harvard's current teaching culture, in which effective classroom guidance is considered a matter of "individual talent, choice, or valor," not something the Faculty of Arts and Sciences (FAS) sufficiently acknowledges or

rewards. . . . Proven skill in teaching is ignored or even stigma-
tized during FAS performance reviews, according to the report.
"Every teaching award earns a warning of how I should not wan-
der off research," the report quotes an anonymous PhD candidate
as saying.

   There are still pockets of the University where winning the Lev-
enson award for teaching as a junior faculty member is considered
"the kiss of death with respect to promotion," the report quotes an
anonymous senior professor as saying. The result, according to the
report, is that "Harvard's academic offerings can alienate students
instead of engaging them."

Many of the products of research are wonderful and absolutely
necessary to our society. And I certainly don't want to seem antischol-
arship or anti-intellectual when I say this, but it doesn't make much
sense if we say to students, "The research scholar is the academic
ideal, but you're not going to get any contact with that person while
you are an undergraduate," and then you say to faculty, "We aren't
going to reward you for outstanding teaching—indeed, if you win an
award for outstanding teaching, it may hurt you in your effort to get
tenure because there are those who might think you are not serious
enough about scholarship."

   One of the nice things about my university is that the faculty members still care about teaching. But not as passionately as they used to.
Following the national trend, we are more and more becoming—or
trying to become—a research university. This trend can be seen in
medical schools, where everyone is looking for the "cure for cancer."
They are increasingly scientists, not practitioners of healing arts. Such
a perspective competes with a focused effort to train skilled medical
caregivers who look after sick and injured people. I had a conversation
with an historian who is writing a book about the GW Medical Center
and is critical of our program because he believes its contribution to
medical scholarship is modest by comparison to those of some of the
other research-focused programs. He gives little credit to the important
fact that our medical center is crafting caring, able doctors! Medical

students come to GW and spend four amazing years, say they love the experience, and then go out and treat actual people. Surely this accomplishment is meritorious and should be celebrated. But the writer continues to insist that we do not do enough research. When institutions also share this view, they confound themselves. Can they do both things equally well?

Have we inadvertently created inefficiency by trying to host in one institution the two seemingly conflicting ambitions of teaching *and* research? We are told that many faculty members do not want to do research but feel compelled to do so in order to keep up with their peers. Left to their own devices, they say, they would be happy to do more work with students and be relieved of the pressure to publish. Places like the Howard Hughes Research Facility, recently built in Virginia, will generate more research productivity than is seen at most universities. Why not create more such centers where staff members can commit themselves to their laboratories, largely undistracted by teaching? There are also existing degree-granting institutions, such as Rockefeller University and the California Institute of Technology, which are very special places where the research is quite remarkable. Also the students.

If the tuition dollars of undergraduates are going to underwrite faculty members whose primary devotion is to research and not to teaching, I wonder if it is fair to the undergraduate parent who pays for a child to be provided with the best education an undergraduate can have. I especially admire small undergraduate colleges like Williams and Amherst; they have extraordinary teaching faculty. They also do research, but their research is done with a clear understanding that it complements and involves the undergraduate experience.

There was a time when Nicholas Murray Butler, the famous Columbia University president who served from 1901 to 1945—considered doing away with the undergraduate program at Columbia. He wanted Columbia to become an exclusively postgraduate institution, with master's and doctoral and professional students only. He was deterred by an outcry from the alumni body. As someone who went to Columbia and loved the undergraduate experience there, I always thought that Butler's idea was terrible. But looking back, in theory at least, it is not the worst proposal I have ever heard, in spite of the fact that I would strongly oppose it for my own alma mater.

In the end, the best college experience is one that the student personally selects to address his or her own strengths. Some students thrive in large research-oriented schools and get a remarkable undergraduate education; others are intimidated or otherwise distracted and have difficulty finding a qualitative undergraduate experience there. I was never offended when I got letters from students saying that, while they have been admitted to GW, they have elected to go to a different school. I could understand why they might have made that choice. At the same time, I knew there was always a large number of people writing to other schools and saying that they had selected GW!

I think many people are uncertain about how to advise their children on the matter of college attendance. In addition, many parents are ambitious for their children and counsel them to go to more competitive institutions than are appropriate for them. For instance, I used to get letters from people wringing their hands because their son or daughter didn't get into GW Law School. I told them that there are many good law schools in our country and explained that at GW, the class would be composed of students who were Phi Beta Kappa performers in college and made 165 on the LSAT. Parents can go through all the usual criticisms of the LSAT and say that their son or daughter, while brilliant, is not good at standardized tests and so on, but in the end, the LSAT is an incredibly accurate indicator of how the test taker will do in law school. It doesn't predict whether students will be good lawyers, good people, excellent parents, loyal friends, or productive public servants; all it does is anticipate their law school performance. Many people go to modest law schools and later make a great contribution to the practice of law! But trying to persuade a parent whose son or daughter has received a 155 on the LSAT that GW is not a good choice for that person is daunting, particularly if the parents themselves are graduates of GW and remember the Law School as the school it was rather than what it has become. In the end, law schools need to depend on these rational ways to sort out whom to admit.

There are many "best" schools—both undergraduate and graduate—all with their own strengths and distinguishing qualities; I would
like to see recognition of that fact become a larger part of the national
understanding. I think it might provide peace of mind to many.

THERE ARE people who go to community colleges for two years and
then transfer to four-year institutions and do as well as or better than
others who did their freshman and sophomore years on four-year campuses. This might indicate that the experience they had in the two-year
colleges prepared them as well as or even better than those who went to
the four-year undergraduate institution from the outset. The community college has the capacity to teach beginning courses competitively
with almost any other institution. It is an interesting notion that has
serious implications and promise for the future.

It seems to me that two-year institutions offer two useful pathways.
One is that people come in, develop skills sufficient to their purposes,
and go out, get jobs, and get on with their lives. Then there are students
who get the two-year degree and, in the process, see that they will be
better served with a four-year degree. They transfer to a four-year institution with advanced standing after two years and continue on a path to
a BA. This method is cheaper than doing all four years at a university,
because community colleges generally have a subvention from taxpayers, and, moreover, since they are devoted to teaching, they are less
expensive to administer than four-year institutions. Those who teach
there teach four and five courses per semester in comparison to faculty
in research-oriented universities, who teach half as many courses. It is
a different business model; the expectation of the community college
teacher is that of a teacher, not a researcher.

I would argue that two-year colleges are as imperative to the health
and welfare of this nation as the research universities are. Indeed, if one
steps back a bit and looks at the economics of American higher education, it may well be that in the future many more students will begin at
a two-year college and then transfer to an upper-division campus where
they can do their junior and senior years and then pursue a graduate or
professional degree.

It is troubling to me that many university faculty don't pay attention to developments such as these and don't become engaged with their own institution to prepare it for what is going to come in the years ahead. Instead, in the struggle to keep things as they are, they wait too long. Eventually, dramatic changes in the university will take place and they will not be as pleasant as incremental changes would have been. I am not a revolutionary, but I believe in constant gradual change, rethinking the college experience, and questioning how we invest our money. For instance, I wonder why the first year of medical school couldn't be taught during the senior year of college. Medical school could then be done in three years: one year of coursework followed by two clinical years. We should be thinking more about such innovations.

Along those same lines, I am torn about the wisdom of teaching beginning languages in a university. It is clear that twenty-first-century students should be able to speak at least one language beyond English. We suffer from not having more Americans who speak Arabic, Russian, Chinese, and many of the many other languages that have increasingly become a factor in our global society. But I am not confident that a student should take a beginning language like Chinese 101 in college, where there is such a limited amount of time and a plentiful offering of challenging courses available. After all, when taking a beginning language, the student spends a lot of time memorizing grammar rules and vocabulary rather than taking courses that may enhance the ability to think and reason. We need to do more with beginning language training in the elementary and secondary schools. We should use what are now summer vacations for intensive language study at home and abroad.

At the college level, we must ask how best to invest one's limited time. We should help students use their undergraduate years more efficiently. For instance, we could have students go to college for twelve months and use the whole year, filling the summers with language study or related educational travel experiences. Of course, this seems a fairly radical—and expensive—notion. But it may actually be cheaper than the way we now do things.

Parents have often said to me that their children seem to be home a lot of the academic year with just a little college thrown in. It certainly seemed that we had much longer semesters when I was in college. For a variety of reasons, we have shortened the academic year. Some of that change had to do with the rise in the cost of heating oil during the Carter administration, when colleges—particularly those in New England—cut an entire week off the fifteen-week semester to save on fuel oil and ended up with fourteen-week semesters. What we have now is fifty-two-week years on our regular calendars and twenty-eight-week years on our academic calendars. In those twenty-eight weeks, we manage to fit in Thanksgiving, Christmas, Rosh Hashanah, Yom Kippur, President's Day, and a whole assortment of other breaks, so students don't even get a full fourteen weeks of five days each. Also, students and professors like to trim a bit by using the last week of classes for exams in order to get a jump start on vacation.

In academe we have many agendas in conflict with one another. If we changed the calendar back to the way it once was, we would be disturbing the lives of all who have become accustomed to this more modest calendar and the accompanying reward structure. And the students—none of whom was even born when semesters ran longer—don't complain about the abbreviated calendar.

THERE IS not necessarily a connection between the outcome we seek and the process we go through on the way there. For instance, we sometimes add degree requirements without paying enough attention to what the degree holder will actually need. This is true in the more vocationally oriented programs. It used to be that nursing programs gave a degree for two years of training. They still do, but now one sees more extensive programs under way and some even leading to the doctorate. Do the new credentials lead to better nursing in our hospitals? We have a serious national shortage of nurses, and we have long been recruiting large numbers of nurses from outside the country. With this shortage of nurses in mind, is this the best time for operational two-year programs to be extended for longer and longer periods?

Too many faculty at four-year state colleges want to be at a school that gives doctorates; teaching in a doctorate-granting institution means that you teach fewer courses, are paid better, and have more status. It is in this way that the reward structure for professors comes into conflict with what we may want them to do. As we have moved more and more to being a research university, my university has reduced the average teaching obligation of faculty. As I have mentioned, we have done this by having more adjunct faculty teach courses. Is this a good thing for the undergraduates, some of whom might have half their courses presented by part-time faculty? Not every university is blessed with a resource pool as we are in Washington. You couldn't do this successfully in a rural location, for instance, where there are, presumably, fewer PhD-credentialed people available in the neighborhood.

At GW, we paid a price for reducing the teaching loads of full-time faculty. I wonder, is the outcome a better university or not? What would it cost if you wanted to have both? GW, like other universities in big cities, has an adjunct-rich environment. New York, Chicago, Boston, and many other cities have people with knowledge, wisdom, and experience to bring into the classroom, and they enjoy doing so along with practicing law, medicine, business, or public service. The universities can use them as part of the teaching staff of clinicians and practitioners. Often this can result in a reduction of required teaching time for full-time faculty so they can do research or write books. The offset is that since adjuncts are part-time, they naturally do not focus on the university. They come in, teach their courses, and go about their lives. The students benefit from what they bring to the classroom but often feel they are not getting enough attention from them as faculty. They usually cannot see the adjuncts when they want to, and adjuncts are not part of the university community in a comprehensive way. There is a tipping point at which if the faculty starts to get too many adjuncts, a price is paid in terms of the participation in the intellectual life of the campus, the construction of curriculum, and the interchange between faculty and students. The question becomes: When have you added so many adjunct faculty that you have changed the nature of the "real" faculty?

The price you pay in this matter can be that you miss the opportunity to enrich the faculty with outside voices and experiences, or you can overload the faculty with people who do not bring enough to the campus community as a whole. At GW we have probably gone to more adjunct faculty than we should. As I have mentioned earlier, my efforts to control that situation involved reinventing the curriculum from a forty-course BA degree to a new, improved thirty-two-course BA degree in order to make the BA degree more normative with other institutions we aspired to be like. In the process, we would use fewer adjuncts, have more full-time faculty teaching courses, and still permit the use of faculty time for other scholarly pursuits. Think of it this way: if you don't want much to drink, you might say to the bartender, "I want a water and scotch." In other words, you want to tone down the scotch. Other times, you might want to order a scotch neat or a regular scotch and water. It's a question of the ratio of one to the other; finding the right ratio is what the issue of adjuncts is all about.

Faculty members say they are concerned that there should be a certain percentage of full-time faculty members in every program. But the university does not have enough money to do everything. We cannot have full-time faculty teach fewer hours while also keeping the ratio of full-time/adjunct at the level the faculty wants, so we add adjunct faculty to compensate for the classes not being taught by the full-time faculty. Everybody wants to go to Heaven, but nobody wants to die! Everyone likes progress. No one likes change.

LEARNING IS one of life's great pleasures. There is nothing more pleasurable than overcoming a lack of understanding or mastering a desired skill. This reminds me of something that happened many years ago, when I was driving with my son Adam. He had been learning how to sound out letters. We came to an intersection and he started to sound out the letters he saw on a sign; *Sss—Ttt—Ohh—Ppp*. Suddenly he pronounced the word "stop." It was a dramatic breakthrough for him; he had figured out a previously mysterious code and saw that he now knew how to read a word! From then on, there was no distracting him; he just started reading. That's the way learning is—world-changing and exciting.

The thought that people who lack an understanding of art, religion, economics, science, and literature are nevertheless university graduates is lamentable to me. Yet we are told that there university alumni who could not name two plays by Shakespeare, much less have read or seen them. I was having a meal with a group of people, and a retired English professor among us asked a student what he was studying. The student replied that he was an English major. The professor started a conversation about Henry James, but it was obvious that the student had no idea who Henry James was. That was a bit shocking. You don't have to like Henry James, and you don't have to have read all of his work to be educated, but, in order to be an English major, you really do have to have to be familiar enough with the name Henry James to get through dinner.

It used to be that there was a shared concept of what an undergraduate degree was. As chair of the local Rhodes Scholarship Selection Committee, I spend a good deal of time looking at the transcripts of student candidates from many different universities. I see extraordinary variances among their records. There are still some universities with core curricula, but in the many universities that don't have required core courses, students have great latitude in choosing what to study to achieve a BA. I am not sure universities are behaving responsibly in permitting quite so much freedom. Presumably, the educated people who teach in universities have some notion about what an undergraduate experience should be. When students graduate, they need to be prepared to be welcomed into the society of educated people. But the way curriculum decisions are made is too often not a robust reflection of that view.

The world doesn't break down into simple pieces the way universities divide up into departments. A liberal arts education allows you to step back and view the world from a many-faceted perspective, but how can you do that if, for instance, you never took a course in comparative religion during your undergraduate study? How can you do that if you don't know any world history, much less your own country's history? How can you do that in the twenty-first century if you have never studied a foreign language? I don't think we are as articulate as we should be when planning university curricula.

The novel *The Da Vinci Code* raised the question of whether Mary Magdalene, as a disciple of Jesus, was present at the Last Supper. Surely, you can't really think or talk about subjects like this without a little knowledge of the Bible and Christianity. I was in China in the company of some university-educated people who spoke English quite well. It was Christmas, and we were singing carols. I knew most of these carols because when I went to school in New York, we learned them in school. A woman heard me singing and said, "You must be a Christian." I said I wasn't, and she said matter-of-factly, "Oh, then you are a Catholic." I said, "No, Catholics are Christians—pre-Reformation Christians." She had no idea what I was talking about. She then asked, "Then what religion are you?" I told her I was Jewish. She was completely silent, so I explained, "My religion is pre-Christian. Before Peter and Paul, Jesus belonged to a religion. I belong to that same religion." She didn't comprehend what I meant, although she is a Christian. I thought, Surely she, as a Christian, should have some inkling of this, because in order to have a New Testament, you have to have the Old Testament—the Hebrew Bible.

Since this happened in China, there could be other cultural factors at work. But I tell the story to express the notion that in order to have a nation, we need a shared body of knowledge. For example, since there are frequently historical and philosophical connections among religions, people who follow a faith need to know something about other faiths. If a student can slide through college without ever having to deal with the history and philosophy of unfamiliar things, it is likely that student will never be educated.

All societies have a sense of what they need from their universities. In Morocco, the business community concluded that the Francophile universities—those that had been heavily influenced by French culture from their days of colonization by France—were producing people whose training was seen as theoretical. It was an example of the familiar tension between scholarship and the use of the mind and hand. The business community tried to get the universities to adapt to their perceived contemporary needs and become slightly more applied. But the Francophile universities couldn't bring themselves to do that.

As a result, the king of Morocco and the royal family of Saudi Arabia founded Al Akhawayn University in 1993. I have been on that university's board for a long time; it is an English-language institution built in Morocco and conceived with much American university land grant philosophy and practice. The faculty members teach in English so that when someone graduates, he or she will speak English as well as French and Arabic. The business community is thrilled with the university because it is now able to find people who can help them in their practical ventures all over the world. They are no longer hampered by the problem of Moroccans speaking only Moroccan Arabic (and French, of course), which is often not well understood outside North Africa. Students come to the university from all over the Middle East.

MANY PEOPLE think that university curricula are the result of clear thinking about what people need to know. I certainly don't want to deny that completely, but it is also important to understand that university curricula are highly political documents. New disciplines have been introduced, and there are several different kinds of politics in the mix now. For instance, Women's Studies, Lesbian and Homosexual Studies, African-American Studies, and other new subjects have all become increasingly important.

Of course, we have to make trade-offs in all aspects of our lives. But we have very gauzy notions when we think about making trade-offs at the college and university levels, and we have become so uncertain about what we believe in, that we have allowed some basic things to be neglected in order to accommodate other, more innovative subjects.

I believe there ought to be a core of liberal arts courses that everybody takes and is enhanced by. Doing so would create a common conversation in the country about what constitutes a liberal arts education. There is no reason why "The Star-spangled Banner" can't be sung in a language other than English. If you sing it in a second language, it is an honor to our country. But everyone in America ought to also be able to sing it in English. It is a *national* anthem and, as such, has a bonding role that calls for a native tongue. I am reminded of some World War II movies in which American soldiers coming back to camp from the front are met by a guard who says, "Stop, who goes there?" The soldiers say they are Americans, and the guard says, "Oh yeah, well, who won the 1942 World Series?" If they answer the question correctly, they are allowed into the camp. These are things that are part of a culture that are handed on and create nationhood and civilization. These are simple examples, but the point I am trying to make is that the undergraduate curricula of our colleges do not have any consistency and so it is impossible to know what it means when a person says that he or she has a certain degree. Thus the experience has diminished its capacity to link us together.

When people begin to develop curricula, you see the kind of trade-offs that might go on in Congress over the Farm Bill, not the kind of academic discourse one might hope for. There are only so many hours that a student can be expected to devote each week to class, and if a judgment is made that art history is not as important as some other topic, it may disappear from the curriculum. In universities, the arts often have to fight to make sure that they aren't pushed aside by brawnier departments. Deciding what a student has to take as a minimum to get a degree becomes an elbowing contest. Every time you introduce a new field, it is important to ask, "What are we taking out?"

THERE IS a cultural transformation going on about which many people are unaware. I used to tell students to read *The New York Times* every day. I told them that if they would do that, at the end of the four years they would understand a lot about what was going on in the world. But now students get their news online and from TV and they don't read columnists. I can rail about that, but I know I am not going to change the evolving sociology of America. The world is simply a different place now, and I don't know to what extent we should try to compensate for substance that has been lost in the process.

Every once in a while, I watch the Jay Leno show and see him do a comedy bit called "Jaywalking" where he asks people on the street simple questions about everyday events that everyone should know

about. The humor of it is that Leno's simple questions and the appalling responses by one passerby after another reveal a great deal of
ignorance and, I guess, make the better-informed viewers feel supe-
rior. Sometimes I experience equally uneducated reactions in my day-
to-day interactions. I no longer feel secure in making a reference to
things that used to be common knowledge; it is discomfiting to receive
a blank stare in response.

Over the years, a variety of new Americans have laid claim to por-
tions of the curriculum. And so what used to be at the core of many
curricula in America—Western civilization—has had to step aside a
little bit to allow in the study of other cultures as well. This is good.
And bad. In thinking about the current debate over the advisability of
putting aside aspects of Western civilization, I am reminded of remarks
made by Judge José A. Cabranes at Columbia University in 1991:

> *Columbia College can take pride in having demanded the most
> of all of us, regardless of background. It can be proud of having
> made all of us quite uncomfortable—uncomfortable as we en-
> countered new and unfamiliar ideas and as we pursued together
> an understanding of the Western heritage.*
>
> *Columbia College did not define its academic program on the
> basis of the ethnicity or the race of any of us. It invited us all, re-
> gardless of our origins and with full respect for our origins, to join
> in the common study of our heritage and to do so with an appre-
> ciation that criticism and reform of our institutions is an integral
> part of the tradition we describe as "Western Civilization."*

We need to learn about other civilizations and that adds to the already large amount we have to learn. But it makes little sense to learn
about another culture while remaining ignorant about one's own. Certainly, we do not learn more by studying less.

My idea of undergraduate education involves combining a core curriculum with enough flexibility and concentration to allow a student
a major. But what we see in the university now is a focus on career-
ism and the need to create a résumé that people think will impress a

future employer. Some of today's students talk about double and triple majoring. This is a form of "product enhancement," an effort by students to create something that will somehow make them competitive in the market and attractive to an employer. It is as if they are creating a shield to carry in front of them. Universities are complicit in this activity, and it seems that this is due partly to the institution's feeling that if it appears noncompetitive to potential students, those students will go elsewhere to seek better value — or better shields.

To some extent universities overdegree and students spend well beyond what is needed. We can say, "That's fine because they will lead richer and better lives because of it." But I'm not so sure that is reflected in the curriculum. We often train for careers and not for better lives.

Two DATA points that drive the university's budget are the number of students and the tuition. You multiply one by the other to get the bottom line, then subtract what you have given away in financial aid, and then add in what you get from fund-raising and endowment. That is your budget. At GW and many other institutions, 80 percent or more of the budget comes from tuition. The city has capped GW's enrollment, so we can't grow. If you can't add more students, you ordinarily look to the tuition. But we have been as aggressive as is sound with tuition. We are now perfectly normative with other institutions. At GW, the percentage of the rise in tuition applies only to the freshman class, not to the sophomores, juniors, and seniors. We freeze tuition at the incoming level for the duration of the undergraduate's tenure at the university. Therefore, the amount of new dollars coming into the university is limited.

Why is the tuition so high? Since there are no stockholders in universities, you are not paying out dividends, so where is the money going? The answer is that universities have an infinite capacity for improvement. We never stop trying to get better, and, in fact, we dare not stop. As I have mentioned, fuel is added to the fire by outside sources like *U.S. News & World Report* that create an artificial competition among institutions for better and more appealing amenities and services.

Consider this hypothesis: small classes are better than large classes.

If there are thirty students in a class, the enrollment could be reduced to fifteen in two classes and almost everyone would automatically assume it was an improvement. But I don't know of any data that demonstrate that the theory is universally true. Certainly, in some disciplines, small must be significantly better. Music lessons are nice one-on-one, for instance. But if you make smaller classes your overall goal, you will be spending more money. You might need two faculty members rather than one to teach thirty students. But if you read about the great teachers at some of the best universities, they may teach four hundred students at a time. There are some faculty and some disciplines that lend themselves quite reasonably to a big group where sixty is better than thirty.

Even if you want to have big classes, the school may not have enough big rooms and may need to build some. But it is often upsetting to faculty if the administration builds big rooms. They begin to think that the administration is trying to manipulate the curriculum by creating a capacity for big classes. The tyranny of on-campus architecture is a neglected issue of discussion.

Clearly, it is not just faculty-student ratios that affect tuition. Take residence halls. In college I had a monkish room with a double-decker bed, a sink, two small desks, a closet, and one window. My roommate, Ted Small, and I did just fine living that way. Today, those kinds of modest dormitories are becoming a thing of the past. The new residence halls are full of amenities. At GW we build kitchens in the rooms, and I suspect that after graduation, some of our students live a meaner existence for a period of time than they did when they were here! There are other extras that students have come to expect, such as exercise rooms, recreational facilities, widely varied menu choices, and so on. These drive up the cost of attendance. Do these things make an important improvement to college life? They certainly add expense.

When people come to see the president about something, whatever it is they are thinking about, they are really talking about money. They might say that the gym needs a new floor or that more student guidance counselors are needed, but what they are really talking about is money.

There is a great reluctance to recognize that; talking about money in the university setting is considered commercial and vulgar. It is so much more agreeable to talk about goals and ambitions. But whatever the goals and ambitions might be, they have to be paid for with money. Because it is the university president who worries about the money, he liberates his colleagues to think yet higher thoughts. I doubt if the faculty has ever thought of me as a liberator of thought!

Faculty in most colleges and universities earn less money than other highly educated people in the society. I don't think this is a necessary or desirable situation, but people do make their own life choices and they knowingly choose to be professors. It is a constant source of wonder and admiration to me that people earn doctorates in English or history knowing that finding employment specifically in those disciplines is as hard as it is. Should we discourage them? Or should we retire more of our senior faculty and create opportunity for younger people to come up the ranks? I have talked about this earlier, but the fact is that, by federal law, *there is no mandatory retirement* in America. Tenure is, therefore, now a lifetime privilege. We are seeing the aging of university faculties. It used to be that tenured faculty would retire at sixty-five. The big accounting firms still retire their partners at fifty-five and sixty to allow others to aspire to promotion. Of course, they compensate their partners well so that they can afford to retire at those ages and take on second careers. But in the military or in some civil service situations, after twenty or twenty-five years, people are obliged to retire. Admirals need to step out so that sailors can advance.

If you had older faculty retiring in greater numbers, there would be more openings for which younger people could compete. Presumably, this would create more opportunities for underrepresented groups such as minorities and women. When I say this, I am not calling for us to be mean to older people! But we *could* be more imaginative than we are. For example, if we have a professor making $70,000 per year and that person has reached age sixty-five and is eligible for a pension of $50,000 per year, why couldn't we provide for Professor Smith to stay on at half-time and count his pension toward his compensation along with $20,000 from the university? Professor Smith would then be making the same amount of money as before for half as much work, and we would be liberating $50,000 with which the university could hire an assistant professor. The older retired faculty member would be teaching a reduced load but still have an income of $70,000, and the assistant professor would be making $50,000 and teaching a full load. The cost to the university would remain constant, while there would now be a professor and a half available to students. At my university, the faculty as a whole doesn't want to do this, and they don't even want to talk about it! Certainly, individual faculty members can do this, but the arrangement happens only randomly. If it were systematic, the institution could serve its goals of teaching and scholarship better.

In general, if one steps back and looks at universities, it is possible to see less expensive ways to run them without hurting the professoriate or the quality of the education being provided to the students. But most of these ways involve changing the way the university goes about its work, and that is where the outcry begins.

UNIVERSITIES ARE often contrarian in outlook. If the president of a university were given the chance to acquire all of Stalin's private papers from the Kremlin, is there any reason why he or she would refuse this opportunity? No one would view such an acquisition as an endorsement of Stalin; they would see it as an opportunity to have a valuable resource available to scholars from all over the world.

But we have read that the president of Southern Methodist University arranged for SMU to become the home of George W. Bush's papers and the faculty objected. There are already two presidential libraries in place in Texas—those of Lyndon Johnson and the first George Bush—and, clearly, the president of SMU saw the Bush acquisition as a way for his university to also become a center of presidential scholarship. But his faculty basically said, "Not so fast! We don't like George Bush, and we're not so sure we want his library or the kind of people the library is likely to bring to our campus." What were these people thinking?

In the old days, academic freedom was not intended for students and outsiders; it was meant only for faculty. That elitist current still runs through academe. For example, I received a call from a faculty member who said that Jimmy Carter was interested in coming to GW to give a talk about his book *Palestine: Peace Not Apartheid*. The book was causing a great deal of controversy because many Middle East scholars found it inaccurate and unsound and others found its title especially provocative. I said, "The man was president of the United States and won the Nobel Peace Prize. Of course he can come to GW to speak. This doesn't mean that we have to allow ourselves to be used just to help a book tour. It wouldn't be right to let him just come in, give a talk, and then walk away. Students and faculty members must be able to ask him questions."

Previous to that, some at Brandeis University had argued that if Carter were to speak there, he would have to debate someone; President Carter declined that suggestion. I don't think a university has to try to embarrass him by bringing in an Alan Dershowitz to debate him, but if he wants to come and give a talk on campus, students and faculty must be allowed access to challenge his presentation.

My response to the faculty member was to tell him to invite President Carter but to point out that we would expect him to meet us halfway. After all, we are a campus, not a rented room. When speakers answer students' questions from the floor, it adds value to discussions, and, of course, universities want to create learning opportunities. The path to understanding among adversaries is open conversation.

17.

PERPETUAL INSTITUTIONS, MORTAL LEADERS

I don't think most people understand the complexity of universities. My reaction to the appointment of the new Harvard president, a woman named Drew G. Faust, is that it could prove to be a stroke of genius. She doesn't have the experience that would normally be considered appropriate. You would not ordinarily put someone in charge of such a massive enterprise who has never done anything comparable. But because of the unnerving events leading to the departure of Lawrence Summers, many candidates did not want the job. Harvard apparently decided to pick someone for rich symbolic as well as practical reasons. And it picked a woman. This has the effect of putting a stake in the heart of what Summers had said about women in the sciences that insulted and incensed some factions of the faculty. This appointment is a historic occasion for Harvard, and it has been said that it wouldn't have happened if it weren't for what Summers had said. But beyond the circumstances of the choice, it seems that Drew Faust brings a healing personality to Harvard.

Different institutions need different things at different times. This is one of the reasons why I am pleased with the choice of Steve Knapp as my successor at GW. My own entrepreneurial bent has been replaced by someone who can address the university's current drive to become more of a research institution. I would like to think that the foundation I have laid down will enable the next chapter to be written by someone who is a faculty insider; part of their club. I hope that he will be able to hold the GW faculty to the performance standard he was accustomed to at his former institution. He may even set a higher bar for them. Great presidents have the ability to reconcile disparate impulses within the institution and to change a series of flashing lights into a steady glow. Also, he has a great reputation as a fund-raiser. I am confident he will do much better than I did.

Universities are perpetual institutions. But the people who are involved in them are mortals who pass away. Current presidents must keep in mind that there will be future presidents of their institution who have not yet been born. Understanding this, all university presidents must be humble and realize that they are only temporary custodians of the institutions they serve. And, most important, a president's decisions must take the future into consideration as much as the present.

In my last year, I spent time contemplating and putting into gear a real estate transaction that, if successfully concluded, will have only a modest effect on GW for ten to twenty years, but at the end of that time, it will have a very consequential impact on the institution and may actually ensure its ability to grow and to flourish a generation or two from now. Crafting the future is heady stuff for any president.

When one looks back at my own alma mater, Columbia University, one can only regret that when the university came to Morningside Heights, it did not acquire land all the way down to the Hudson River. No doubt there wasn't the money to do so, but what a less crowded campus Columbia would be today if that had been possible! It is said that one of my GW predecessors decided not to buy property from Foggy Bottom down to the Potomac River because he did not want to encumber the university with debt. When I was told that story, I wondered, "What! Was he a Communist?" But no, he was only following the conventional wisdom of his time.

Most of the people in universities, particularly students who are there for a defined period of time, are focused on what is happening right now—that is, when they arrive and while they are there. Faculty are included in this group. Although they have some strong feelings about the university, they seem to see it more as a platform for their personal careers and show little evidence of thinking far into the institution's future. The president of the university has to be looking twenty, forty, and fifty years ahead at all times.

Suppose a gift of $100 million—not earmarked—has been given to a university. A gift of that size has the potential to create a profound effect. The president could decide to put that much into the endowment and watch it throw off $5 million per year for the operating budget. This would permit the administration to prudently invest $100 million, to draw on an asset at the present time, and also to let it serve as a protection against inflation or shortfalls in the future. A fairly predictable outcome can be ensured with this tactic, and it is a sound and sensible way to go.

Another way to proceed would be for the president to put a portion of that amount into the endowment but spend $50 million right now with dramatic effect in order to build new facilities or hire new professors and use it immediately in a variety of good ways. With this option, the administration would be using $50 million to urge the university forward in a way it could not without the money. Of course, there are those who would say that this would not be a sound thing to do, that the president's duty is to invest and hold on to the money.

I am not a believer in a pure invest-and-hold strategy for a university. I do believe in prudence, however, and my university's endowment has increased by $1 billion during my tenure. But I think that while a university needs those assets, it also needs to apply available resources on a regular basis. Among other things, building new facilities leads to heightened morale and a sense of accomplishment on campus. Buildings are more than brick and mortar; they are symbols of the possible and as such are a reassuring sight. Excellent facilities are an affirmation of the good work that is being carried out on campus and an encouragement of more.

A president has to listen to concerns about how to allocate resources, but the worst thing I can imagine is a leader—who has a clear vision of where the institution needs to go—being easily persuaded to take it in another direction by advocates of a different worldview. It would be a nightmare to end up taking the institution in a wrong direction after abandoning one's own vision. When I have made blunders, I think they have been mostly my own, rather than mistakes I have made because I took advice I didn't believe in.

But it is harder to go your own way in university settings than in others because of the expectation on campuses of collegiality and consultation. I have already discussed a situation in which I allowed myself to be swayed by faculty in my selection of a new dean. But I had to deal with the problem by myself. At least if I had been wrong about *my* choice of dean, I would have been more comfortable accepting the blame! It was a lesson to me, and I never let someone else cajole me into a choice I didn't feel right about again. Of course, I still got it wrong now and again on my own.

The term "bold university president" seems almost an oxymoron. Leadership in universities is very much about persuasion, compromise, knowing when to accede. You've got to know when to hold and when to fold. Obviously, there are some dramatic presidents, but not many. John Silber comes immediately to mind as one of those; he redefined Boston University by taking it forward in tangible ways. He substantially upgraded its academic programs, its faculty, its student spaces and amenities, and its physical plant. He raised the university to a new level. A greater percentage of that university's student body now sees it as its first choice, not just a university in Boston that isn't Harvard, MIT, or Tufts, where they might have preferred to go.

People generally aren't certain or clear about what they want from university presidents. We sort of know what we want from military generals and captains of industry, whereas university presidents suffer more from multiple, even contrary expectations. For instance, if Senator Joseph McCarthy is attacking the university, we would want a strong defender of freedom of speech and the rights of universities. But if there is internal controversy, the faculty generally wants someone who is accommodating to their views and perceived needs. They want a lion dealing with the world and a lamb addressing them.

Simply stated, university leadership is contrarian and complex. Because many of a president's faculty constituents have lifetime contracts, his or her capacity to reward or deny is minimal. Therefore, a president's toolbox is largely filled with ways to try to be persuasive. If people don't want to be persuaded, there is a problem, especially since faculty are people who are generally skilled in argumentation and don't necessarily accord any special status to department chairs, deans, and presidents. There is no normal chain of command. Most professors think they know how the institution should be run, and any expenditure that does not go their way is wrong. This is another variation on the theme of subgroup maximization; in other words, the dean of the School of Engineering might feel no compunction about cannibalizing the rest of the university in order to strengthen and grow his own school. Institutions with multiple competing divisions have internal as well as external rivalries.

Sometimes I have a mental image of professors as a nest of robins calling out, "Go get worms, feed us, and then go get more!" This is interesting, because when a person is being interviewed for the presidency, the search committee, which always includes faculty, asks the candidates' views of curriculum, academic issues, and other subjects. These are the very subjects that the faculty members will never want to hear about again from the president when he or she inhabits the office. It reminds me of a long-ago group interview I had for a university presidency. At the end of the interview, as I was being pulled away to catch a plane, a faculty member shouted out a last-minute question from the back of the room: "What are your views of academic freedom?" As I was exiting, I called to him, "I'm in favor of it!" I don't know how the room reacted; I was off to the airport by then.

THE NATURE of the university is more complex and, in many ways, more vulnerable than that of other types of enterprises. Two years after the departure of its president in 2005, American University in Washington was still without a president. And there was still no indication that the job would be filled any time soon. Having no president after two years makes no sense. If the university were a publicly held corporation, would the stockholders be content with a search for president or CEO that goes on for more than two years? Would they be content with an interim president who might be reluctant to act as if he or she had been given the job already?

I know of a case in which a professor at a very good eastern university was given a sabbatical and went off to spend a year at a fabulous university in California. During that visiting year, he was offered a two-year appointment at the California university but was told that he would not come up for tenure there until the contract ended. He asked his home university to give him a two-year leave to go to the university in California. This would mean that, in effect, his position in the first university would have to be frozen until it was a certainty that he would get tenure and depart for California. It didn't make sense for the first university to agree to hold the position open so the faculty member could come back if he failed. The administration declined to go along with this idea, and the professor decided not to leave the first university!

Leaving positions open indicates that the university does not really care about the quality of the department. Making a personnel decision in favor of a well-liked person over and above the interest of the institution is simply not businesslike. Industry certainly does not take this kind of soft approach. In universities, lines are not always drawn clearly. Many of the hiring decisions have to do more with personality and politics than with performance potential. While this approach has a caring quality about it, it makes running a university less efficient and usually more expensive than is necessary. If a university president raises money for an endowed chair in a particular discipline and then the department takes two to three years to fill the job, the benefactor is justified in asking "Why are you so slow to fill this position after you were so eager to get the money for it?"

UNIVERSITIES ARE partners in the future of the nation. If our country is going to flourish, particularly in the coming century, when we will see India and China moving forward strongly, we will have to continue to compete on many levels. In order to do so, we will have to trade with the rest of the world and we will have to have a highly educated, highly trained, sophisticated population. Our citizens will have to know our country's history, culture, and civilization and have an appreciation for and knowledge of others as well. We certainly need to find ways of solving problems of health care and infrastructure, but at the heart of all of our most pressing issues is that of the quality of our schools and our universities. They are a source of talent, workers, and ideas. They are at the center of our national wealth, and they ensure our ability to sustain ourselves both domestically and internationally.

Being a university president is a waiting game that calls for time, opportunity, people coming and going, birth and death; you can't change institutions quickly. They all have a certain tensile strength, and if you bend them too quickly, they break. But if you bend them slowly and patiently, you can sometimes get them to yield. Leadership has a lot to do with people having faith in you, which means that you have to have been part of their lives and they have to have a reason to trust you. I have spent a lot of time going to weddings and funerals and marking occasions in people's lives both happy and sad, sending congratulatory notes, and sending cheesecakes and flowers to celebrate their accomplishments, because I think you have to bond with people if you want them to be there with you.

THE DAY the new president of GW was announced, the two of us appeared together at a press conference. I said:

> Over the years, I've talked with thousands of parents who have expressed the wonderful, yet mixed emotions attached to sending their children off to college. Today, I begin the process of sending my university off to its next president. Like any proud parent, I am filled with joy, a little sadness, and a great sense of satisfaction for all that has been accomplished to get us to this point. That GW has attracted a candidate of the caliber of Dr. Steven Knapp is a testament to our combined efforts to help GW become one of the truly great institutions of higher education. I look forward to working with Dr. Knapp in the coming months to ensure a smooth

transition. And I look forward to our university's future success under his leadership.

I won't lie; I had a tear in my eye when I said this. And there were more of those during the months in which I was saying good-bye to the very full life I had led for so many years.

AMONG OTHER things, I have been challenged as a university president to inquire not only "What is education for?" but also "What are the aims of an educational institution?" The inquiry is interminable; society is habitually engaged in revising its cultural givens and exploding as myths any notion or modality that comes from the past—the past being any time between the creation of the cave paintings at Lascaux and what took place last night. The aims of an educational institution must be the creation and maintenance of a sound equilibrium in the face of social and intellectual fragmentation on campus—or academic tribalism. In other words, the institution must first aim at creating the preconditions that make learning and teaching possible and then decide what is worth learning and teaching.

Making these decisions is at the heart of the matter and the soul of the problem, especially in a democracy that accepts pluralism as a matter of course and is skeptical about the existence of any single cultural or traditional canon of learning. Our decisions can achieve only a temporary equilibrium of intellectual interests and commercial realities. Plato and Paglia might be invited to the dance today, but perhaps others will be invited tomorrow. Like a good professor, a university president rewrites his or her notes yearly and may have to discard them at the end of the academic year, writing new ones for the next.

I may complain about universities and the difficulties they present, but in the end, they are the most spectacular institutions in the world, and being president is one of the most extraordinary pleasures and privileges there is. Certainly this is true of my life. I secretly marvel that people have been willing to pay me for what I have done for a living for so long. Most important, at the end of my tenure, I find pleasure in thinking of what we—administration, faculty, and staff together—have accomplished. For this I am eternally grateful. I have always liked the epitaph "He got a lot of stuff done," although I might add as my own epitaph "He got a lot of good stuff done with the help of a lot of good people and he had a wonderful time doing it."

Before I left office, I received this note from an acquaintance:

In my line of work, I meet lots of people of accomplishment. Some of them are utterly pretentious, vain about the place they have come to occupy in the world. Happily, some of them are unspoiled, honest, and decent. And it always makes me feel better about humanity when I meet someone like yourself who has actually taken an important institution and made it better, and managed to stay true to his values.

What I see at GW is a university that has improved dramatically over the past twenty years, but, more important, one that is also imbued with the personality of someone who is not afraid to invest real emotion in a project.

It can never be said that I failed to invest real emotion in my job. I gave it everything I had. And I left unindicted.

ACKNOWLEDGMENTS

Editor, cheerleader, and straw boss:

Mark Gompertz

Guiding light—made contributions to the manuscript, remembered some of the stories and people, tolerated the working on weekends, read and commented on the manuscripts at each stage:

Francine Zorn Trachtenberg

Consulting editor on earliest chapters:

Anne Harding Woodworth

Scheduler and coordinator:

Helene Interlandi

Reviewers of early drafts:

Anne Glickman
Gerry Kauvar
Lewis Paper
David Bruce Smith
Stanley Trachtenberg

Research and fact-checking:

A. Paige Blumer

Sandy Holland
Steven Keating

Photographs:

Jessica McConnell, GW photographer

About the Authors

STEPHEN JOEL TRACHTENBERG served for thirty years as a university president. He is now president emeritus and university professor at The George Washington University, where he teaches courses on the university presidency in America. He is also an adviser to Korn/Ferry International, where he is helping to find the next generation of university leadership. He has a BA from Columbia, a MPA from Harvard, and a JD from Yale. Trachtenberg is also the recipient of fifteen honorary degrees. A swell guy. But not much of a dancer.

TANSY HOWARD BLUMER is a writer who specializes in memoirs. She lives in Washington, D.C.